Gramsci, Culture and Ant

Gramsci, Culture and Anthropology

Kate Crehan

University of California Press

BERKELEY • LOS ANGELES

University of California Press
Berkeley and Los Angeles, California

Published by arrangement with
Pluto Press
345 Archway Road, London N6 5AA

Library of Congress Cataloging-in-Publication Data
Crehan, Kate A. F.
   Gramsci, culture, and anthropology / Kate Crehan.
      p. cm.
   Includes bibliographical references and index.
   ISBN 0–520–23601–7 (cloth : alk. paper) — ISBN 0–520–23602–5
(paper : alk. paper)
      1. Gramsci, Antonio, 1891–1937. 2. Culture. 3. Social classes.
   4. Ethnology. I. Title.

GN357 .C74 2002
306—dc21

                                                            2002074224

10   9   8   7   6   5   4   3   2   1

Designed and produced for Pluto Press by
Chase Publishing Services, Fortescue, Sidmouth EX10 9QG
Typeset from disk by Stanford DTP Services, Towcester
Printed in Canada by Transcontinental Printing

Contents

Reading Gramsci

General Editor: Joseph A. Buttigieg

Antonio Gramsci (1891–1937), little known outside communist circles at the time of his death, is now one of the most frequently cited and widely translated political theorists and cultural critics of the twentieth century. The first wave of interest in Gramsci was triggered by the publication, in Italy, of his prison writings, starting with the letters, which appeared in 1947, and continuing with the six volumes of the thematic edition of the notebooks, the last of which was brought out in 1951. Within the space of a few years, hundreds of articles and books were written explicating, analysing and debating Gramsci's concept of hegemony, his revisionist views on the history of Italy's unification, his anti-economistic and anti-dogmatic version of Marxist philosophy, his theory of the state and civil society, his anti-Crocean literary criticism, his novel approach to the study of popular culture, his extensive observations on the role of intellectuals in society, along with other aspects of his thought. Although long dead, Gramsci became more than an object of dispassionate study; the intensity of the discussions surrounding his work and the often heated struggle over his legacy had, and continue to have, a profound effect on the political culture and cultural politics of postwar Italy.

During the late 1960s and the 1970s Gramsci's name and ideas started circulating with increasing frequency throughout Europe, Latin America, and North America (and, to a lesser extent, elsewhere too). The various currents associated with Eurocommunism and the 'New Left' that accompanied the swell of interest in what came to be known as 'western Marxism' contributed immensely to Gramsci's rise to prominence during this period. In the anglophone world, the publication, in 1971, of Quintin Hoare and Geoffrey Nowell Smith's superbly edited *Selections from the Prison Notebooks* made it possible for scholars to move from vague and general allusions to Gramsci to serious study and analysis of his work. Gramscian studies were further bolstered by various editions in diverse languages of the pre-prison writings – which, among other things, drew attention to the valuable essay on the Southern Question – and by the publication, in Italy, of Valentino Gerratana's complete critical edition of the *Quaderni del carcere* (1975).

Gramsci's influence became even more pronounced in the 1980s with the spread of cultural studies, the growing fascination with the question of 'power', and the greater attention that scholars from different disciplines were devoting to the relations among culture, society, and politics. The rapid decline of interest in Marxist thought following the events of 1989 had no effect on Gramsci's 'fortunes'. By that time, as Stuart Hall was among the first to point out, Gramsci had already 'radically displaced some of the inheritances of Marxism in cultural studies'. Indeed, Gramsci's ideas have come to occupy a very special position in the best known of post-Marxist theories and strategies by the political left. Furthermore, the ubiquitous concern with the concept of civil society during the past 15 years has rekindled interest in Gramsci's reflections on the subject. Likewise, many of the issues and topics that currently preoccupy a broad spectrum of academic intellectuals – subaltern studies, post-colonialism and North–South relations, modernity and postmodernity, the relation between theory and praxis, the genealogy of Fascism, the socio-political dimensions of popular culture, hegemony and the manufacturing of consent, etc. – have motivated many a reading and rereading of Gramsci's texts.

In the 50 years since Gramsci first became an 'object' of study, his theories and concepts have left their mark on virtually every field in the humanities and the social sciences. His writings have been interpreted, appropriated, and even instrumentalized in many different and often conflicting ways. The amount of published material that now surrounds his work – John Cammett's updated *Bibliografia gramsciana* comprises over 10,000 items in 30 languages – threatens to overwhelm even the trained scholar and to paralyse or utterly confuse the uninitiated reader. Yet the sheer size of the Gramscian bibliography is also an important indication of the richness of Gramsci's legacy, the continuing relevance of his ideas, and the immensity of his contribution to contemporary thought. In many respects, Gramsci has become a 'classic' that demands to be read. Reading Gramsci, however, is not quite an easy undertaking; his most important writings are open-ended, fragmented, multidirectional explorations, reflections, and sketches. His prison notebooks have the character of a cluttered, seemingly disorganized intellectual laboratory. The well-trained scholar, no less than the first-time reader, would welcome an expert guide who could point to the salient features of Gramsci's work and bring into relief the basic designs underlying the surface complexity of different parts of his massive oeuvre. Similarly, a critical exposition of the most important existing treatments of Gramsci's works, together with a discussion of the potential usefulness of his insights to certain current lines of inquiry in the humanities and social sciences, would enable readers of Gramsci to appreciate better why (and in what ways) his ideas have a bearing on discussions about some of the most pressing social, cultural, and political issues of our time.

The multifaceted character of Gramsci's writing and the rich diversity of critical and theoretical work it has inspired cannot be treated effectively in a single, comprehensive study. A series of monographs, each dealing with a specific aspect of his work (but also cognizant of the many threads that link its various parts), would be a much more useful companion to the reader who is seeking to become better acquainted with Gramsci's legacy. Each volume in the 'Reading Gramsci' series is devoted to a theme that is especially prominent in Gramsci's work or to a field of study that has been strongly influenced by his ideas.

Abbreviations

1   INTRODUCTION

If one wants to study a conception of the world that has never been systematically expounded by its author-thinker, detailed work is required, and it has to be conducted with the most scrupulous accuracy and scientific honesty ... The search for the leitmotiv, the rhythm of the thought, more important than single, isolated quotations.

(PNII: 137)

This book is about the concept of culture in the writings of Antonio Gramsci and the potential relevance of Gramsci's approach to culture for contemporary anthropologists. The basic question it addresses is: what might anthropologists, and others interested in issues of culture, have to gain from reading this early twentieth-century Italian Marxist? Its aim is not so much to answer this question as to provide readers with the information they need to decide for themselves.

In the 30 years since the publication of the first major English edition of Gramsci's prison notebooks, Gramsci has become a name much cited by anthropologists. However, as Michel Foucault noted in a 1984 letter to the Gramsci scholar Joseph Buttigieg, Gramsci remains an author who is cited more often than he is genuinely known.[1] Most anthropologists it would seem get their Gramsci second-hand. A key interpreter of Gramsci for anthropologists is Raymond Williams; the section on hegemony in Williams' *Marxism and Literature* is probably the gloss on this much-argued-over Gramscian term most commonly cited by anthropologists. A reliance on interpreters and secondary sources is understandable given the nature of Gramsci's major work, the prison notebooks. For while these notebooks are without doubt one of the masterpieces of twentieth-century Marxism and have given rise to a vast literature,

1. 'Un auteur plus souvent cité que réellment connu', see PNI: xix (the first volume of Buttigieg's English translation of the complete prison notebooks, of which two volumes have so far been published; a list of the abbreviations I have used to refer to the different editions of Gramsci is given on p. x).

they are also a collection of fragments; a series of individual Notes[2] on related topics, some as short as a few sentences, some article length, that were never organized by Gramsci into a systematic whole. My hope is that this book will help provide a way into Gramsci's writings for those who would like to engage seriously with his thought but are not quite sure where to start.

I have chosen to organize this book around the concept of culture, firstly because this complicated and often slippery term is so central both to anthropology and to Gramsci's overall intellectual project, but secondly because what culture means in Gramsci's writings is often very different from what it has commonly meant in anthropology. Exploring this divergence and examining some of its implications is one of the book's major concerns. It is not, however, its only concern: this is also a book about the concept of class. Those who cite Gramsci's writings on culture are not always sufficiently aware that for Gramsci the notion of culture is always inextricably entangled with that of class. Culture for Gramsci is, at least in part, how class realities are *lived*. As I shall argue in subsequent chapters, an important part of the value of Gramsci's writings on culture is that they provide us with an insightful approach to the whole issue of class and inequality that is undogmatic, nuanced and never economically reductionist.

My intention, however, is not to force my particular interpretation of Gramsci on the reader. Rather I have attempted to provide an introduction to Gramsci's writings on culture that, while supplying the necessary context, allows him, as much as possible, to speak for himself. Given how daunting many readers find the prison notebooks, so that they turn instead to Gramsci's interpreters, I decided to structure the central chapters of this book almost as a Gramsci reader that would include extensive passages from Gramsci's own writings. My aim is to give readers the opportunity to judge for themselves what Gramsci understands by culture, and the place of culture within his overall project. My hope is that having read this book readers will both want to go on to read more of Gramsci and be in a better position to decide for themselves what Gramsci has to offer those interested in questions of culture. But let me not be too disingenuous. I would not have written this book if I did not think that Gramsci does indeed have much to offer anthropologists, so let me say a little more about what that might be.

2. 'Note' when capitalized refers to one of the Notes in the prison notebooks.

Why Should an Anthropologist Read Gramsci?

All too often anthropologists seem to assume, at least implicitly, that when Gramsci refers to culture he means what they mean by culture. Drawing attention to just how different Gramsci's concept of culture is can be a useful way of beginning to defamiliarize what is perhaps an over familiar term in anthropology. Reading Gramsci, and tracing out his complex and sometimes shifting definitions of culture, can offer the attentive anthropological reader a fresh approach to one of the discipline's fundamental concepts. Gramsci, read carefully, calls into question a number of basic assumptions as to the nature of 'culture' that seem to be deeply embedded in anthropological notions of culture. But also, I want to suggest, Gramsci's writings on culture can help anthropologists and anthropology as a discipline to think freshly about class, currently a rather unfashionable way of theorizing inequality.

One of the core concerns around which anthropology developed as a discipline was the need to understand societies encountered by an expanding West, societies that seemed to represent forms of social organization quite different from the West's own capitalist and market-based ones. While that concern certainly had its dark side, and the quest for knowledge was always entangled with a desire for control, anthropology can be considered as one of the very few disciplines that has always taken social worlds beyond those of the triumphant West seriously, and has attempted, albeit often unsuccessfully, to understand these 'other' worlds in their own terms. The 'othering' of various, often colonized societies has frequently, and justifiably, been much criticized in recent years. It is true, for instance, as Johannes Fabian has argued, that there was historically a powerful tendency in anthropology to map differences in social organization onto some broad evolutionary trajectory, so that, for example, hunters and gatherers existing in the contemporary world might be taken as representing the primordial past of humanity.[3] Nonetheless, while it may have been flawed in practice, this attempt to see the world from standpoints other than those of Western capitalist rationality seems to me to represent one of the major contributions of anthropology as a discipline. For example, freed from any evolutionary assumptions, it can potentially offer an interesting vantage point from which to examine the hegemonic (to use the

3. Fabian's 1983 *Time and the Other* is a particularly thoughtful and powerful critique.

Gramscian term) and taken-for-granted certainties of what is commonly referred to nowadays as our 'globalized' world. All too often the term globalization seems to involve the assumption that capitalism and democracy, as these have developed in certain societies in the North, represent a *telos* to which every human society everywhere is (or should be) aspiring.

Associated historically with anthropology's definition of its object of study as the elucidation of 'other' worlds were two powerful tendencies; firstly, a tendency to treat these worlds as bounded wholes that could be understood in isolation from the larger political, economic and social contexts, such as those of various colonial encounters, within which they were embedded, and secondly, a tendency to celebrate and even romanticize them. Both of these can be seen as the other side of the insistence that these non-Western, non-capitalist worlds should be taken seriously and not judged simply in terms of their lack of recognizable Western forms of social organization. As Malinowski put it in the Introduction to *Argonauts of the Western Pacific*, when laying out his version of what became arguably the defining anthropological research method, participant observation, non-Western societies should not to be seen as 'the sensational, wild and unaccountable world[s] of "savages"', but rather as 'well ordered communities, governed by law, behaving and thinking according to consistent principles' (1984[1922]: 9–10). This stress on the order and logic of apparently 'savage' societies has been a persistent theme in much anthropology.

The idea behind participant observation is that through living for extended periods of time in close daily contact with a small group of people the anthropologist comes to see the world they inhabit through their eyes. In the case of colonial anthropologists this necessarily had a tendency to undermine any unquestioned acceptance of the colonialist world view. It is true that colonial anthropologists always remained a part of the colonial elite, and that the larger intellectual project within which they worked had to an important extent emerged out of the realities of colonialism; nonetheless, at the same time that intellectual project had built into it certain tensions and contradictions. It is not coincidental that Jomo Kenyatta, later to become the first president of an independent Kenya, studied anthropology with Malinowski at the London School of Economics. Anthropology may indeed have been entangled with the rationalization and legitimation of colonialism but it also created an interesting space within which critiques of colonialism, rooted in views of the colonial world which saw that world from the vantage point of the colonized, could emerge. However, the focus on the perspective of the subordinated, and the need to assert the legitimacy of that perspective in the face of an often dismissive colonial regime, could lead to anthropologists writing overly celebratory and sometimes romanticized accounts of the 'other' worlds they studied.

Gramsci's analytical starting point was very different from that of academic anthropology. Not only was he not an anthropologist, he was first and foremost a political activist whose primary concern was to bring about political change in Italy. Prior to his imprisonment by Mussolini's Fascist regime, he had been one of the leaders of the Italian Communist Party. He was certainly deeply interested in mapping the cultural worlds of those he termed subaltern, the peasants and other non-elite groups, but his interest stemmed from his awareness that to have any chance of success a revolutionary movement needs to be genuinely popular with the mass of the population. For Gramsci any would-be revolutionaries need to understand the cultural realities they are bent on transforming, apart from any other reason because counterhegemonies, capable of challenging in an effective way the dominant hegemony, emerge out of the lived reality of oppressed people's day-to-day lives. Any such embryonic counterhegemony would, as he saw it, necessarily emerge as an incoherent jumble requiring the work of intellectuals to provide it with coherence and intellectual rigour, but unless they engaged with such raw material those intellectuals, no matter how brilliant and committed, were doomed to irrelevance.

Gramsci's concern here is clearly a very different one from those that gave rise to the discipline of anthropology. Nonetheless, Gramsci's writings can be enormously illuminating for anthropologists. His approach to the analysis of the cultural worlds of peasants and other non-elite groups, for instance, provides anthropologists with potentially thought-provoking accounts of those worlds that, while taking them very seriously, never romanticize or sentimentalize those who inhabit them, nor overestimate the logical coherence of the narratives such worlds produce. Very importantly, Gramsci always recognized that subaltern groups are not homogeneous, that they have their own hierarchies and inequalities, and that it cannot be assumed that all the members of a particular subaltern group see the world in the same way. Gramsci was also aware that however isolated and seemingly remote such communities may appear, they are in fact embedded in larger political and economic realities. Their heterogeneity and their embeddedness raise the question of what analytical framework we should use to understand these other, often marginalized worlds.

There has always been an interesting tension associated with the anthropological project of searching out, through participant observation, how the world appears from some other vantage point than that of a hegemonic, Western rationality. To what extent can, or should, anthropologists writing about different places, and different ways of seeing things, use the maps of the social world those they study themselves use? Should they use local categories and terms, local accounts of why the world is as it is, or should they translate these local, sometimes parochial social maps into the analytical maps of the larger world they inhabit as professional intellectuals? There is, of course, no one simple answer to this question; it all depends on the specific context. Gramsci's usefulness here, I would suggest, derives from his insistence that ultimately the most important question is that of power: who has power and who does not? who is the oppressor and who the oppressed? and what are the specificities of the relations of oppression? If we want to understand how power works in a small rural community in Sardinia, for instance, we need to understand both the larger forces that bind Sardinia and Italy itself into more encompassing economic and political entities, and how the realities of power are experienced and named by individuals within the community itself. For Gramsci, neither the larger, nor the local understanding on its own is adequate because in isolation neither is capable of producing effective, plausible political narratives; and as a committed activist, Gramsci's ultimate concern is with understandings of the world that can mobilize the oppressed to overcome their oppression. The problem here is that accounts of power that identify its larger structural underpinnings tend not to resonate with those they must mobilize, while narrow, parochial accounts are unable to see the larger forces at work. It should also be noted that for Gramsci, any adequate account of power is also an account of class.

In the context of analysis of societies of the South,[4] I would argue, Gramsci's insistence that the key relation is that of oppressor and oppressed is a useful corrective to the common assumption that the primary opposition in these societies is one between tradition and

4. The currently preferred term for what used to be called the Third World, or the developing world.

modernity. In Chapter 3 I develop the argument that this assumption is bound up with the concept of culture as this came to be understood within the anthropological mainstream. But the characterization of a whole range of conflicts in postcolonial societies and those of the South generally in terms of a fundamental opposition between the 'traditional' and the 'modern' is also popular within those societies themselves. In any society in the South there are likely to be some who argue that their society needs to become 'modern' and leave the old traditional ways behind, while others insist that modernity is a false god in the name of which authentic 'tradition' is being lost, and that there should be a return to 'tradition'. What is generally agreed, it would seem, by many intellectuals and non-intellectuals in both North and South, is that mapping the contemporary world involves understanding this basic opposition between the 'traditional' and the 'modern'. Within anthropology, which has always prided itself on the attention it pays to people's own accounts of their world, the fact that this opposition is used by the very people the anthropologist is trying to understand tends to legitimize it. But does the fact that those within a given society use these categories in constructing their accounts of their world, necessarily mean that this is indeed the best way of 'naming' what is going on? There is much in Gramsci that can help us as anthropologists to think through this particular issue.

As an anthropologist I remain convinced that the discipline has developed important areas of expertise over the course of its history, even if some of this expertise remains entangled with some less helpful legacies. In sum, why anthropologists should read Gramsci, I would suggest, is because he can help us free ourselves from some of the unhelpful baggage that the anthropological concept of culture tends to carry, often in subtle, implicit ways, while simultaneously suggesting potentially productive ways, that build on our disciplinary expertise, of thinking about culture and class. He provides us, that is, with suggestive, sometimes provocative, insights into how we might rethink the whole complex terrain of culture, class and inequality. The value of Gramsci's approach is, firstly, that it recognizes the reality of fundamental, systematic inequalities, while rejecting any crude economic reductionism. Secondly, there is Gramsci's insistence that we take seriously the complexity and specificity of the cultural worlds different people inhabit – and pay serious attention to their own mappings of those worlds.

Organization of the Book

The two chapters of Part I provide context. Chapter 2 gives a brief sketch of Gramsci's life and discusses the relationship between his life and his writings, explaining the profoundly political nature of his intellectual project in the prison notebooks. Gramsci, writing in his prison cell, may appear to have been removed from active political life, but for him his intellectual work and his writings in prison were a way of continuing to engage in the political events of his time. His concern in his notebooks was to provide the rigorous analysis of inequality and injustice that is a crucial part of any struggle for social transformation; societies can only be transformed if we understand them. Chapter 3 focuses on the concept of culture in anthropology. I should say at once that my discussion here is a very partial and limited one. All I have tried to do is to draw attention to some assumptions about the nature of culture and cultures, associated, I would argue, with the history of the emergence of anthropology as a discipline, that have played an important shaping role in how many (although not all) anthropologists have approached questions of culture. While the ways in which anthropologists approach issues of culture may have been transformed in recent years, and many might argue that these assumptions belong to the history of the discipline rather than to its present practice, it seems to me that fragments of these older understandings of culture often continue to haunt the work of contemporary anthropologists.

The three chapters of Part II attempt to map out Gramsci's very different approach to culture and its inextricability from the issue of class. I have tried to do this using, as far as possible, Gramsci's own words. This has meant including relatively extensive extracts from Gramsci's writings; the chapters in fact take the form of something like an annotated reader with passages from Gramsci organized thematically. The themes around which I have structured the three chapters are: culture and history; subaltern culture; and intellectuals and the production of culture. Throughout the book, but particularly in these chapters, I have deliberately kept footnotes to a minimum with the idea of keeping the reader focused on what Gramsci himself has to say rather than immediately moving to the debates among Gramsci scholars. Also with the aim of focusing the attention of the reader on Gramsci's own mapping of the terrain of culture, I have largely refrained in these chapters from drawing attention to exactly how his maps differ from those of anthropologists, leaving this for the final chapter. My hope is that having provided this kind of structured introduction to Gramsci's writings, as well as a generous sampling of the writings themselves, the interested reader, who may well quarrel with some of my readings of Gramsci, will move on to reading the now numerous editions of different selections of his writings now available in English.[5] A full list of these is provided at the beginning of the bibliography.

In the final chapter I turn to how Gramsci has been used by anthropologists, looking at how he entered the anthropological conversation and at the interesting role played here by Williams' *Marxism and Literature*. I go on to look at the theorization of culture and class in the work of Eric Wolf, an anthropologist central to the renewal of a political economy approach. Finally, I turn to two examples of recent uses of Gramsci by the anthropologists Matthew Gutmann and Roger Keesing. Throughout this chapter my concern is to think through how anthropologists might engage in more substantive ways with this often challenging and difficult theorist; how Gramsci might become known and not merely cited.

Let me end this introduction with a few brief acknowledgements. First and foremost I want to thank Joseph Buttigieg who suggested the idea of a book about Gramsci and anthropology and has been enormously supportive throughout the book's gestation. Both he and Frank Rosengarten read the manuscript; I have benefited greatly from their deep knowledge of Gramsci and his writings. The anthropologists Shirley Lindenbaum, Steven Striffler, Michael Blim and Steven Caton also read the manuscript and gave me many helpful suggestions. I also benefited very much from the comments of Bruce Knauft and the other, anonymous, reader, both of whom read the manuscript for the University of California Press. From the City University of New York I received a PSC-CUNY grant which gave me some precious time to work on the project.

5. In common with many others who write on Gramsci in English, I have relied on the English translations of Gramsci's writings. Almost none of Gramsci's writings remain untranslated into English. For those readers interested in Italian debates on Gramsci, there is a series of volumes edited by Martin James (2001) from Routledge which provides a wide selection of previously untranslated essays on Gramsci by Italian scholars.

Part I

Contexts

2 Gramsci's Life and Work

It seems to me that it is not difficult to find splendid formulas for
life, but it is difficult to live.

(PLII: 33)

This chapter sketches out some of the main contours of the political
and intellectual landscape within which Gramsci and his work need
to be located. Gramsci, like all theorists, was the product of a
particular time and place; and his writings are deeply entangled in
that historical moment. If his work is to be relevant and useful to
anthropologists concerned with different times and places, it is
necessary to untangle some of those threads and look at their relationship to the larger intellectual and political contexts in which he
lived and worked. It is also important to look at the kind of theorist
he was and at the form his writings took. Why, for instance, are the
prison notebooks so fragmentary? Was it simply because of the con-
straints of writing them while incarcerated in a Fascist jail, or were
there deeper reasons to do with the very nature of his intellectual
project? Let me begin, however, with a brief account of his life,[1] and
his place in Italian history.

'Times of Iron and Fire'

Writing to his mother soon after his arrest, Gramsci reflected that
being forced to confront poverty and hardship as a child, as he had
been, had certain advantages. He feared that the more comfortable
circumstances in which his niece, Edmea, was being raised might

---

1. For those interested in a fuller account there are three full-length biog-
raphies of Gramsci in English, by Giuseppe Fiori (1990), Alastair Davidson
(1977) and Dante Germino (1990). Fiori's *Antonio Gramsci: Life of a
Revolutionary*, first published in Italian in 1965, is a straightforward life
that draws heavily on the reminiscences of those who knew Gramsci.
Davidson's *Antonio Gramsci: Towards an Intellectual Biography* explores in
considerable detail Gramsci's intellectual and political development and
his place within the history of Italian communism. It also includes a
detailed account of Gramsci's childhood in Sardinia. Germino's *Antonio
Gramsci: Architect of a New Politics* pays particular attention to Gramsci's
early life and his pre-prison writings.

end up 'creating in her a certain softness and a certain sentimental-
ity that are not to be recommended in these times of iron and fire
in which we live' (PLI: 77) Gramsci's times were certainly ones of
'iron and fire'.

Antonio Gramsci was born in 1891 in Sardinia, the fourth of seven
children of a minor civil servant. He was always a frail child and,
probably as a result of Potts disease (tuberculosis of the spine), he
grew up hunchbacked. His adult height was less than five feet. When
Gramsci was seven his father fell foul of local political intrigues and
was imprisoned for embezzlement for almost five years. The family
was thrown into poverty and after completing elementary school,
the far from robust nine-year-old Gramsci was obliged to go to work
to help eke out the family income. He was able to resume his
schooling two years later but the family's finances remained
precarious throughout his childhood. His father emerged from
prison a broken man and only worked sporadically after his ordeal;
in later life Gramsci recalled his mother's extraordinary hard work
and single-minded devotion to her family. In 1911, Gramsci won a
small scholarship to attend university in Turin, the heart of the
rapidly expanding Italian automobile industry. Apart from a few
visits to see his family, he was never to return to Sardinia.

Gramsci's family may have been poor when he was growing up,
but his background was not a peasant one. On his father's side he
came from the stratum that provided minor state bureaucrats. His
mother's family were a little lower on the social scale but reasonably
prosperous, and she, unlike the majority of Sardinian women at that
time, was literate and a keen reader. The sale of a small piece of land
she had inherited was crucial to the family's survival during its years
of hardship.

Gramsci, however, certainly saw peasant life close up as a boy and
in later life, probably as a result of his early experiences, had a clear,
unsentimental attitude to its realities that avoided both romanti-
cization and demonization. One of his class mates at the *lycée* in
Cagliari (Sardinia's largest city), which he attended for a couple of
years before leaving for Turin, recalled his irritation with Sardinian
authors who exoticized and romanticized their homeland. 'Sardinia
wasn't all waterfalls, sheep-folds, vendettas, and mothers weeping
over their dead sons, he objected. It was also miners working
hundreds of feet under the earth for Belgian capital, and getting in
exchange not hospitals, not schools and blankets, but military intervention the moment they dared to ask for anything at all' (Fiori,

1990: 56). Even before leaving Sardinia, Gramsci had begun reading socialist publications supplied by his older brother, Gennaro. He had also begun reading the neo-Hegelian philosopher, Benedetto Croce, one of the most influential Italian intellectuals of the twentieth century, and Croce's writings exercised a profound influence over the young Gramsci. Later, as he got deeper into the ideas of Marx, Gramsci became increasingly critical of Croce but he remained for Gramsci the pre-eminent Italian philosopher of his time and in the prison notebooks Gramsci frequently engages in explicit or implicit debate with Croce and Crocean idealism.[2]

Once in Turin, Gramsci became increasingly involved in socialist politics and began writing for various socialist newspapers. The university scholarship he had been awarded was tiny so that he was forced to rent the cheapest rooms, often having to go without heat, and unable to afford anything but the most meagre diet. The effects of these poor living conditions were particularly serious in Gramsci's case because of his generally weak health. Throughout his life Gramsci was plagued by ill heath and recurrent health crises. The rigours of his childhood and his iron determination, however, had instilled in him work habits that enabled him to keep going even when ill until, pushed beyond its limits, his body would simply collapse.

Gramsci's academic studies came to focus on the study of language and literature, and his analytic approach right through the prison notebooks remained deeply marked by his training in philology.[3] But while Gramsci never lost his fascination with language, his political involvement increasingly crowded out his academic work. By 1916 he had abandoned his formal studies towards a degree and was devoting himself full-time to politics. He was also writing a regular column for the socialist newspaper *Avanti!* In addition he contributed regular theatre reviews; throughout his life Gramsci remained fascinated by literature, both high and low, in all its forms. In 1917, in the wake of an unsuccessful insurrection in Turin and the subsequent arrest of most of the prominent leftists, Gramsci

2. Frank Rosengarten, the editor of Gramsci's prison letters puts it this way: '[Croce] was for Gramsci what Hegel had been for Marx, an exponent and systematizer of idealist thought in relation to whom Gramsci worked out the basic features of his own historical-materialist conception of life' (PLI: 85).
3. See Joseph Buttigieg's Introduction to PNI for an extended discussion of Gramsci's philological approach.

became secretary of the Turin Section of the Italian Socialist Party (PSI) and editor of the socialist newspaper, *Il Grido del Popolo*. Like many other European leftists, Gramsci and his Italian colleagues were caught up in the whirling excitement of the Russian Revolution and what seemed to be an unstoppable revolutionary tide washing over the whole European continent. In 1919, by which time *Il Grido del Popolo* had ceased publication, Gramsci together with a group of like minded socialists, Angelo Tasca, Umberto Terracini and Palmiro Togliatti (all later to be prominent members of the Italian Communist Party), founded *L'Ordine Nuovo* (The New Order) to which they gave the subtitle, A Review of Socialist Culture. Within a year, however, *L'Ordine Nuovo* had become much more than this; it became in fact the journal of the Turin factory council movement. This movement saw factory councils based in the huge Fiat plants as potentially providing an equivalent to the Soviets (the organizations of workers and soldiers that gave the Soviet Union its name) that were seen as the basis of the new revolutionary Russia. The years 1919 to 1920 in Turin saw an epic struggle between the Fiat management and their workers with a month-long strike by the metal workers during which they occupied the factories, and a ten-day general strike throughout Turin to which the state responded with a massive show of force. The outcome was a crushing defeat for the Turin workers and their factory councils, and the consolidation of the Fiat management's power. The reasons for this defeat, and whether a different political strategy on the part of the Turin socialists could have prevented it, is one of the questions shaping Gramsci's intellectual project in the prison notebooks.

By the beginning of 1921 the growing split within the PSI, and its perceived lack of support for the Turin strikers, had convinced those on the left of the Party, including Gramsci, that they needed to break with the Party and form an Italian Communist Party (PCd'I). By this time, however, the great revolutionary tide of the immediate postwar period was ebbing and the PCd'I, from its founding in January 1921 until it was finally driven completely underground in 1926, was always a party on the defensive, attempting to hold out against the new Fascist tide flowing across Europe, but from a position of weakness rather than strength. In early 1922 Gramsci was selected by the PCd'I as their representative on the executive committee of the Communist International in Moscow and he spent the next 18 months in the Soviet Union. Close to physical collapse on his arrival he was sent to a sanatorium to recuperate. While there he met and fell in love with Julca ('Giulia') Schucht, a Russian woman of German descent whose family had spent many years in exile in Italy during the Czarist period. They married in 1923 and two sons were born in 1924 and 1926. After Gramsci left Moscow, however, husband and wife had only a few, scattered months together, as Gramsci and the PCd'I worked feverishly to maintain the Party under the growing fascist threat. Gramsci never saw his second son.

In October 1922, while Gramsci was in Moscow, Mussolini and the Fascists came to power in Italy after the fascists had staged what became known as the 'March on Rome'. As the Fascists tightened their hold on power and increasingly abandoned all pretence of maintaining parliamentary democracy, the space for any opposition shrank, with communists, and anyone perceived as being in any way leftist, being arrested, driven into exile or murdered by Fascist vigilantes. Just how little respect Mussolini had for legal niceties may be obvious in hindsight but in the early twenties as he was consolidating his power it was by no means so clear. Gramsci returned to Italy in May of 1924 shortly after having been elected as a parliamentary deputy, which, in theory, should have protected him from arrest. In November 1926, in spite of his supposed immunity, Gramsci was arrested and put on trial the following year, together with 21 other PCd'I leaders. The outcome of the trial was never in doubt; Mussolini was determined to silence the PCd'I and all those on trial knew they could expect long prison sentences. During the trial the Prosecutor famously demanded that in the case of Gramsci, 'We must prevent this brain from functioning for twenty years.' In the event Gramsci received one of the longest sentences: 20 years, 4 months and 5 days.

Gramsci had long accepted that he was, as it were, engaged in a war; one side representing the interests of capital and the Fascists, the other those of the subordinated and the subaltern. He had also accepted that he might well end up a casualty of that war. As he wrote to his mother while awaiting trial, 'Just think, it's about ten years now that I've been in an atmosphere of struggle and that I have become sufficiently tempered; I could have been killed a dozen times and instead I'm still alive: this in itself is a point of incalculable gain' (PLI: 116). But while Mussolini might have succeeded in confining him in prison, Gramsci was determined that, to the extent that it was possible, he would use the time productively and study; prison would not stop his brain functioning. The very first letter in the two-volume collection of his prison letters is to his landlady. After apologizing for the trouble and inconvenience he has caused her, Gramsci first asks her to send him some of his underclothes and then, at much greater length, details which of his books he wants her to send him. During his long years in prison he was able to obtain all those books not forbidden by the prison authorities (not allowed, for instance, was anything by Marx or Engels) thanks to the generosity of Piero Sraffa. Sraffa was an Italian economist and a good friend of Gramsci's, as well as a communist sympathizer, who moved to Britain in 1927. He arranged for Gramsci to have an account with a Milan bookshop for which Sraffa paid. Getting permission to write in his cell was harder for Gramsci and it was not until January 1929 that he finally obtained this and was able to begin what would become the prison notebooks.

Gramsci's health, always precarious, was continually undermined by the prison regime and by the time he was released in April 1937, after an international campaign on his behalf and having had his sentence shortened a little by various amnesties, he was near death. He had already been moved from prison to a series of clinics and he died at Quisisana clinic in Rome a few days after his formal release, having suffered a cerebral haemorrhage. At his side was his sister-in-law, Tatiana Schucht, who had been his main support during his prison years. His wife, who was herself often in fragile health, had remained in Moscow with their children throughout his imprisonment. It was Tatiana who supplied Gramsci with the notebooks in which he wrote. She also provided him with whatever other small comforts the prison authorities would allow; something that sometimes led to tussles between Tatiana and Gramsci when he felt that she had overstepped the mark of what was appropriate for a prisoner. Gramsci was adamant that he would not beg his jailors for any special favours, while insisting equally firmly on what he considered to be his rights as a prisoner under the penal code. Gramsci continued to work on the notebooks until the middle of 1935 by which time his health had finally deteriorated to a point where it was no longer possible for him to write. It was Tatiana who, together with his final cell-mate, ensured that the prison notebooks were first smuggled out of the prison, accompanying him to the various clinics, and then transported for safe keeping to Moscow.

To understand Gramsci's project in the prison notebooks it is important not to lose sight of either the committed political engagement out of which they emerged or the circumstances in which they were composed. They were above all an intervention, of the only kind possible for Gramsci in his prison cell, in what he saw as the fundamental struggle between the interests of capital and the interests of those oppressed by the dominant capitalist order. Power might take the form of the iron fist of Mussolini's Fascists or the gentler, gloved hand of bourgeois democracy, but these were both forms of *capitalist* power. The rest of this chapter traces out some of the main contours of the overall intellectual project of the prison notebooks, looking at Gramsci's relationship to Marxism, the kind of theorist he was, and why the prison notebooks took the form they did.

'History in All its Infinite Variety and Multiplicity'[4]

A few months after his arrest and imprisonment, and long before he obtained permission to write in his cell, Gramsci wrote a letter to Tatiana in which he sketched out a provisional plan of the studies he hoped to carry out. 'I am obsessed', he said, using (a little ironically) a phrase from Goethe, 'by this idea: that I should do something *"für ewig"* [for eternity] ... I would like to concentrate intensely and systematically on some subject that would absorb and provide a center to my inner life' (PLI: 83). He went on to outline four topics of study: Italian intellectuals; comparative linguistics; Pirandello; and the serial novel and popular taste in literature. All four subjects he saw as at root concerned with 'the creative spirit of the people in its diverse stages and degrees of development ...' (PLI: 84). While the prison notebooks explore more topics than these, and the study of Pirandello did not in fact materialize, running through the notebooks is indeed a concern with 'the creative spirit of the people'; or, to put it in slightly different terms, with how the Italian people (both intellectuals and the mass of the people), at different times and in different places, have understood and imagined the circumstances in which they live, and the role of those imaginings in Italian history.

What Gramsci is laying out here in this preliminary sketch for his prison studies is in fact very much a cultural project – as long as we understand culture in a broad sense. Gramsci's interest in cultural questions is present in even his earliest writings. According to Buttigieg, the *L'Ordine Nuovo* group's concern with cultural issues

---

4. 'The experience on which the philosophy of praxis is based cannot be schematised; it is history in all its infinite variety and multiplicity, ...' (SPN: 428).

(recall that *L'Ordine Nuovo* described itself as a 'Review of Socialist Culture') was largely the result of Gramsci's influence. In subsequent chapters I discuss the concept of culture and some of its many different meanings, as well as mapping out Gramsci's usage of this complex and slippery term. First, however, it is necessary to provide an overview of the kind of thinker Gramsci was, and of his general approach to the questions that interested him.

A good place to begin is Gramsci's concern to do something '*für ewig*'. Is it not rather odd that this committed political activist should describe, albeit with ironising quotation marks, his study plans in terms of Goethe's notion of disinterested '*für ewig*' scholarship? Relevant here is Gramsci's profound awareness that however much a theorist may wish to break with the past and with old ideas and language, the new is always a response to the past and cannot but remain linked to that past. Paradoxically, the new, however revolutionary it may in fact be, must (if it is to be intelligible) be expressed, at least initially, in existing language and concepts. Gramsci, who was always concerned that his ideas should be as accessible as possible, often adopted a strategy of taking an existing term and, as it were, stretching and even subverting its meaning. Gramsci, so to speak, brushes language 'against the grain', to borrow one of Walter Benjamin's metaphors.[5] Here in a more playful but similar fashion Gramsci deliberately chooses a Goethean phrase, *für ewig*, saturated with the associations of German idealism that Gramsci, like Marx, rejected, and gives it a twist so that it actually calls into question the whole idea of a lofty, disinterested scholarship beyond the tainted world of politics.

Gramsci is, however, by the term '*für ewig*' also drawing attention to an important distinction between his journalistic writings up to his imprisonment which had been, as he put it in another later letter to Tatiana, 'written for the day' (PLII: 66), and his more in-depth studies. The difference was between writing often polemical articles in the context of the day-to-day struggles within first the Socialist Party, then the Communist Party, both of which were riven by often bitter debates over strategy and tactics; and the less pressured exploration of issues in a broader and generally more 'scholarly' way that the isolation of prison allowed.[6] Gramsci was always very aware

5. Anne Showstack Sassoon explores this aspect of Gramsci's analytical strategy very interestingly in 'Gramsci's Subversion of the Language of Politics' (Sassoon, 2000).
6. See PNI: 9–11 for Buttigieg's helpful discussion of the '*für ewig*' letter.

that there is a big difference between analysis that is concerned with gaining a fundamental, theoretical understanding of political, social and economic realities (often of the past, which affords the luxury of hindsight) based on careful scholarship, and the strategizing demanded by the far messier world of day-to-day politics. For him, these two forms of analysis are equally necessary. What is especially important is to understand the ways in which they interact with each other. As he was to write in one Note on historical studies:

> [S]uch analyses cannot and must not be ends in themselves (unless the intention is merely to write a chapter of past history), but acquire significance only if they serve to justify a particular practical activity, or initiative of will. They reveal the points of least resistance, at which the force of will can be most fruitfully applied; they suggest immediate tactical operations; they indicate how a campaign of political agitation may best be launched, what language will best be understood by the masses, etc.
>
> (SPN: 185)

In other words, the '*für ewig*' analysis Gramsci, the committed activist, had in mind was important in so far as it could inform contemporary political struggles, but while it might *suggest* political strategies, it should not be seen as providing any kind of predetermined answers. It is, therefore, in this sense a little removed and 'disinterested'.

If Gramsci's initial ideas for what he might study in prison are in a broad sense concerned with issues of culture, what culture meant to Gramsci needs to be understood within a Marxist framework. For Gramsci culture and class have their roots in the same basic power relations. Gramsci's Marxism may be, as I shall try to show, an extremely flexible one that has little if anything in common with the rigid dogmas that came to characterize the Stalinism of the later Soviet Union, nonetheless it is important to stress that Gramsci saw his intellectual project in the prison notebooks as rooted in Marxism, just as his political activity prior to his arrest had been. Gramsci took it as axiomatic, for instance, that it is the fundamental economic relations in society, which Marx termed the infrastructure or base, that provide the dynamic of history. Not that he saw there as being any simple one-to-one relationship between the economic structure and the concrete social realities that develop in particular societies at particular times. For Gramsci this relationship is precisely the problem that needs to be studied, the fundamental question is, as he put it, 'how does the historical movement arise on the structural base? ... This is furthermore the crux of all the questions that have arisen around the philosophy of praxis' (SPN: 431–2). Philosophy of praxis is the term Gramsci often uses in the prison notebooks to refer to Marxism. He took the term from Antonio Labriola (1843–1904), one of the earliest and most original Italian Marxist scholars, whose work had a considerable impact on Gramsci's Marxism. Gramsci used a number of circumlocutions so as not to arouse the suspicions of the prison censors who read everything he wrote – such as referring to Lenin (whose full name was Vladimir Ilich Lenin) as Ilich – and the term philosophy of praxis has often been explained as one of these. This has been strongly rejected, however, by some Gramscian scholars who argue that it in fact describes very precisely Gramsci's understanding of Marxism.[7] What is indisputable is that while Gramsci had little direct access to Marx's writings in prison, Marx is present throughout the notebooks. The *Theses on Feuerbach*, *The Communist Manifesto*, *A Contribution to the Critique of Political Economy*, and *The Holy Family* seem to have been especially important to Gramsci.

While Gramsci saw basic economic relations as the ultimate shapers of society and, contrary to the assumptions of many commentators, as Buttigieg emphasises, devoted a good deal of space in the prison notebooks to economic issues, he was also highly critical of the often crude economistic determinism so prevalent among his generation of Marxists. The following comment captures his scorn for this kind of reductionism.

In its most widespread form as economistic superstition, the philosophy of praxis loses a great part of its capacity for cultural expansion among the top layer of intellectuals, however much it may gain among the popular masses and the second-rate intellectuals, who do not intend to overtax their brains but still wish to appear to know everything, etc. As Engels wrote, many people find it very convenient to think that they can have the whole of history and all political and philosophical wisdom in their pockets at little cost and no trouble, concentrated into a few short formulae.

(SPN: 164)

7. This argument is developed persuasively in the Introduction to the complete German edition of the prison notebooks (Haug et al., 1994). This section of the Introduction has been published in an English translation in Haug (2000).

One way Gramsci conceptualized the character of any given political event, social relation, social group, etc., was in terms of whether or not it was 'organically' linked to that which was fundamental, in other words the basic economic structure of society. 'Organic' was a very important term in Gramsci's vocabulary. He continually contrasted the organic with that which was not organic as in these examples (in all cases the emphasis is mine). The first two are both from a Note on 'The Organisation of Education and of Culture'.

> The crisis of the curriculum and organisation of the schools ... is to a great extent an aspect and a ramification of the more comprehensive and general *organic* crisis.
>
> (SPN: 26)

> It may also be observed that deliberative bodies tend to an ever-increasing extent to distinguish their activity into two '*organic*' aspects: into the deliberative activity which is their essence, and into technical-cultural activity in which the questions upon which they have to take decisions are first examined by experts and analysed scientifically. This latter activity has already created a whole bureaucratic body, with a new structure; for apart from the specialised departments of experts who prepare the technical material for the deliberative bodies, a second body of functionaries is created – more or less disinterested 'volunteers', selected variously from industry, from the banks, from finance houses. This is one of the mechanisms by means of which the career bureaucracy eventually came to control the democratic regimes and parliaments; now the mechanism is being *organically* extended, and is absorbing into its sphere the great specialists of private enterprise, which thus comes to control both regimes and bureaucracies. What is involved is a necessary, *organic* development which tends to integrate the personnel specialised in the technique of politics with personnel specialised in the concrete problems of administering the essential practical activities of the great and complex national societies of today. Hence every attempt to exorcise these tendencies from the outside produces no result other than moralistic sermons and rhetorical lamentations.
>
> (SPN: 27–8)

Perhaps Gramsci's best known use of 'organic' is in his distinction between organic and traditional intellectuals. This is discussed at length in Chapter 6; here I just want to give a couple of quotations to illustrate Gramsci's use of the concept of 'organic' in this context.

> It can be observed that the *'organic'* intellectuals which every new class creates alongside itself and elaborates in the course of its development, are for the most part 'specialisations' of partial aspects of the primitive activity of the new social type which the new class has brought into prominence.
>
> (SPN: 6)

> It should be possible both to measure the *'organic quality'* [*organicità*] of the various intellectual strata and their degree of connection with a fundamental social group, and to establish a gradation of their functions and of the superstructures from the bottom to the top (from the structural base upwards).
>
> (SPN: 12)

To grasp the essence of what Gramsci's understands by 'organic' it is helpful to remember Gramsci's training in philology and the meaning of 'organic' in philology: 'Belonging to the etymological structure of a word; not secondary or fortuitous' (*OED*). This distinction is central to Gramsci's Marxism, allowing him to distinguish between that which is indeed shaped by fundamental economic forces and all the varied and unpredictable contingencies of history. Of course, this neat distinction never maps in any simple way onto the messy confusion of reality, but it can provide a helpful guide through that confusion.

For Gramsci the insights of Marx and Engels are starting points, ways of framing the important questions, but coming up with answers to those questions for particular contexts requires the hard work of careful analysis of the relevant empirical realities. There is a limit to what theory alone can tell us about actual societies. 'The experience on which the philosophy of praxis is based cannot be schematised; it is history in all its infinite variety and multiplicity ...' (SPN: 428).

Certain fundamental economic realities may open up certain possibilities but whether or not those possibilities will be acted upon can never be known in advance. For this to happen such possibilities need to be recognized and embodied in actual political movements. One of the thinkers in whom Gramsci was particularly interested, and wrote about at length in the prison notebooks, was the great Italian political theorist of the Renaissance, Niccolò Machiavelli.[8] What fascinated Gramsci about Machiavelli was above all how Machiavelli could be seen as the theorist of a particular historical path (the creation of an Italian national state) which Italy could have taken at the time of Machiavelli but did not. He put it this way in a letter to Tatiana, commenting on the flood of articles on the four-hundredth anniversary of Machiavelli's death:

> I was struck by the fact that none of the writers on the centenary made a connection between Machiavelli's books and the development of the States in all of Europe during the same historical period ... they did not see that Machiavelli was the theoretician of the national States ruled by absolute monarchies, i.e. that he in Italy theorized about what in England was energetically accomplished by Elizabeth, in Spain by Ferdinand the Catholic, in France by Louis XI, and in Russia by Ivan the Terrible, even though he was not and could not be acquainted with some of these national experiences, which in reality represented the historical problem of the epoch that Machiavelli had the genius to intuit and present systematically.
>
> (PLI: 153)

It is this sense of history as a field of possibilities that explains Gramsci's emphasis on the importance of both ideas and political will. Turning historical possibilities into actualities demands the recognition of these possibilities and the articulation of them in the form of persuasive narratives capable of moving large groups of people and convincing them that certain actions are not only possible, but desirable, or inevitable, or the will of God, or the logic of history, etc., etc. Nothing is inevitable in history,

> In reality one can 'scientifically' foresee only the struggle, but not the concrete moments of the struggle, which cannot but be the results of opposing forces in continuous movement ... In reality one can 'foresee' to the extent that one acts, to the extent that one applies a voluntary effort and therefore contributes concretely to creating the result 'foreseen'. Prediction reveals itself thus not

8. Benedetto Fontana's *Hegemony and Power: On the Relation between Gramsci and Machiavelli* is an excellent exploration of Gramsci and Machiavelli.

as a scientific act of knowledge, but as the abstract expression of the effort made, the practical way of creating a collective will.

(SPN: 438)

If an idea is shared by enough people it becomes, as it were, a material force. *L'Ordine Nuovo* carried on its masthead the slogan, 'pessimism of the intellect, optimism of the will'. Gramsci had taken this from the French socialist Romain Rolland, and it sums up nicely Gramsci's political philosophy. While it is crucial to have a clear-headed and totally realistic analysis of any political situation, effective political action, particularly on the part of those outside the ruling elite, demands a political will that believes in the possibility of success.

Every philosopher is, and cannot but be, convinced that he expresses the unity of the human spirit, that is, the unity of history and nature. Indeed, if such a conviction did not exist, men would not act, they would not create new history, philosophies would not become ideologies and would not in practice assume the fanatical granite compactness of the 'popular beliefs' which assume the same energy as 'material forces'.

(SPN: 404)

Another way of describing this transformation of ideas and beliefs into 'material forces' capable of acting in history is as their circulation beyond a limited group of intellectuals to the point where they become part of a general culture.

Gramsci himself inhabited the broad Marxist culture of his time, and like any culture, this one had its own characteristic forms of expression and vocabulary. Understanding what the concept of culture in general means to Gramsci involves inhabiting, at least to some degree, his general intellectual landscape. Throughout this book, therefore, from time to time I deliberately use what may seem to some readers some rather old-fashioned Marxist language precisely because it is within that intellectual landscape that Gramsci thought and wrote.

I want now to return to the point I made earlier about Gramsci 'brushing language against the grain'. To me one of the most interesting aspects of Gramsci's approach to the analysis of society is the way he continually questions and problematizes large, abstract concepts such as 'culture', 'nation', 'state', and 'democracy'. For Gramsci the meaning of such concepts is always contingent on the context in which they are being used and the particular questions that are being asked. This was true even of the young Gramsci. In 1918, for instance, we find him writing in one of his early newspaper articles:

> So why Camillo Prampolini's cheap irony about the 'interpreters' of the proletariat who can't make themselves understood by the proletarians? Because Prampolini, with all his good sense and rule of thumb, thinks in abstractions. The proletariat is a practical construct: in reality there are individual proletarians, more or less educated, more or less equipped by the class struggle to understand the most refined socialist concepts.
>
> (SCW: 32)

Later in the prison notebooks Gramsci argues that one of the primary contributions of Marxism as a theory of society is its rejection of impressive sounding, but ultimately empty, capitalized abstractions, such as 'Man in general'.

> [T]he philosophy of praxis ... is consciousness full of contradictions, in which the philosopher himself, understood both individually and as an entire social group, not only grasps the contradictions, but posits himself as an element of the contradiction and elevates this element to a principle of knowledge and therefore of action. *'Man in general', in whatever form he presents himself, is denied and all dogmatically 'unitary' concepts are spurned and destroyed as expressions of the concept of 'man in general' or of 'human nature' immanent in every man.*
>
> (SPN: 404–5, my emphasis)

In another Note on the topic of language, Gramsci draws attention to the problem of 'national' boundaries:

> [T]he linguistic fact, like any other historical fact, cannot have strictly defined national boundaries ... history is always 'world history' and ... particular histories exist only within the frame of world history ... the national language cannot be imagined outside the frame of other languages that exert an influence on it through

innumerable channels which are often difficult to control. (Who can control the linguistic innovations introduced by returning emigrants, travellers, readers of foreign newspapers and languages, translators, etc.?)

(SCW: 181)

In his analysis of contemporary Italian society and Italian history Gramsci is always concerned with understanding actual, empirical realities in all their shifting confusion, not with forcing them into rigid, predetermined theoretical boxes. It is not that Gramsci rejects theory; he believed passionately that those who wish to change the world must understand it and that this required theory. What he had no time for was theory that had become detached from the concrete reality of actual history. In a Note entitled 'Against Byzantinism' Gramsci writes:

The problem arises of whether a theoretical truth, whose discovery corresponded to a specific practice, can be generalised and considered as universal for a historical epoch. The proof of its universality consists precisely 1. in its becoming a stimulus to know better the concrete reality of a situation that is different from that in which it was discovered (this is the principal measure of its fecundity); 2. when it has stimulated and helped this better understanding of concrete reality, in its capacity to incorporate itself in that same reality as if it were originally an expression of it. It is in this incorporation that its real universality lies, and not simply in its logical or formal coherence, or in the fact that it is a useful polemical tool for confounding the enemy ... every truth, even if it is universal ... owes its effectiveness to its being expressed in the language appropriate to specific concrete situations. If it cannot be expressed in such specific terms, it is a byzantine and scholastic abstraction, good only for phrase-mongers to toy with.

(SPN: 201)

For Gramsci concepts like the 'proletariat', the 'peasantry', or the 'nation' are always 'practical constructs' that can help the theorist understand concrete reality, not actual entities *in* that reality. For instance, towards the beginning of 'Aspects of the Southern Question', which is in essence an argument for the need for an alliance between workers and peasants, Gramsci stresses that there is no such thing as *the* peasant in Italy, only different groups of peasantry with their own particular histories which have shaped them in different ways. He writes, for instance, 'the peasant question is historically determined in Italy; it is not the "peasant and agrarian question in general", in Italy the peasant question, through the specific Italian tradition, and the specific development of Italian history, has taken two typical and particular forms ...' (SPWII: 443). Gramsci goes on in the course of the essay to map out in careful detail the complicated terrain of rural Italy which any political group seeking to mobilize specific groups of peasants needs to understand.

Essentially, for Gramsci the phenomena of which useful theoretical concepts are, as he puts it, 'an expression' are never bounded entities in any simple or straightforward way. Rather, they are shifting, overlapping sets of relationships whose boundaries change according to the standpoint from which they are being viewed. It is important to be clear here. Gramsci did not believe in a structureless world in which all is always in flux. Writing his notebooks as he did while sitting in a Fascist jail cell, with every page subject to the stamp of the censor, he could hardly have been oblivious to the reality of certain power structures and clearly he was not. As he wrote in 'Elements of Politics', '[I]t is precisely the first elements, the most elementary things, which are the first to be forgotten ... The first element is that there really do exist rulers and ruled, leaders and led' (SPN: 144). For Gramsci the 'ruled' and the 'led' included workers (or proletarians) and peasants, and in certain contexts he considered that it *is* indeed appropriate to refer to the proletariat, or peasants as a group. He ends 'Aspects of the Southern Question', for example, as follows: '... only two social forces are essentially national and bearers of the future: the proletariat and the peasants' (SPWII: 462).

Having sketched out some of the broad contours of Gramsci's Marxism, I want in the final section of this chapter to say something about the form of the prison notebooks. Just what kind of text did Gramsci end up creating '*für ewig*'?

'... Something "*Für Ewig*"'

Once he had obtained permission to write in his cell Gramsci was soon, despite frequent bouts of ill health, working intensively on his notebooks. By the time he had finally become too ill to continue there were over 30 notebooks. In writing the notebooks, however, Gramsci did not simply fill one and then go on to the next. He used different notebooks to work on different topics and often worked on a number of them simultaneously; however, it is not always obvious why a particular Note is in one notebook rather than another. They are very much a series of notes, not a finished work, nor even a collection of finished works. All the Notes, in Buttigieg's words, remain provisional, and it is clear 'that no parts of the notebooks were intended (much less deemed ready) for publication by their author' (PNI: x). What we have in the prison notebooks is essentially something like the fragments of a great tapestry, where all the different pieces seem to be part of a single whole, but it is not immediately apparent just how they fit together.

Their fragmentariness is one of the reasons for the 'difficulty' of the prison notebooks. It is probably the main reason why the anthropologists who use them tend to draw on secondary sources, such as Raymond Williams or Stuart Hall, rather than the notebooks themselves. One explanation that is often given for their fragmentariness is the conditions under which they were composed: writing in a Fascist jail, having to ask his jailors for permission every time he wished to work on a notebook with each page being scrutinized and stamped by the prison censors, deprived of access to a scholarly library so that he was frequently forced to rely on his memory of crucial sources, is it any wonder that Gramsci was reduced to making a series of provisional notes?

There is certainly some truth in this. Gramsci was always a meticulous scholar. The academic education he had acquired had been hard won and he had enormous respect for the careful, painstaking labours of the serious scholar. In letters to Tatiana he was characteristically dismissive of his early journalistic pieces, writing in one: 'In ten years of journalism I wrote enough lines to fill fifteen or twenty volumes of 400 pages each, but they were written for the day and, in my opinion, were supposed to die with the day. I have always refused to permit the publication of a collection of them, even a limited one' (PLII: 66). Similarly he described his 'Aspects of the Southern Question', the essay on which he was working at the time of his arrest – subsequently widely recognised as, to quote Buttigieg, 'an extremely valuable contribution to sociopolitical theory in its own right' (PNI: 22) – as 'my very hasty and quite superficial essay' (PLI: 83), again in a letter to Tatiana. The prison notebooks themselves are full of similar caveats as to their provisional nature. Gramsci was implacably hostile to any kind of dilettantism and the last thing he was interested in producing were any kind of 'inspired' but ungrounded reflections, however brilliant these might be. This hostility comes across strongly in a letter Gramsci wrote to Giuseppe Berti, who was interned with Gramsci on the Island of Ustica in the months immediately following Gramsci's arrest. Berti and Gramsci, together with a number of the other political prisoners, had set up a school for the prisoners on Ustica, and after Gramsci had been transferred to Milan, Berti wrote to him asking for advice on the running of the school. Gramsci responded with a characteristic brusqueness: 'I find it difficult to give you advice or even dish out, as you put it, a series of "inspired" ideas. I believe that inspiration should be dropped into a "ditch" and instead one should apply the method taught by the most particularized experiences and the most dispassionate or objective self-criticism' (PLI: 119). In approaching the prison notebooks it is important to distinguish between the caveats of a scrupulous scholar, always aware of how far short he was falling of his idea of rigorous scholarship, and what Gramsci in fact achieved in the notebooks. And here understanding the nature of Gramsci's project in the prison notebooks, and the way he approached questions in which he was interested, is just as important in explaining their fragmentary character as the difficult conditions under which they were composed.

In the notebooks Gramsci deals with a wide range of topics that had expanded far beyond those laid out in the original letter to Tatiana. The way Gramsci's project developed as he began working on it is closely related to the kind of Marxist Gramsci was. Marxism was for him a science of history in which, as he in wrote in one Note, 'one cannot separate politics and economics from history, even the specialised aspects of political science and art and of economic science and policy ... the general concepts of history, politics and economics are interwoven in an organic unity ...' (SPN: 431). Gramsci's basic project in the notebooks was the exploration of that organic unity in the specific context of Italy, although understanding Italy necessarily involved understanding Italy's relationship to larger global contexts. But, of course, tackling such a vast project could only be done by breaking it up into smaller, more manageable pieces. One of the ways Gramsci did this was by picking out certain topics, such as 'intellectuals' or 'popular culture', as he did in his early letter to Tatiana, and assembling a series of Notes on each topic. Gramsci's practice of working on a series of notebooks simultaneously, keeping different notebooks for different topics was one strategy he used to order his reflections. In a letter in which he asked

Tatiana to send him some more notebooks he stressed that these should not have 'too many pages – 40–50 at the most – so that they do not turn into increasingly jumbled, hodgepodge miscellanies. I would like to have these small notebooks precisely for the purpose of rearranging these notes, dividing them by topic and thus system-atising them' (PNI: 37). At the same time he was always aware of the 'organic' links between the different topics, and that reflections on one topic might well, from a slightly different vantage point, fall under another.

The basic fact that Gramsci saw himself as ultimately dealing with an 'organic unity', together with his rigorous scholarly standards, also tended to lead to any one topic expanding to include ever more lines of inquiry. A letter he wrote to Tatiana in August 1931 (PLII: 50–3) is very revealing about his view of the exacting demands of any scholarship worth the name. He begins by pointing out how at a certain stage serious work on a topic moves 'into a phase of docu-mentation and then to a phase of work and elaboration that requires large libraries'. He goes on to give Tatiana an example of how a topic rapidly expands to almost unmanageable proportions. This passage is worth quoting in full since it provides a good illustration of Gramsci's approach to the topics in which he was interested. The example Gramsci chose was Italian intellectuals, itself part of his interest in the state and in 'the historical development of the Italian people'. He writes:

> Even if one restricts the essential lines of the research, it still remains formidable. One must inevitably go back to the Roman Empire and to the first concentration of 'cosmopolitan' ('imperial') intellectuals, which results from it; and then study the formation of the Papal-Christian organisation that imparts to the heritage of imperial intellectual cosmopolitanism a European castelike form, etc. Only in this way, in my opinion, can one explain that it was not until after the eighteenth century, that is, after the beginning of the first struggles between Church and State over jurisdictionism that one can speak of 'national' Italian intel-lectuals; until then, Italian intellectuals were cosmopolitans, performed an anational, universalistic function (either for the Church or for the Empire), helped to organize other national States as technicians or specialists, offered 'executive personnel' to all of Europe, and did not become concentrated as a national category, as a specialized group of national classes. As you can see,

this subject could result in a whole series of essays, but for that intensive scholarly research has to be undertaken. The same thing applies to other studies. You must also keep in mind that the habit of rigorous philological discipline that I acquired during my university studies has given me perhaps an excessive supply of methodological scruples.

(PLII: 52)

One way of looking at the series of Notes that make up the prison notebooks is to see their form as a means by which Gramsci was able to overcome his 'methodological scruples'. Throughout the notebooks we find caveats like this one:

Look over this argument carefully. In general, remember that all these notes are provisional and written as they flow from the pen: they must be reviewed and checked in detail because they undoubtedly contain imprecisions, anachronisms, wrong approaches, etc. which do not imply wrongdoing because the notes have solely the function of quick memoranda.

(quoted in PNI: 33)

In the frequent reminders of this kind Gramsci seems to be as much reassuring himself as warning us, his readers, that this is not the final word, that there is always more that could be said, that looked at from a different vantage point things might look different and so on. This open-endedness makes the prison notebooks, on the one hand, difficult to pin down definitively – something that has frustrated some commentators[9] – but, on the other, enormously rich and suggestive for those wanting to draw on Gramsci in different times and different places. The note form adopted by Gramsci does, however, make the notebooks extremely difficult to summarize in any satisfactory way. Ultimately, grasping the nature of Gramsci's project in the prison notebooks requires reading the notebooks themselves.

A final important characteristic of Gramsci's analytical style that I want to mention is his profoundly dialogic approach: Gramsci

9. Even the generally insightful editors of the *Selections from the Prison Notebooks* complain, for example, that 'Gramsci did not succeed in finding a single, wholly satisfactory conception of "civil society" or the State' (SPN: 207).

writes as a participant in a continuing conversation. He refers to this fact about himself in a 1930 letter to Tatiana:

> If you are sending her [Giulia Schucht, Gramsci's wife[10]] this [letter] as well, she'll read about my wish, which expresses a real psychological need that I cannot suppress. Perhaps it is because my entire intellectual formation has been of a polemical order; even thinking 'disinterestedly' is difficult for me, that is, studying for study's sake. Only occasionally, but rarely, does it happen that I lose myself in a specific order of reflections and find, so to speak, in the things themselves enough interest to devote myself to their analysis. Ordinarily, *I need to set out from a dialogical or dialectical standpoint, otherwise I don't experience any intellectual stimulation.* As I once told you, I don't like to cast stones into the darkness; *I want to feel a concrete interlocutor or adversary ...*

> (PLI: 369, my emphasis)

In the notebooks Gramsci engaged with many interlocutors. In his writings he was debating with, challenging, answering and so on, a vast array of different people, who ranged from the writers of mediocre articles in the newspapers and journals to which Gramsci had access in prison, to major intellectual figures, such as Croce. Sometimes, particularly given that Gramsci was engaging in this conversation more than 60 years ago, and that a number of the debates have disappeared into the mists of history, this can make reading the prison notebooks a little like hearing just one side of a telephone conversation. In my mapping out of Gramsci's discussions of 'culture', therefore, I have tried to provide some information about some of the relevant 'interlocutors and adversaries'.

Throughout this chapter I have stressed Gramsci's Marxism, which I have argued underpins the whole of his approach. But, as I have also argued, Gramsci's Marxism was anything but rigid and dogmatic; it was a Marxism that saw the whole domain of ideas, beliefs and discourse generally, not as some mere epiphenomenon of the economic infrastructure but as an integral, or to use Gramsci's term, an organic part of it. Let me end this chapter, therefore with an extract from a Note discussing how specific

---

10. Giulia Schucht suffered from various health problems and corresponded somewhat irregularly with Gramsci, something that was a source of great anguish to him.

concepts shape reality. This Note also provides a good example of Gramsci's adversarial style. In this instance his interlocutor is Bertrand Russell, the philosopher.

One can also recall the example contained in a little book by Bertrand Russell. Russell says approximately this: 'We cannot, without the existence of man on the earth, think of the existence of London or Edinburgh, but we can think of the existence of two points in space, one to the North and one to the South, where London and Edinburgh now are.' It could be objected that without the existence of man one cannot think of 'thinking', one cannot think at all of any fact or relationship which exists only in so far as man exists. What would North–South or East–West mean without man? They are real relationships and yet they would not exist without man and without the development of civilisation. Obviously East and West are arbitrary and conventional, that is historical, constructions, since outside of real history every point on the earth is East and West at the same time. This can be seen more clearly from the fact that these terms have crystallised not from the point of view of a hypothetical melancholic man in general but from the point of view of the European cultured classes who, as a result of their world-wide hegemony, have caused them to be accepted everywhere. Japan is the Far East not only for Europe but also perhaps for the American from California and even for the Japanese himself, who, through English political culture, may then call Egypt the Near East. So because of the historical content that has become attached to the geographical terms, the expressions East and West have finished up indicating specific relations between different cultural complexes. Thus Italians often, when speaking of Morocco, call it an 'Eastern' country, to refer to its Moslem and Arab civilisation. And yet these references are real; they correspond to real facts, they allow one to travel by land and by sea, to arrive where one has decided to arrive, to 'foresee' the future, to objectivise reality, to understand the objectivity of the external world. Rational and real become one.

(SPN: 447–8)

3 Anthropology and Culture: Some Assumptions

To reconstruct a megatherium or a mastodon from a tiny bone was Cuvier's special gift, by it may also happen that from a piece of a mouse's tail one might reconstruct a sea serpent.

(PLI: 302)

Preliminaries

This chapter focuses on the notion of culture in anthropology. If we as anthropologists are to draw on Gramsci's writings on culture, it important not only to be clear as to what Gramsci means when he refers to culture, but also as to what may be involved in our own anthropological uses of the term; what unstated assumptions might there be underpinning anthropological notions of culture? Let me stress at the outset that in no sense is this chapter a history of how the concept of culture has been used in anthropology. My concern is far more modest. I simply want to draw attention to certain assumptions about the nature of 'culture' which seem to me to have haunted that history. It may seem to some that in doing this I am setting up an ahistorical and oversimplified straw being that does scant justice to the complex and rich history of the discipline – a history in which there have been a wide range of understandings of this entity 'culture'. And it is true that I do ignore much of the diversity and debate. Also, I have deliberately chosen to focus on anthropologists who have taken the elucidation of culture as central to the anthropological project. I am certainly not arguing that the assumptions I have identified define anthropology's notion of culture in any exhaustive way. There are many other legacies and other intellectual lineages that could be traced out. All I have tried to do is to draw attention to some assumptions with long histories that seem to me to have persisted in interesting ways through the many theoretical upheavals undergone by anthropology over the last 40 years. Not in the work of all anthropologists, of course, but in enough – albeit often in shadowy, unacknowledged ways – to make this exercise worthwhile.

So what are these assumptions? They are firstly, that cultures are in some sense *systems*, not necessarily homogeneous and conflict-free ones, but ones that nonetheless constitute patterned wholes of some kind; secondly, that 'cultures', again in some sense, constitute discrete and bounded entities; and thirdly that the societies around whose study anthropology emerged as a discipline (in modern parlance, societies of the South) are characterized by a fundamental opposition between 'tradition' and 'modernity'. It is true that nowadays these assumptions may not have the same power that they once had, indeed they may often be explicitly renounced, but nonetheless, I would argue, they can still be found lurking in the shadows. The importance of this in the context of a discussion of Gramsci's understanding of culture is that, as we shall see in Part II, they are all assumptions stemming from a radically different understanding of 'culture' from that of Gramsci. The problem for anthropological readers of Gramsci is that it is all too easy to assume that when Gramsci speaks of 'culture' he is referring to 'culture' as this has commonly been understood within their discipline. To appreciate just how different Gramsci's approach to culture is, it is helpful, therefore, to begin by clarifying some of the common-sense[1] baggage the notion of culture in anthropology often carries, particularly since, being common sense, it tends to be implicit rather than explicit. This is not to say of course that *all* anthropology carries such baggage. Nonetheless, to switch metaphors, there are still ghosts that have not yet been laid and it is these ghosts that are the concern of this chapter.

To illustrate some of the ways in which the three assumptions I have identified underpin some of the dominant anthropological approaches to the issue of culture, I have focused particularly on three anthropologists, Clifford Geertz, Marshall Sahlins and Sherry Ortner. I chose these three because all of them have written extensively on culture and all have produced highly influential accounts of the anthropological enterprise. While the meaning of culture in anthropology cannot be reduced to what it has meant in the work of Geertz, Sahlins and Ortner – and even here I focus only on certain of these authors' writings – they articulate some dominant currents of thought in anthropology in a particularly clear way. These three anthropologists also represent two anthropological generations.

---

1. See Chapter 5 pp. 110–15 for a discussion of the important Gramscian category of 'common sense'.

Geertz and Sahlins, born in 1923 and 1930 respectively, were both graduate students in the 1950s, while Ortner, born in 1941, who started out as one of Geertz's students, did her graduate work in the turbulent 1960s. I touch more briefly on some British anthropologists, as well as drawing on a popular textbook designed to introduce anthropology to students. Introductory textbooks necessarily tend to provide an oversimplified, and often slightly out-of-date picture of a discipline, but such simplification can have the virtue of stating clearly some of the basic assumptions left unstated in writings aimed at a more advanced readership. The final section of the chapter looks at two works published in 1997, *Routes* by James Clifford and an essay by Liisa Malkki, both of which suggest that residual traces of these assumptions can still be found in contemporary anthropology.

A Complicated Word

All anthropologists would likely agree that culture has been one of the discipline's central concepts. In a much cited essay, 'Thick Description', first published in 1973, Clifford Geertz described culture as the concept 'around which the whole discipline of anthropology arose' (Geertz 1973a: 4), a claim many anthropologists would probably accept. At the same time, just how the term culture has been defined has varied hugely. In the 1950s A. L. Kroeber and Clyde Kluckholm collected over a hundred anthropological definitions of culture. Things get even more complicated if we include culture's wide field of meaning beyond anthropology. Indeed, Raymond Williams, in his invaluable *Keywords*, termed culture 'one of the two or three most complicated words in the English language'; in part, 'because it has now come to be used for important concepts in several distinct intellectual disciplines and in several distinct and incompatible systems of thought' (1983: 87). Nonetheless, as regards anthropology, it is possible, within all the twists and turns of meaning associated with the notion of culture over the history of the discipline, to trace out certain persistent assumptions. In focusing on a few shared assumptions, and their persistence, my account necessarily ignores important areas of disagreement and debate, as well as the ways in which these have shifted over time.

To understand the different meanings 'culture' came to have within the discipline of anthropology it is helpful to look at the larger history of the word and at how certain shifts in meaning were related to broader historical contexts.[2] The history of particular concepts, and how they come to mean what they do at particular moments and particular times, can never be divorced from larger historical contexts. It is important to look carefully at why it is seen as necessary, at those moments and those times, that this particular aspect of social reality should be *named*. Concepts, especially those relating to social life, emerge out of debate, contestation, and generally as in some sense answers to perceived problems; a concept's history shapes it in various ways. On the one hand, the meanings a concept acquires are never completely fixed, rather they tend to evolve continuously; on the other hand, earlier meanings may cling to it and affect its later usage. In other words, there is a continual reciprocal interaction between the context that calls concepts into being and within which they come to be used, and the relatively stable meanings that they acquire over time, which have their own power. This power derives from the fact that human beings necessarily perceive their world as defined, not totally but to an important extent, by the names or concepts they have inherited.[3]

The word 'culture' in English began as 'a noun of process: the tending *of* something, basically crops or animals' (1983: 87, Williams' emphasis), a meaning that is still present in words like 'agriculture' or 'horticulture'. Later, 'culture' also began to be used to refer to a process of human development and this became its main sense until the beginning of the nineteenth century. Very gradually, however, beginning as early as the late seventeenth century, in ways that are difficult to trace precisely, 'culture' began to acquire some of its modern senses. Another term that emerged during the eighteenth century, and that was originally closely linked to the concept of culture, was 'civilization'. By the end of the eighteenth century the word 'civilization', as Williams puts it, 'has behind it the general spirit of the Enlightenment, with its emphasis on secular and progressive human self-development' (1983: 58). Well into the nineteenth century 'civilization' and 'culture' were used as synonyms. It is specifically at the end of the eighteenth century and the beginning of the nineteenth, however, that 'culture' assumes its modern meanings in English, which were strongly influenced by

2. My discussion here relies heavily on Williams' *Keywords*.
3. The power bound up with the naming of social reality is discussed in Crehan, 1997a: 30–5.

what the terms *culture* and *Cultur* (later spelt *Kultur*) were coming to mean in French, and in German respectively.

The emergence of this new cluster of meanings can be linked to the seismic historical events taking place throughout Europe at this time. This is the historical period when Enlightenment thinking was erupting throughout Europe, the French Revolution was overturning old hierarchies, and a little later, Napoleon at the head of the revolutionary French army was marching through Europe remaking national borders. Partially as a response to Enlightenment ideas, a very different current of thought emerged that became associated with the Romantic Movement. In place of the secular rationalism of the Enlightenment, Romantic thinkers celebrated the emotions, irrationality, and authentic 'tradition'. In addition, and closely linked with both Romantic and Enlightenment currents of thought (although in complicated and varying ways in different countries and at different times) various forms of nationalism emerged, all of which asserted the rights of 'nations' to their 'national territories'. One of the new senses that 'culture' acquired in the context of this swirling, historical maelstrom was the one that came to be the central anthropological meaning, namely culture understood as 'a people's way of life'. The genealogy of culture as a particular people's way of life is worth dwelling on a little since the anthropological notion of culture, I would argue, is shot through with traces of this history.

A key figure here is the German Romantic philosopher Johann Herder. In his unfinished *Ideas on the Philosophy of the History of Mankind* (1794–91), Herder attacked the Enlightenment teleology that saw all human history as leading up to its final culmination in 'civilized' European culture, insisting rather – and this was his radical departure – that we should not speak of 'culture' in the singular, but of cultures. For Herder, different nations and different time periods had different cultures; and within a single nation there were different cultures associated with different social and economic groups. In this usage 'culture' ceases to be a synonym for 'civilization', becoming instead an alternative, even an antonym. Used first by the Romantics, particularly in reference to what were seen as 'national' and 'traditional' cultures (which tended to be seen as in some sense constituting organic wholes), it came later to be used to contrast older, more 'authentic' cultures, centred on the needs of human beings, with what was often seen as the soulless, mechanical character of emerging industrial 'civilization'. I shall return to this characteristic Romantic opposition later in this chapter.

Just to make things more complicated, however, there were also those who continued to use 'culture' and 'civilization' as synonyms until late in the nineteenth century. Interestingly, one of the most often cited definitions of culture in anthropology textbooks, Edward Tylor's in *Primitive Culture,* published in 1871 and commonly taken to be one of the ur-texts of modern anthropology, reads in its original form: 'Culture or Civilization, taken in its wide ethnographic sense, is that complex whole which includes knowledge, belief, art, morals, law, custom and any other capabilities and habits acquired by man as a member of society.' Tylor's definition here draws on another German theorist, G. F. Klemm, whose *General Cultural History of Mankind* (1843–52) was concerned with the development of human society from its earliest emergence to its culmination in 'freedom'. 'Culture' as a synonym for 'civilization' fell out of usage in the twentieth century and as it did so civilization also tended to be silently dropped from Tylor's definition when it was quoted by anthropologists.

In addition to its two main meanings as 'a general process of intellectual, spiritual and aesthetic development' (Williams, 1983: 90), and as a way of life, whether of specific groups or of humanity in general, 'culture' acquired yet another meaning in the late nineteenth and early twentieth centuries. Culture became also the *products* of intellectual and especially artistic activity. Nowadays for many people 'culture' means primarily music, literature, painting and sculpture, theatre and film. This extension can be seen as culture in the sense of 'a general process of intellectual, spiritual and aesthetic development' being expanded to include all those things that are taken as representing this development and that help to bring it about.

Given these complex and sometimes contradictory clusters of meaning, it is important to resist the temptation to fix on one of them as the 'correct' one. Rather, as Williams says:

[I]n general it is the range and overlap of meanings that is significant. The complex of senses indicates a complex argument about the relations between general human development and a particular way of life, and between both the works and practices of art and intelligence.

(Williams, 1983: 91)

As I hope will emerge in Part II, it is precisely this complex argument that is at the heart of Gramsci's explorations of culture. Within anthropology, however, particularly in the United States, the dominant meaning of culture has been the one that originated with Herder and Klemm, culture as 'a way of life' – an understanding of culture which has deep roots in German Romanticism. Bound up with this anthropological notion of culture are the three assumptions which I have already mentioned: that cultures are in some sense systematic; that they are bounded; and that there is a fundamental and structuring dichotomy between 'tradition' and 'modernity'. In the next two sections I trace out the presence of these assumptions in selected texts by Geertz, Sahlins and Ortner, and in some popular anthropology textbooks. I also touch on an influential collection of essays by Victor Turner. In the final section I turn to some contemporary anthropological writings. Let me reiterate that this is a very partial account focused solely on the constants I have identified. In no way does this brief and highly schematic discussion do justice to the sophisticated and nuanced ways in which many individual anthropologists have explored issues of culture. Let me also stress that I am not claiming that these assumptions are necessarily wrong, my aim is simply to map out something of the common ground shared by otherwise rather different anthropologists as to the nature of 'culture' as an object of anthropological study.

'... The Informal Logic of Actual Life'

That cultures are in some sense patterned wholes has been fundamental to the anthropological notion of culture as 'a way of life', however that may have been understood. Roger Keesing, for instance, in his 1974 *Annual Review of Anthropology* survey article of current theories of culture in anthropology, argues that the many different, and often conflicting, 'recent rethinkings of "culture"' can be seen as falling into four broad types: cultures as adaptive systems, cultures as cognitive systems, cultures as structural systems and cultures as symbolic systems. Whatever else they may disagree about, anthropologists as different as Marvin Harris, David Schneider, Claude Lévi-Strauss and Clifford Geertz, all apparently agree that cultures are in some sense *systems*. These cultural systems may well have been seen as containing conflicting and contradictory elements, and indeed many anthropologists have focused precisely on conflict and contradiction but this has tended to be treated as existing either within distinct cultural entities, or between them.

Geertz, one of the most influential anthropologists of the last 30 years, has certainly approached cultures as patterned wholes. For Geertz culture is primarily a domain of beliefs and ideas. Having, for instance, described culture in 'Thick Description' as the concept 'around which the whole discipline of anthropology arose', he goes on to explain his usage of the concept of culture:

> The concept of culture I espouse, and whose utility the essays below [in his *Interpretation of Cultures*] attempt to demonstrate, is essentially a semiotic one. Believing, with Max Weber, that man is an animal suspended in webs of significance he himself has spun, I take culture to be those webs, and the analysis of it to be therefore not an experimental science in search of law but an interpretive one in search of meaning.
>
> (1973a: 5)

In an earlier essay reprinted in *Interpretation of Cultures* (the collection of Geertz's essays in which 'Thick Description' first appeared) Geertz amplifies his definition, although without the metaphorical embellishment:

> [T]he culture concept to which I adhere ... denotes an historically transmitted *pattern* of meanings embodied in symbols, a *system* of inherited conceptions expressed in symbolic forms by means of which men communicate, perpetuate, and develop their knowledge about and attitudes towards life.
>
> (1973b: 89, my emphasis)

A culture for Geertz, that is, involves a '*pattern* of meanings', 'a *system* of inherited conceptions'. All the bits and pieces that go to make up a culture can be seen as in some sense constituting a coherent and systematic whole. As he puts it later in 'Thick Description', 'the proper object' of cultural analysis is 'the informal *logic* of actual life' (1973a: 17, my emphasis).

Another towering figure in the recent history of the discipline is Marshall Sahlins. Sahlins began his career as a cultural ecologist, although shifting later to a more structuralist approach derived in large part from Lévi-Strauss, and the question of how the relationship between culture and history should be theorised has always loomed large in his work. The general theme of his 1985 collection of essays, *Islands of History*, is summed up in 'the assertion that what anthropologists call "structure" – the symbolic relations of cultural order – is an historical object' (1985: vii).[4] Throughout these essays Sahlins is at pains to demonstrate that an anthropological approach to the history of the islands in question (Hawaii, Fiji and New Zealand) that stresses the shaping role of culture can nonetheless encompass, and theorize, change. A key problem for him is 'the dual existence and interaction between the cultural order as constituted in the society and as lived by the people: structure in convention and in action, as virtual and as actual' (1985: ix). What is not in doubt is that there is 'a cultural order'. What he wants to emphasize is that 'the different cultural orders studied by anthropology have their own historicities' (1985: 53). That anthropologists study 'different cultural orders' is taken for granted. As he writes in one of the essays, 'Structure and History', 'Human social experience is the appropriation of specific percepts by general concepts: an ordering of men and the objects of their existence according to *a scheme of cultural categories* which is never the only one possible ...' (1985: 145, my emphasis). Sahlins is quick to make the point here that there is nothing inevitable about a particular culture, but at the same time he seems to assume that a scheme of some sort is inevitable. A little earlier in the same essay he writes: 'Hawaiian history is throughout grounded in structure [for Sahlins, structure = culture, see note 4], the *systematic* ordering of contingent circumstances' (1985: 144, my emphasis). Like Geertz, Sahlins assumes that cultures, or cultural orders, have their own logics.

> In the decades following Cook's fatal visit, Hawaiian chiefs and commoners, men and women, ritual tabus and material goods, were all engaged in practical exchange with Europeans in ways that altered their customary meanings and relationships. And always the functional revaluations appear as *logical* extensions of traditional conceptions.
>
> (1985: 140, my emphasis)

---

4. In line with this assertion the entry for culture in the Index to *Islands of History* reads: 'see structure'.

Cultures change over time, but they do so in terms of their own logics.

My point here is not that 'cultures' do not have their own logics, or are not 'systematic' and 'patterned', it is simply that for both Geertz and Sahlins this is something that can be assumed: both of them take this as a starting point from which they go on to explore the analytical questions in which they are interested.

Cultures as Bounded Entities

I want now to move on to the assumption that cultures constitute discrete entities, an assumption that necessarily poses the question of where and how these different entities are bounded. It is helpful here to go back to Herder and the origins of the notion of culture as a particular way of life. The crucial shift in meaning initiated by Herder was the notion of cultures rather than culture. Replacing the idea of a single developmental process culminating in the achievement of 'culture' was the assertion that there exist numerous different 'cultures'. The larger impulse from which this claim emerged is nicely caught in this passage from his unfinished *Ideas on the Philosophy of the History of Mankind*, written in the last years of the eighteenth century, but which has a very modern ring to it.

> Men of all the quarters of the globe, who have perished over the ages, you have not lived solely to manure the earth with your ashes, so that at the end of time your posterity should be made happy by European culture. The very thought of a superior European culture is a blatant insult to the majesty of Nature.
>
> (quoted in Williams, 1983: 89)

In this work Herder, as the anthropologist Eric Wolf puts it, 'undertook to write a universal history of humanity [cf. G. F. Klemm's *General Cultural History of Mankind*] but transformed the project into a synthetic presentation of the multiple histories of particular peoples' (1999: 28). This insistence that different peoples have different cultures, their own ways of seeing and doing things, can be seen in part as a reaction against the universalizing claims of the Enlightenment thinkers with their stress on humanity as an undifferentiated whole with a single history moving towards a single goal guided by universal human reason – a way of thinking which some saw as having led to the excesses of the French Revolution. As one émigré aristocrat, Joseph de Maistre (1753–1821), also interestingly one of the founders of sociology, wrote: 'The constitution of 1795, just like its predecessors, was made for *man*. But there is no such thing as *man* in the world. I have seen Frenchmen, Italians, Russians ... But as for man, I declare I have never met him in my life' (quoted in Wolf, 1999: 28). As Napoleon's revolutionary army spread out over Europe, remaking it in its own Enlightenment image, resistance, particularly among German intellectuals, frequently took the form of various nationalist claims, according to which different 'peoples' all have a right to their own autonomy. At the same time the ideas and language of nationalism also drew on Enlightenment thinking; the Enlightenment legacy of a discourse of universal human rights and the discourse of Romanticism are entangled in complicated ways. It is in this complex historical context that the anthropological understanding of culture as referring, in the words of one best-selling text book, 'to the way of life of some group of people' (Bailey and Peoples, 1999: 15) has its roots. The key innovation, as I have stressed, is that rather than there being simply culture, there are *cultures*.

It is also important to note that the nationalist notions sweeping Europe at this time lent a particular character to how these different cultures were imagined, with cultures essentially being thought of as bounded wholes of the same broad type as nationalities. A culture, like a nationality, tended, for example, to be seen as referring to a specific people, often associated with a specific territory, and who were characterized by a particular world view, expressed through a common language. The point here is not that all cultures were necessarily assumed to share all these features, but that this cluster of associations was to some extent carried along, even if only implicitly, with the notion of culture as this developed its distinct anthropological meanings. In other words, the circumstances of its birth can be seen as having shaped the notion of culture 'around which anthropology as a discipline arose' in certain ways and as leaving embedded in it certain persistent traces. Two further brief quotes from Geertz's 'Thick Description' illustrate this underlying idea of cultures as bounded universes of the same type as nations, to which individuals 'belong' in the same way they do to a particular nation. Geertz is explaining here what he means by actor-oriented interpretations of other cultures.

What it [i.e. actor-oriented interpretation] means is that descriptions of Berber, Jewish, or French culture must be cast in terms of the constructions we imagine Berbers, Jews, or Frenchmen to place upon what they live through, the formulae they use to define what happens to them.

(1973a: 15)

Geertz concludes his argument here: 'In short, anthropological writings are themselves interpretations, and second and third order ones to boot. (By definition, only a "native" makes first order ones: it's *his* culture)' (1973a: 15).

So far in this chapter I have concentrated on North American cultural anthropology, but what of British social anthropology? Has it had a comparable notion of 'cultures' as coherent and bounded wholes? I would argue that while there may have been important differences of emphasis, as is signalled by the term *social* as opposed to *cultural* anthropology, the concept of culture has also been central to British anthropology, and while there may have been differences in just how culture was conceptualized – and indeed a reluctance to use the term – the basic assumptions that what anthropologists are concerned with is the analysis of coherent systems with their own logics that 'belong to' specific groups is common to both anthropological traditions. There is not the space to go into this issue in detail here but let me mention briefly by way of illustration two classic texts both published in the mid-sixties, just prior to the 'rethinking' of anthropology that began to upset so many of the old certainties in the late sixties and on into the seventies.[5] Both come out of the British social anthropology tradition. One is Victor Turner's *The Forest of Symbols: Aspects of Ndembu Ritual*, still regarded as one of the classics of symbolic anthropology, and the other is John Beattie's best-selling text book, *Other Cultures: Aims, Methods and Achievements in Social Anthropology*. It is worth noting that while Turner was very much a product of the British anthropological tradition he taught for a number of years at Chicago, and that Beattie spent a year at Stanford while working on *Other Cultures*. From the discipline's earliest years there was continual interaction between British and American anthropologists and there was always an important

5. Two key works here are Hymes, 1969, in the United States and Asad, 1973, in Britain.

dialogue between the two traditions. In more recent years American and British anthropology have become ever more entwined.

To begin with Turner; the subject of all the essays which make up *The Forest of Symbols* is defined as 'aspects of the ritual system of the Ndembu people of northwestern Zambia ...' (1967:1) In the essay 'Ritual Symbolism, Morality, and Social Structure among the Ndembu' Turner refers to the relationship between the Ndembu ritual system and Ndembu life in general. 'In an Ndembu ritual each symbol makes visible and accessible to purposive public action certain elements of Ndembu culture and society.' He goes on to explain that 'a single symbol may stand for many things. This property of individual symbols is true for ritual as a whole. For a few symbols have to represent *a whole culture* and its material environment' (1967: 50, my emphasis). A little later in the same essay Turner writes, 'The positional meaning of a symbol derives from its relationship to other symbols in a totality, a *Gestalt*, whose elements acquire their significance from the system as a whole' (1967: 51). Turner sees his task as an anthropologist, therefore, as the explication of a particular symbolic system which can be taken as representing the culture of this group, the Ndembu, as a totality. And this symbolic system has its own logic: 'The semantic structure of *mudyi* [the milk tree, one of the Ndembu's basic symbols] may itself be likened to a tree. At the root is the primary sense of "breast milk" and from this proceeds *by logical steps* series of further senses' (1967: 53, my emphasis). Turner's focus is very much on Ndembu ritual and Ndembu culture as a bounded whole to which all Ndembu belong and all non-Ndembu do not.

Beattie, at the beginning of his book, discusses the distinction between social anthropology and cultural anthropology. Citing Tylor's classic definition Beattie provides a paraphrase.

> In its broadest sense, 'culture' refers to the whole range of human activities which are learned and not instinctive, and which are transmitted from generation to generation through various learning processes. Often the physical products of human activity are included under the term as 'material culture'.
>
> (1964: 20)

This makes cultural anthropology a bit too inclusive and unwieldy for Beattie, and he wants to limit the subject matter of anthropology to a part of this large domain of culture. 'Men's social institutions and values, social anthropology's central concern, occupy only a small part of this range' (1964: 20). However, as the title of his book makes clear, for Beattie, as for Geertz, what anthropologists study are 'other cultures'. For reasons having to do in part with the difference between an anthropology that developed in the context of a formal empire (British social anthropology), and one that developed out of a rather different kind of encounter between an advancing American society and various native peoples, British anthropologists may have had a special concern with the formal institutions (still often existing, at least in name) of those they studied, but culture was still a central concern. Beattie goes on to make a distinction between a tendency for American anthropologists to study 'cultural traits', rather than being concerned with 'the analysis of cultures or societies as, in some sense, *systematic wholes*' (1964: 21, my emphasis), which is what he implies British social anthropologists study. Beattie stresses how the differences between the two traditions are ones of emphasis, 'they do not imply... that social anthropologists and cultural anthropologists study two different kinds of thing' (1964: 21). Ultimately, it seems to me, what is at issue here is not so much a difference between whether or not an anthropologist studies culture but rather how the concept of culture itself is being understood. What is clear is that for Beattie, as for Turner, what anthropologists should be concerned with are systematic wholes or bounded cultures.

In recent years the concept of cultures as bounded wholes has been much criticized. Anthropologists nowadays often spend a lot of time emphasizing the fluid, shifting nature of cultural boundaries and how different cultures overlap and intermingle, but a focus on difference, on the existence of 'other cultures', however fluid and shifting these may be, remains a basic concern for most anthropologists. Anthropology is, after all, a discipline that grew up specifically around a focus on how things looked from a perspective other than that of the West and modernity, and on how things were done in these other worlds. That concern may have been implicated in the whole colonial enterprise and the rise of a Western, capitalist-based hegemony, and may have been to some extent the product of an imperialist endeavour, but it was a concern that, albeit in a way shot through with contradictions, took the non-West seriously and tried in some measure to understand those societies in their own terms. Understandably, anthropologists have on the whole been anxious to hold on to this attention to difference, to a view of the contemporary, 'globalized' world that attempts to see how things look from a perspective other than that of its hegemonic centres. In the next section I look at some recent examples of this concern, and this way of framing the anthropological project, but for the moment I want to focus on an earlier moment in the anthropological story, the 1980s.

Sherry Ortner in a much-cited survey of anthropological theory written in the mid-eighties expressed a characteristic anxiety in her critique of the then very influential political economy approach in anthropology. What worried her was what she saw as the abandonment of anthropology's traditional concern with 'other worlds' beyond the North in the name of the recognition of the power of world capitalism. Her objection was this:

> Specifically, I find the capitalism-centred view of the world questionable, to say the least, *especially for anthropology*. At the core of the model is the assumption that virtually everything we study has already been touched ('penetrated') by the capitalist world system, and that therefore much of what we see in our fieldwork and describe in our monographs must be understood as having been shaped in response to that system. Perhaps this is true for European peasants, but even here one would want at least to leave the question open. When we get even further from the 'center,' however, the assumption becomes very problematic indeed. *A society, even a village, has its own structure and history*, and this must be as much part of the analysis as its relations with the larger context within which it operates ...
>
> The problems derived from the capitalism-centred worldview also affect the political economists' view of history. History is often treated as something that arrives, like a ship, from outside the society in question. Thus we do not get the history *of* that society, but the impact of (our) history *on* that society. The accounts produced from such a perspective are often quite unsatisfactory in terms of *traditional anthropological concerns: the actual organization and culture of the society in question* ...
>
> The political economists, moreover, tend to situate themselves more on the ship of (capitalist) history than on the shore. They say in effect that we can never know what *the other system, in its unique, 'traditional,' aspects*, really looked like anyway ...
>
> To such a position we can only respond: try ... *The attempt to view other systems from ground level is the basis, perhaps the only basis,*

of anthropology's distinctive contribution to the human sciences. It is our capacity, largely developed in fieldwork, to take the perspective of the folks on the shore, that allows us to learn anything at all – even in our own culture – beyond what we already know.

(1984: 142–3, my emphasis)

As the statements I have emphasized make clear, this passionate defence of the 'traditional concerns' of anthropology is very much framed in terms of the study of other societies, each with its own culture and its own structure and history. For Ortner it is this that constitutes 'anthropology's distinctive contribution to the human sciences'. She stresses the autonomy of individual societies, that 'a society, even a village', is, as it were, a system unto itself, which has a prior existence independent of any larger power contexts in which it may be enveloped. Let me reiterate that my point is not that this stress on autonomy is necessarily wrong, I simply want to draw attention to how the focus of the anthropological project here is on what is contained within the boundaries of these separate systems. Only after these autonomous systems have been understood can the anthropologist move on to analyse their interlinkages. This framing of the anthropological project as the study of autonomous systems with their own histories generated by their own internal dynamics has indeed, as Ortner emphasizes, been an important and distinctive feature of anthropology as a discipline.

Ortner defines her own preferred approach in anthropology as a 'practice approach'. Drawing (as so many anthropologists have done) on Raymond Williams' discussion in *Marxism and Literature* of Gramsci's concept of hegemony, Ortner writes: 'What a practice theory seeks to explain, then, is the genesis, reproduction, and change in form and meaning of *a given social/cultural whole*, defined in – more or less – this sense [i.e. as Williams in *Marxism and Literature* defines hegemony]' (1984: 149, my emphasis). I shall return in Chapter 7 to the interesting part played by *Marxism and Literature* – particularly this section on hegemony – in anthropology's encounter with Gramsci. For the moment I just want to draw attention to Ortner's insistence on 'a given social/cultural whole' as the proper topic for anthropologists, albeit not the whole of a world capitalist system, and her apparent confidence that Gramsci's theorization of hegemony can be harnessed to this project.

So far in this chapter I have looked at how the anthropological concept of culture tends to carry with it an assumption of logical coherence, and some notion of boundedness, as well as a stress on the autonomy of local systems that need to be understood in their own terms. In the next section I want to look at another cluster of assumptions which have to do with a common identification by anthropologists in the societies they study of a central opposition between 'tradition' and 'modernity', even if they do not use these precise terms.

Culture and the Notion of Tradition

From when it was first expanded to refer to a specific way of life, which as I have stressed happened in a particular historical context, the concept of culture was entwined with an opposition between tradition and modernity. Wolf puts it this way in *Envisioning Power*: 'Revolutionary and Imperial France asserted dominance over Europe in the name of rationalism, secularism, and equality; the Germanies responded with traditionalizing and "spiritual" countermovements in the name of "culture"' (1999: 64). At the end of his book Wolf elaborates on some of the threads bound up with this notion of culture understood as 'an organic whole imbued by a common spirit':

> Against such rhetoric [arguing for a universal order based on Reason and rational governance by the sovereign state] and the claims and cosmological visions implied in it, the opponents of the expanding Third Estate invoked ancient customs and rights, authenticity, hallowed truth, tradition, and faith. In their hands 'folklore' and 'custom' became 'culture,' meaning not just another set of practices and discourses but an organic whole imbued by a common spirit. This formulation allowed its proponents to become spokesmen for that organic and spiritual unity and to challenge those at home and abroad who advocated universal progress and free advancement. In the process they made themselves defenders of the culture against the onslaught of civilization, denying to the universalizers anything like culture of their own. The universalizers, in turn, wished to dissociate themselves from an outdated and nonprogressive 'culture' and adopted instead styles of dress and comportment, educational innovations, reading habits, and other patterns of behavior and thought represented as in the realm of universal Reason.

(1999: 287)

No anthropologist nowadays would subscribe to this Romantic notion of culture, although this kind of Romanticism is still alive and well in popular understandings of anthropology, such as those to be found in mass circulation magazines and television programmes. Even among anthropologists, however, the association of culture with 'tradition', albeit in a far weaker and more nebulous sense, is a persistent one. It is worth looking a little more closely at this term 'tradition'.

The *Oxford English Dictionary* gives the following general definition:

> A long established and generally accepted custom or method of procedure, having almost the force of a law; an immemorial usage; the body (or any one) of the experiences and usages of any branch or school of art or literature, handed down by predecessors and generally followed. In quot. 1818, an embodiment of an old established custom or institution, a 'relic'.

This notion of tradition is enormously powerful; claims in the name of tradition – as long as such a claim is considered to be authentic – carry considerable moral weight, especially if the claim is being made by a group that is accepted as having its own 'culture'. In the United States, Native Americans would be a good example. That, within certain limits, Native American people have an inalienable right to live according to their own 'cultural traditions' is generally accepted both by the state and by what we might call a common consensus. What can be debated is whether a specific practice is indeed part of that tradition, or whether the practice falls within the permitted limits. It is agreed, for instance, that polygyny, regardless of how 'traditional' it may have been, does not fall within those limits. In other words, there is something like a recognized domain within which the claims of cultural tradition are seen as sovereign, even if the boundaries of this domain can be argued over. It is worth noting how the notion that people have a 'right' to their culture draws on a universalist discourse of 'rights'. The discourse of 'tradition and culture' emerged very much out of the shadows cast by its apparent opposite, the discourse of 'rationalism, secularism, and equality', and the two discourses have always had an uneasy dependence on each other, with each being defined in part by reference to *not* being its opposite.

Whatever else 'tradition' be may thought to be, one of its strongest associations is with the past. It represents, in the words of the *OED*, 'long established custom', 'immemorial usage', and in general, the older a tradition can be shown to be, the greater its claim to respect. In recent years, especially since the publication of Eric Hobsbawm and Terence Ranger's *Invention of Tradition* (a deliberately paradoxical title), many scholars have focused on how much that is said to be part of 'tradition' is often of far more recent coinage, and far from being long established custom, has frequently been invented. A recently *invented* tradition would seem on the face of it to be something of a contradiction in terms, as well as being a 'tradition' that has forfeited its automatic claim to respect *as a tradition*, even if it may claim respect on other grounds. At the same time the fact that people seem to be so keen to claim authority in the name of tradition is an indication of the power of such a claim.

The persistent, if often implicit, association of culture with tradition has marked how culture has tended to be imagined in anthropology. Culture, for instance, tends to be approached as something – ideas, beliefs, practices, institutions, whatever – that already exists. Whatever it is, it tends to be seen as something handed down from generation to generation. A particular culture is seldom imagined as something that has been consciously created. Like an 'authentic' tradition, an authentic 'culture' is not thought of as invented. These underlying assumptions can perhaps be most simply illustrated by looking at how culture is defined in Bailey and Peoples' widely used anthropology textbook, *Introduction to Cultural Anthropology*. The purpose of a text book after all is, at least in part, to state clearly all those basic presuppositions which those already socialized into a discipline tend to take for granted.

After providing an overview of anthropology in their initial chapter, in their second chapter, entitled 'Culture', Bailey and Peoples move on to an explication of the anthropological concept of culture. They begin by writing that 'a useful and popular way to define culture is: the culture of a group consists of shared, socially learned knowledge and patterns of behaviour' (1999: 16). They go on to expand on the various terms of their definition over several pages, from which I have selected a few passages. What I want to draw attention to here is how running through their discussion are firstly, a tight bundling of culture and tradition, and secondly, the assumption that culture is something received from previous generations and passed on to the next. The emphasis throughout is mine.

Shared

By definition culture is collective – it is shared by some group of people. 'Shared by some group of people' is deliberately vague ... The people who share *a common cultural tradition* may be quite numerous and geographically dispersed ... When we say people share culture we usually mean at least one of two things. First, the people are capable of communicating and interacting with one another without serious misunderstanding and without needing to explain what their behavior means. Second, people share a common cultural identity: *they recognise themselves and their culture's traditions as distinct from other people and other traditions ... The identification of a cultural tradition with a single society is sometimes convenient because it allows us to use phrases like "American culture" and "Indian culture."* ...

Socially Learned

... To say that a culture is learned is to deny that culture is trans-mitted to new generations genetically, by biological reproduction. *Culture ... is something that the people born into that group acquire while growing up among other members. ... the knowledge and behavior that any generation has acquired is passed down to the next generation, which transmits it to the third generation and so on. ...* people alive today live largely (but not entirely) off *the knowledge acquired and transmitted by previous generations* ...

Knowledge

What is most important about cultural knowledge is not its Truth Value, but that ... the knowledge leads people to behave in ways that work at least well enough to allow them to survive and reproduce themselves and *transmit their culture.*

(Bailey and Peoples, 1999: 16–18)

Judging from this account of culture, culture like tradition is understood as something that, by definition, is not consciously created or invented. Invented culture, like invented tradition, rings false.

The entanglement of the concept of culture with the notion of tradition played an important role in shaping the subject matter of anthropology as a discipline. Many have drawn attention to anthropology's emergence in the context of an expansionist, colonizing West's encounters with non-Western societies: making sense of these 'others' was always central to the anthropological enterprise. But what is less often discussed is how this enterprise was also directed towards the elucidation of 'the other' of modernity itself. In the nineteenth century, as capitalism was remaking the world, modernity came to mean that transformation. If tradition stands for continuity, modernity is change. In a famous passage in *The Communist Manifesto* Marx and Engels provided a memorable image of the defining dynamism of the new capitalist world being born – a dynamism, incidently, that they by no means viewed as simply negative.

> Constant revolutionizing of production, uninterrupted distur-
> bance of all social conditions, everlasting uncertainty and
> agitation distinguish the bourgeois epoch from all earlier ones. All
> fixed, fast-frozen relations, with their train of ancient and
> venerable prejudices and opinions, are swept away, all new-
> formed ones become antiquated before they can ossify. All that is
> solid melts into air ...

> (Marx and Engels, 1998 [original edition,1848]: 38)

Whatever else might be imagined as the subject of anthropology, until recently it was seldom this dynamic modernity. There have, of course, been exceptions. *The Kalela Dance* by Mitchell (1956), an analysis of African mine workers' reimagining of their colonial world through dance, is an interesting early example.[6] In the main, however, anthropology's province was understood to be the 'fixed, fast-frozen relations, with their train of ancient and venerable prejudices and opinions' which were either being swept away and

---

6. Particularly in its early years, a number of the anthropologists of the Rhodes-Livingstone Institute in then Northern Rhodesia (of whom Mitchell was one), engaged in interesting ways with issues of industrialization and urbanization in the context of Northern Rhodesia's rapidly developing mining towns. Nonetheless, it is striking how, especially after the departure of the Institute's first director, Godfrey Wilson, in 1941, this concern with modernity increasingly tended to be framed in terms of problems of 'detribalization', with Africans being seen as essentially tribal beings (see Crehan 1997b for an account of the Rhodes-Livingstone Institute and the concept of the 'tribe').

needed to be recorded before their inevitable, if sad, demise, or were maintaining a stubborn resistance to the march of progress. In the academic division of labour out of which both sociology and anthropology emerged as recognized disciplines, with all the attendant institutional trappings, it was sociology that was given the task of making sense of modernity, while anthropology's remit was the elucidation of the worlds existing outside that modernity. Originally this remit included both societies existing spatially beyond the capitalist West, and those existing prior to the emergence of societies with recognized histories. In other words, anthropology's job was the study of those who were seen, as Wolf's ironic 1982 title puts it, as 'the people without history'. Johannes Fabian (1983) has stressed how distance in space was often equated with distance in time; hunters and gatherers, for instance, might be described as living a stone-age life that showed modern 'man' how he had lived in the remote past. While they may not have had history – the idea that societies without written records can be considered to have 'proper' histories has only slowly established itself within the discipline of history – what such peoples were considered to have was culture. Nowadays there are probably few anthropologists who are not concerned in some way or another with the effects of modernity. However, this concern, I would suggest, is still often framed in terms of the effects of modernity *on* some cultural entity or entities.

So far in this chapter the anthropologists, and the particular pieces on which I have focused, might be said by some to belong more to anthropology's past than to its present. What about more recent work that explicitly critiques the older formulations of 'culture'? It is certainly true that there are many anthropologists writing today who approach questions of culture rather differently, and I shall have more to say about some of them in Chapter 7. Nonetheless, I would argue, persistent residues of the assumptions I have identified are still to be found, sometimes even in the work of some of those most associated with new anthropological approaches. To illustrate this I want to turn in the final section of this chapter to a recent book by James Clifford, an anthropologist whom many regard as having radically challenged accepted anthropological notions of culture. I also look, more briefly, at an essay by another anthropologist whose work challenges a number of the discipline's orthodoxies, Liisa Malkki.

Of Hybrids and Hybridity

Writing Culture, a collection of essays edited by James Clifford and George Marcus published in 1986, is often identified as marking an important change of course in anthropology. After *Writing Culture*, for many anthropologists it seemed that fieldwork – that central pillar of anthropological methodology – would never look quite the same. Both Clifford and Marcus can be considered major figures in contemporary anthropology but it is Clifford on whom I want to focus here, and in particular on one of Clifford's most recent publications: *Routes: Travel and Translation in the Late Twentieth Century*, a collection of essays published in 1997 which contains many powerful insights and suggestions for the reimagining of the anthropological project.

In *Routes* Clifford, as he explains in the prologue, wrestles with the concept of culture.

> *Routes* continues an argument with the concept of culture. In earlier books, especially *The Predicament of Culture* (1988), I worried about the concept's propensity to assert holism and aesthetic form, its tendency to privilege value, hierarchy, and historical continuity in notions of common 'life.' I argued that these inclinations neglected, and at times actively repressed, many impure, unruly processes of collective invention and survival. At the same time, *concepts of culture seemed necessary if human systems of meaning and difference were to be recognised and supported.* Claims to coherent identity were, in any event, inescapable in a contemporary world riven by ethnic absolutism.
>
> (1997: 2–3, my emphasis)

While Clifford is unhappy with the concept of culture – in part because of its 'propensity to assert holism', in other words the assumption of cultures as bounded entities – he is unwilling to abandon it. Not only does he see the existence of 'cultures' in the contemporary world as an inescapable reality; the concept of culture in his view is important because it names 'human systems of meaning and difference'. For Clifford it would seem, as for Geertz, cultures are systems; and culture is at the heart of the anthropological project – as he puts it a little later in *Routes*, 'culture and its science, anthropology ...' (1997: 25). The problem for contemporary anthropologists, as he sees it, is that cultures in the modern world confront new complexes of power relations:

> In the twentieth century, cultures and identities reckon with both local and transnational powers to an unprecedented degree. Indeed the currency of culture and identity as performative acts can be traced to their articulation of homelands, safe spaces where the traffic across borders can be controlled ... Cultural action, the making and remaking of identities, takes place in the contact zones, along the policed and transgressive intercultural frontiers of nations, peoples, locales. Stasis and purity are asserted – creatively and violently – *against* historical forces of movement and contamination.
>
> (1997: 7)

This has resulted, in Clifford's view, in the emergence, in anthropology and elsewhere, of new theoretical paradigms.

> The new paradigms begin with historical contact, with entanglement at intersecting regional, national, and transnational levels. Contact approaches presuppose not sociocultural wholes subsequently brought into relationship, but rather *systems* already constituted relationally, entering new relations through historical processes of displacement.
>
> (1997: 7, my emphasis)

Note that while the notion of sociocultural wholes is rejected, what replaces it are 'systems already constituted relationally'. However, while cultures are still, it seems, to be understood as constituting systems of some kind, something has happened. As he puts it in the first essay in *Routes*, 'Traveling Cultures',

> Anthropological 'culture' is not what it used to be. And once the representational challenge is seen to be the portrayal and understanding of local/global historical encounters, co-productions, dominations, and resistances, one needs to focus on hybrid, cosmopolitan experiences as much as on rooted, native ones.
>
> (1997: 24)

The terms 'hybrid' and 'hybridity' have become popular ways of referring to the fact that many people in contemporary societies do not seem to belong to a single 'culture'. It is a term Clifford uses repeatedly in the essays in *Routes*, at one point describing himself as one of those 'who have worked towards a recognition of hybrid, relational cultural processes' (1997: 176). Hybrid is a very powerful and resonant word, implying far more than simple difference, and it is worth spending a moment examining some of these implications. Firstly, hybrid is a term rooted in biology rather than culture. According to the *Oxford English Dictionary*, its primary meaning is: 'the offspring of two animals or plants of different species, or (less strictly) varieties; a half-breed, cross-breed, or mongrel'. Even when used figuratively as an adjective it remains a word signalling an origin in distinct entities, 'derived from heterogeneous or incongruous sources; having a mixed character; composed of two diverse elements; mongrel' (*OED*). Hybrid entities, it would seem, are composed of elements that somehow do not belong together. Very importantly, even as a metaphor, I would argue, hybridity is never completely free from the taint of the biological. Clifford himself is anxious to escape the associations with the organic of the term 'culture', arguing against 'the organic, naturalizing bias of the term "culture" – seen as a rooted body that grows, lives, dies, and so on' (1997: 25). And yet his favoured term hybridity seems to me also to carry a powerful 'organic, naturalizing bias' of its own – albeit one related to the distinctiveness of species rather than to the life cycle.

So what exactly is it that makes a *culture* 'hybrid'? Clifford refers in *Routes* to his first book, published in 1982, which 'grappled with how New Caledonian Kanaks survived a peculiarly violent (and ongoing) colonial regime, finding in hybrid Christianity new ways to be different' (1997: 175). At approximately the same period as these New Caledonian Kanaks were coming up with their forms of Christianity, a number of Roman Catholic theologians were attempting to marry elements of Marxist theory with Christian theology (which could certainly be considered two 'heterogeneous or incongruous sources') to produce what they termed liberation theology. Liberation theology has been both lauded and castigated but never, to my knowledge, has it been referred to as a hybrid Christianity. Clearly some incongruities are more troubling than others. And, interestingly, it is those elements that are seen as belonging to subordinate 'cultures' – the colonized rather than the colonizing, the minority rather than the majority – that seem to signal most clearly their 'alien' origin. The New Caledonian Kanaks' cultural innovations result in a hybrid Christianity rather than a hybrid Kanak culture.

Underpinning the metaphor of hybridity, it seems to me, is a persistent assumption of the existence of distinct cultures, elements of which may intermingle in all kinds of ways but which nonetheless somehow remain rooted in that culture to which they 'belong'. Clifford's original oral presentation of 'Traveling Cultures' was followed by a discussion, parts of which were included in the version published in *Routes*. One of the participants in this discussion, Keya Ganguly, drew attention to precisely this lingering assumption of distinct and rooted cultures in 'Traveling Cultures', asking Clifford:

> When you extend the metaphor of bifocality to call for a comparative study of, for example, Haitians in Haiti and Haitians in Brooklyn, New York, don't you make the kind of reifying move that Appadurai critiques as the othering of others? By locating them as Haitians in a continuous space between Haiti and New York, Indian in India and Indian in New York, are you reinscribing an ideology of cultural difference? Being a child of Indian immigrants, I find it very difficult to identify myself with that sort of ideology of difference ... for instance, I choose to be identified with Philadelphians rather than with Indians from Bombay.
>
> (1997: 45)

Clifford's answer to Ganguly included the following statement of his position:

> I will admit to a specific localizing of 'Haitian' difference when I speak of Haiti simultaneously in Brooklyn and the Caribbean. I would hope this does not reinscribe an ideology of absolute cultural difference. I would also want to hold onto the notion that there are different cultures that are somewhere(s), not all over the map.
>
> (1997: 45)

What Clifford appears anxious to deny is any assertion of *absolute* cultural difference, but he does, it seems, want to hold on to the notion of different cultures rooted in particular geographical locations. This is particularly significant given his framing of the anthropological project. At the beginning of 'Traveling Cultures' he writes: 'My aim, initially, is to open up the question of how cultural analysis constitutes its objects – societies, traditions, communities, identities – in spatial and through specific spatial practices of research' (1997: 19). Earlier, in the Prologue to *Routes*, Clifford has already positioned himself vis-à-vis the Marxist tradition, citing Gramsci approvingly:

> These essays are written under the sign of ambivalence, a permanently fraught hope. They discover, over and over, that the good news and the bad news presuppose each other. It is impossible to think of transnational possibilities without recognizing the violent disruptions that attend 'modernization,' with its expanding markets, armies, technologies, and media. Whatever improvements or alternatives may emerge do so against this grim backdrop. Moreover unlike Marx, who saw that the possible good of socialism depended historically on the necessary evil of capitalism, I see no future resolution to the tension – no revolution or dialectical negation of the negation. Gramsci's incremental and shifting 'war of position,' a politics of partial connections and alliances, makes much more sense.
>
> (1997: 10)

Just what Gramsci meant by 'war of position' – which he contrasted with 'war of manoeuvre/movement' – has been much argued over,[7] but basically Gramsci is using military metaphors to characterize different moments of political struggle. There are times when some form of open, frontal attack is appropriate, and others when this is impossible and struggle takes the form of something like trench warfare. For Gramsci, however, as for Marx, the ultimate actors in history are not 'societies, traditions, communities, identities', they are *classes*, and it is always classes that are the, again ultimate, contenders in Gramsci's 'war of position'. There is nothing wrong in principle, of course, with Clifford's taking Gramsci's formulation, 'war of position' and using it to illuminate what he refers to in the passage immediately preceding this one as 'the politics of hybridity'. What I am not clear about, however, is just who or what has replaced classes as the ultimate contenders in this war. Is it societies, traditions, communities, identities? None of these would seem to fit

---

7. Sassoon (1987: 193–204) provides a careful discussion of the term 'war of position'. See SPN: 120, 229–35, 238–9 for Gramsci's use of 'war of position'.

very well. *Routes* itself 'tracks the worldly historical routes which both constrain and empower movements across borders and between cultures' (1997: 6), which suggests a fundamental role for 'cultures', however fractured and porous these may be, in the unfolding narratives with which Clifford's cultural analysis is concerned.

In sum, while Clifford stresses that 'Anthropological "culture" is not what it used to be', the notion of culture that runs through *Routes* remains one that continues to be haunted by some of the ghosts of anthropology past. Very significantly, particularly in relation to Gramsci's approach to culture, 'cultures' remain for Clifford a primary object of analysis. As Part II will show, this is not true for Gramsci.

Another anthropologist whose work has explored some of the realities of the contemporary world in interesting ways is Liisa Malkki. The fieldwork for her 1995 study, *Purity and Exile: Violence, Memory, and National Cosmology among Hutu Refugees in Tanzania*, was done in what in our brutal and bloody times is becoming an increasingly common 'somewhere' inhabited by millions: the refugee camp. Like Clifford's, Malkki's work is rich and insightful but it too, I would argue, is haunted from time to time by some ghosts of anthropology past. Here I have chosen to focus on Malkki's 1997 essay, 'News and Culture: Transitory Phenomena and the Fieldwork Tradition', in which she discusses the relationship between the different kinds of knowledge produced by anthropologists and by journalists. For the purposes of this chapter what interests me about this essay is not so much Malkki's thoughtful pondering on the relation between anthropology and journalism, but how she frames her discussion. For instance, I am struck by Malkki's defensiveness about her choice of a refugee camp as a field site. At the beginning of her essay she grounds her own essay in some recent work by the much respected, elder stateswoman anthropologist, Sally Falk Moore, in which Moore argues for the importance of studying change rather than continuity. Malkki goes on to state as one of the central questions of her essay:

> In the face of long traditions of studying cultures as more or less stable, durable processes of order-making that retain and reproduce their constitutive patterns over time, what do we do with fleeting, transitory phenomena that are not produced by any particular cultural grammar?
>
> (Malkki, 1997: 87)

A little later she reiterates how 'The transitory phenomena I am trying to identify are not readily analyzed in relation to "systems of meaning," "codes" or "canons"' (Malkki, 1997: 87). What I find interesting here is Malkki's apparent acceptance, at some level, that it is 'the transitory phenomena' she is interested in that are the anomaly; in 'normal' circumstances, it would seem, cultures *can* be thought of as 'more or less stable, durable processes of order-making' with their own 'cultural grammar'. Summarizing this tradition in anthropology she writes:

> Whatever their actual training or place of work, anthropologists today know that the dominant traditions of their discipline have been heavily oriented toward identifying and classifying patterns of culture, holistic principles of social organization, customary practices, oral traditions, bodies of law, systems of rules and pro-hibitions – in short phenomena that are understood to have withstood the test of time. In our fieldwork, as well as our writing, we have long been oriented to look for the repetitive, the persistent, the normative – durable forms.

> (Malkki, 1997: 89–90)

We might expect that a critical anthropologist writing in the late 1990s would identify this assumption of continuity, which treats cultures as machineries of reproduction, as perhaps problematic, but Malkki's concern seems rather to be limited to a defence of her own focus on the transitory.

> It is obviously not inherently 'wrong' to look at durable forms or structures – and it would be nonsense to argue that durable structures and practices do not exist. The point is, simply, that the analytical centering of durable structures (or at least structures we *think of* as durable) moves other phenomena out of view – transitory, nonrepetitive, anomalous phenomena.

> (Malkki, 1997: 91, Malkki's emphasis)

In her Conclusion Malkki reflects self-critically on what she sees as failures in her own fieldwork practices which she links to some of the anthropological baggage she carried with her into the field. By way of illustration she provides 'two instances of a community of memory – or perhaps better; a community of imagination –

instances that conventional anthropological practices of field research might never produce as objects of scholarly attention' (Malkki, 1997: 99). The first of these was when she visited a Hutu political leader, Gahutu Rémi, in his refugee camp compound.

> He had one round, mud house devoted to books – agronomy books, religious texts, dictionaries, and some novels (among them, I noted a copy of Stendhal's *The Red and the Black*). I should have had a longer, more careful conversation with him about his books – Stendhal and the other authors with whom he had communed – instead of seeing him so closely in relation to his geographical and 'cultural' context.
>
> (Malkki, 1997: 99–100)

The second instance is a news report from the Gulf War which reported that in the course of the bombing of Baghdad, 'books were found in the rubble of a man's house. One of them was a well-read, dedicated copy of *The Catcher in the Rye*' (Malkki, 1997: 100). Malkki's discomfort here is interesting. What does she mean exactly when she regrets seeing Rémi 'so closely in relation to his geographical and "cultural" context'? Is there not lurking in the shadows here some residual notion of cultures as bounded entities, some assumption that Rémi's essential culture is Hutu, or maybe African, and that by definition European or American culture, to paraphrase Geertz, 'are not his' (see above p. 43). Rémi's appropriation of the products of Western culture, therefore, turns him into some kind of hybrid. On the one hand, Malkki recognizes the falsity of this, yet, on the other hand, she also seems to find a copy of *The Red and the Black* in a 'round, mud house' in East Africa, and Salinger in the ruins of a bombed house in Baghdad, incongruities that need investigation. It is worth thinking about why it is that they seem so much more out of place than would a copy of, say, the Mahabharata found in the home of a European or American political figure. Sometimes it seems as if we who can claim a home in 'Western culture' have culture in the singular, while the rest of the world are boxed up into their own, unique, cultures. It is interesting how those who fill their apartments in New York, or their town houses in Islington, with Third World artefacts and play world music on their stereos are never referred to as hybrid beings adrift between cultures.

Anthropology may have been rethought in recent years, and it is certainly true that, as Clifford says, 'Anthropological "culture" is not what it used to be'. But nonetheless, it seems to me, there are still some hovering ghosts that have stubbornly resisted exorcism. It is these ghosts with which I have been concerned in this chapter. My intention, as I have already stressed, was never to provide a history of the concept of culture in anthropology. All I have tried to do is draw attention to certain persistent assumptions associated with how anthropologists – albeit not all anthropologists, there have always been interesting countertendencies – have tended to approach 'culture' as an object of study. These assumptions are that cultures are in some sense patterned wholes with their own logics (and that it is the business of anthropologists to tease out these logics), that cultures, again in some sense, constitute some kind of bounded wholes (however porous their boundaries), and that there exists a basic opposition between 'tradition' and 'modernity'. One of my reasons for writing this book was that it seems to me that Gramsci, if read seriously, can perhaps help us exorcise some of these ghosts that continue to haunt the discipline. For one thing, as we shall see in Part II, Gramsci's approach to culture is radically different from that of mainstream anthropology.

None of the assumptions I have identified are to be found in Gramsci. Firstly, for Gramsci, the cultural worlds of subalterns are anything but systematic. Rather, this Sardinian raised among peasants saw subaltern culture as an incoherent jumble that had been piled up over time in a piecemeal fashion (see particularly Chapter 5). He had no patience with those, such as the folklorists of his day, who advocated its preservation. Secondly, for Gramsci the primary object of study is never specific 'cultures', it is always power, more specifically particular constellations of power relations in particular times and places. What he is interested in is not stable, bounded cultural wholes, but *relationships* and how these create fluid and shifting social entities; where exactly a social theorist should draw the boundaries depends upon the particular question being asked. Thirdly, as a consequence of his focus on relations of power, for him the basic opposition in any society is not that between the traditional and the modern but that between the dominant and the dominated. In Gramsci's view, societies are not mosaics of different cultures, hybrid or otherwise, rather they are constellations of different power groups, with the fundamental entities being classes – as long, that is, as we understand the concept of class in an open, non-doctrinaire way.

The next three chapters trace out in some detail just what Gramsci's approach to culture is. Each chapter takes a particular set of questions about culture as its focus and gathers together relevant passages from his writings that speak to those questions. Chapter 4 examines the problem of culture and history; Chapter 5, the nature of subaltern culture; and Chapter 6, the production of culture and the role of intellectuals in this. Given the rich complexity of Gramsci's writings, and the difficulty I referred to in Chapter 2 of summarizing his thought in any adequate way, what these chapters attempt to do is to map out the terrain that 'culture' – which necessarily entails a discussion of class – occupies in his writings. In these chapters I have tried, as far as possible, to let him speak for himself. I have included, therefore, numerous extended extracts from his writings rather than attempting to paraphrase these. My aim has been to enable the reader to engage directly with Gramsci himself rather than with my version of his project – or those of his many interpreters. This aim has also meant that I have not framed these chapters in terms of the anthropological assumptions about culture on which this chapter focused, merely pointing out from time to time the absence of these assumptions in Gramsci. For the next three chapters my hope is that the reader will concentrate on following Gramsci's contour lines in mapping the cultural terrain. Once this map has been traced out, we will be ready to return in Chapter 7 to the question of the significance of Gramsci's approach to culture for anthropologists.

Part II

Gramsci on Culture

4 Culture and History

> What is the point of reference for the new world in gestation? The
> world of production; work.
>
> (SPN: 242)

When reading Gramsci it should never be forgotten that he was an
activist and his central concern was the radical transformation of
capitalist society. While for Gramsci the ultimate actors in that transformation were classes, issues of culture were for him always at the
heart of any revolutionary project since culture is, as it were, how
class is lived. And how people see their world and how they live in
it necessarily shapes their ability to imagine how it might be
changed, and whether they see such changes as feasible or desirable.
A concern with culture runs through all his writings from the very
earliest to the final prison notebooks but it is important never to lose
sight of the fact that ultimately his interest in questions of culture
stemmed from a revolutionary political project. His concern was
above all with cultural *change*; with, on the one hand, how what he
saw as progressive cultural shifts could be facilitated and how, on
the other, cultural forces he saw as reactionary could be overcome.
He could be very scornful of 'the admirers of folklore, who advocate
its preservation' (SPN: 197). Gramsci's basic concern was: how might
a more equitable and just order be brought about, and what is it
about how people live and imagine their lives in particular times and
places that advances or hampers progress to this more equitable and
just order? I begin with this point because, as the last chapter
explored, this is a very different question to ask of culture than those
that the shapers of the modern discipline of anthropology (who were
fighting other intellectual battles) characteristically asked.

This chapter and the next two attempt to map out some of the
key contours of the terrain occupied by the slippery and problematic concept 'culture' in Gramsci's writings, and to do this as much
as possible by letting Gramsci speak for himself. The first section of
this chapter gathers together some early passages from the pre-prison
writings in which Gramsci first defines what he means by culture.
These are then followed by a series of extracts from the prison

notebooks all of which engage in some way with the broad question of how ways of understanding and living in the world come into being; how and why they do, or do not, persist; and how they are, or might be, transformed. In other words, the problem of culture and history. A key theme is the profound, and complex, relationship between culture and basic economic relationships. As I have already stressed, from first to last Gramsci remains a Marxist – albeit always an extraordinarily open and flexible one – for whom the fundamental actors in history are classes. While his Marxism underwent various shifts over time, his basic commitment to the centrality of class never wavered.

It is equally important to stress, however, that 'culture' is never seen by Gramsci as merely an epiphenomenon, or simple reflection of more fundamental economic relations. While he retains even in his final writings the language of base and superstructure, in practice he transcends this over-simple metaphor of stacked layers. Crucial here is Gramsci's concept of the organic, which I discussed in Chapter 2 (see pp. 23–4). Ultimately for Gramsci, whether particular ideas, beliefs, legal systems and all the other supposedly *super*structural and 'cultural' elements should in fact be seen as an organic part of a society's basic economic structure is a question that can only be answered in the context of particular social formations at particular times. Indeed, many of the passages in Gramsci that deal with culture can be read as his continual wrestling with the problem of how this organic relationship is to be understood in particular historical contexts. Linked to this is the final point I want to emphasize before moving on to the Gramsci extracts: 'culture' in Gramsci never represents any kind of autonomous domain. Just as he does not oppose culture to some more fundamental economic base, neither does he oppose it to history. Culture is for Gramsci rather a precipitate continually generated in the course of history. In other words, the ways of being and of living in the world that we think of as culture can be seen as particular forms assumed by the interaction of a multitude of historical processes at particular moments of time. Gramsci's whole approach to culture, therefore, is very far from any kind of traditional anthropological mapping out of distinct and bounded 'cultures'.

Culture in the Pre-Prison Writings

In 1917 the young Gramsci was at the beginning of his journalistic career and still to some extent under the influence of Croce. In

December of that year he wrote an article in the socialist newspaper *Avanti!* in response to an earlier piece by a union organizer critical of Gramsci's proposals for a workers' cultural association. Here he defines culture as follows:

> I give culture this meaning: exercise of thought, acquisition of general ideas, habit of connecting causes and effects. For me, everybody is already cultured because everybody thinks, everybody connects causes and effects. But they are empirically, primordially cultured, not organically. They therefore waver, disband, soften, or become violent, intolerant, quarrelsome, according to the occasion and the circumstances. I'll make myself clearer: *I have a Socratic idea of culture; I believe that it means thinking well, whatever one thinks, and therefore acting well, whatever one does.* And since I know that culture too is a basic concept of socialism, because it integrates and makes concrete the vague concept of freedom of thought, I would like it to be enlivened by the other concept, that of organization. Let us organize culture in the same way that we seek to organize any practical activity. Philanthropically, the bourgeoisie have decided to offer the proletariat the Popular Universities. As a counterproposal to philanthropy, let us offer solidarity, organization. Let us give the means to good will, without which it will always remain sterile and barren. It is not the lecture that should interest us, but the detailed work of discussing and investigating problems, work in which everybody participates, to which everybody contributes, in which everybody is both master and disciple.
>
> (SCW: 25, my emphasis)

This introduces two themes that continue to run through Gramsci's pre-prison writings on culture and throughout the prison notebooks. Firstly, culture is understood as thought in action, as a means by which people are able actively to understand their place within the reality within which they live. Gramsci's insistence here, for instance, that 'everybody is already cultured because everybody thinks, everybody connects causes and effects', prefigures his later prison writings on intellectuals where he writes, 'All men are intellectuals, one could therefore say: but not all men have in society the function of intellectuals ... There is no human activity from which every form of intellectual participation can be excluded: *homo faber* cannot be separated from *homo sapiens*' (SPN: 9). The second theme in the *Avanti!* article to note is the stress on the importance of organisation. Left to themselves people (and here, of course, Gramsci is concerned with workers) are 'empirically, primordially cultured, not organically'. What is needed is for progressives to organize and develop this embryonic proletarian culture.

In January 1916, almost two years before he wrote this article, Gramsci had written a piece for another socialist newspaper, *Il Grido del Popolo,* under the heading 'Socialism and Culture', in which he had expanded on the nature of 'culture' and its relationship to revolutionary change. It is worth quoting from this article at some length since while it clearly represents a young Gramsci, with some echoes of Croce, the theme of 'culture' as providing people with the tools not merely to understand but to change the world remains central to Gramsci's intellectual project in the prison notebooks. It also provides a good introduction to the flavour of Gramsci's writing and shows how early he had developed his very distinctive, direct, combative style. As in the previous extract Gramsci begins by disputing an understanding of culture as passive knowledge.

We need to free ourselves from the habit of seeing culture as encyclopaedic knowledge, and men as mere receptacles to be stuffed full of empirical data and a mass of unconnected raw facts, which have to be filed in the brain as in the columns of a dictionary, enabling their owner to respond to the various stimuli from the outside world. This form of culture really is harmful, particularly for the proletariat. It serves only to create maladjusted people, people who believe they are superior to the rest of humanity because they have memorized a certain number of facts and dates and who rattle them off at every opportunity, so turning them almost into a barrier between themselves and others ... But this is not culture, but pedantry, not intelligence, but intellect, and it is absolutely right to react against it.

Culture is something quite different. It is organization, discipline of one's inner self, a coming to terms with one's own personality; it is the attainment of a higher awareness, with the aid of which one succeeds in understanding one's own historical value, one's own function in life, one's own rights and obligations. But none of this can come about through spontaneous evolution, through a series of actions and reactions which are independent of one's own will ... Above all, man is mind, i.e. he is a product of history, not nature. Otherwise how could one explain the fact, given that there have always been exploiters and exploited, creators of wealth and its selfish consumers, that socialism has not yet come into being? The fact is that only by degrees, one stage at a time, has humanity acquired consciousness of its own value and won for itself the right to throw off the patterns of organization imposed on it by minorities at a previous period in history. And this consciousness was formed not under the brutal goad of physiological necessity, but as a result of intelligent reflection, at first by just a few people and later by a whole class, on why certain conditions exist and how best to convert the facts of vassalage into the signals of rebellion and social reconstruction. This means that every revolution has been preceded by an intense labour of criticism, by the diffusion of culture and the spread of ideas amongst masses of men who are at first resistant, and think only of solving their own immediate economic and political problems for themselves, who have no ties of solidarity with others in the same condition. The latest example, the closest to us and hence least foreign to our own time, is that of the French Revolution. The preceding cultural period, called the Enlightenment ... was a magnificent revolution in itself and, as De Sanctis acutely notes in his *History of Italian Literature,* it gave all Europe a bourgeois spiritual International in the form of a unified consciousness, one which was sensitive to all the woes and misfortunes of the common people and which was the best possible preparation for the bloody revolt that followed in France ...

The same phenomenon is being repeated today in the case of socialism. It was through a critique of capitalist civilization that the unified consciousness of the proletariat was or is still being formed, and a critique implies culture, not simply a spontaneous and naturalistic evolution. A critique implies precisely the self-consciousness that Novalis[1] considered to be the end of culture. Consciousness of a self which is opposed to others, which is differentiated and, once having set itself a goal, can judge facts and events other than in themselves or for themselves but also in so far as they tend to drive history forward or backward. To know oneself means to be oneself, to be master of oneself, to distinguish oneself, to free oneself from a state of chaos, to exist as an element of order – but of one's own order and one's own discipline in

1. Novalis was the pen-name of Freidrich von Hardenberg (1772–1801) German Romantic poet and novelist called the 'Prophet of Romanticism'. All footnotes to the extracts from Gramsci's writings are mine.

striving for an ideal. And we cannot be successful in this unless we also know others, their history, the successive efforts they have made to be what they are, to create the civilization they have created and which we seek to replace with our own. In other words, we must form some idea of nature and its laws in order to come to know the laws governing the mind. And we must learn all this without losing sight of the ultimate aim: to know oneself better through others and to know others better through oneself.

(SPWI: 10–13, my emphasis)

Culture here is defined as the work of self-knowledge, but not a narrowly individualized self-knowledge, rather a critical self-knowledge focused on understanding one's relations to others, including one's 'rights and obligations' in relation to them, and one's place in history. Having explained what culture means for him, Gramsci at once goes on to reject the idea of consciousness as emerging 'spontaneously' since if an awareness of social realities was automatic, 'how could one explain the fact, given that there have always been exploiters and exploited, creators of wealth and its selfish consumers, that socialism has not yet come into being?' Gramsci, in common with Marx and others in the Marxist tradition, is often accused of thinking teleologically and believing that socialism is somehow inevitable and that all human history can be seen as leading up to this final end point. It is important, therefore, to clarify just where Gramsci stands here, and since the accusation of teleology is so often seen as one of the most damning of all those levelled against Marx and Marxism, a clarification of Gramsci's position deserves a short section of its own.

Gramsci and Teleology

Gramsci most certainly did not have a teleological view of human history and had little time for those who did. His dismissive attitude comes out clearly in the prison notebooks, as when he castigates those who oppose on principle any form of political compromise:

For the conception upon which the aversion is based can only be the iron conviction that there exist objective laws of historical development similar in kind to natural laws, together with a belief in a predetermined teleology like that of a religion: since favourable conditions are inevitably going to appear, and since these, in a rather mysterious way, will bring about palingenetic events, it is evident that any deliberate initiative tending to predispose and plan these conditions is not only useless but even harmful.

(SPN: 168)

Gramsci in fact spent a good deal of time before he was imprisoned struggling against this kind of misguided intransigence within his own party. And in the prison notebooks he devotes many pages to the dismissal of Bukharin's *The Theory of Historical Materialism: A Manual of Popular Sociology*[2] precisely because he saw it as reducing Marxism to a rigid, teleological dogma. Even in the very early *Il Grido del Popolo* article he recognized the basic problem that while certain groups may appear to outside observers to be exploited, they themselves do not necessarily see things that way, frequently manifesting in the eyes of those outside observers a strange, and irritating, resistance to assuming their historical duty of rising up against their oppressors. At the same time, however, Gramsci in this article clearly assumes some kind of forward march of human progress within which the development of new forms of consciousness by subjugated peoples, as they become aware of their conditions of subjugation, is a crucial component. Gramsci's view is not teleological, however, since he does not see the development of these new forms of consciousness as in any way inevitable. As he puts it in the prison notebooks, 'Politics in fact is at any given time the reflection of the tendencies of development in the structure, but it is not necessarily the case that these tendencies must be realised' (SPN: 408). Neither is Gramsci an economic determinist. He writes, for instance,

It may be ruled out that immediate economic crises of themselves produce fundamental historical events; they can simply create a terrain more favourable to the dissemination of certain modes of thought, and certain ways of posing and resolving questions involving the entire subsequent development of national life.

(SPN: 184)

2. Nikolai Bukharin (1888–1938) was a prominent Russian communist executed by Stalin after one of the great show trials of the 1930s. In *The Theory of Historical Materialism* he attempted to provide a popular account of Marxism aimed at a non-scholarly audience.

In the following passage from the notebooks Gramsci explains clearly his unequivocal rejection of teleology and the crude historical determinism adopted by some of the followers of Marx, stressing instead the importance of human will, even, as the editors of the *Selections from the Prison Notebooks* point out, using the voluntaristic concepts of Henri Bergson – albeit giving them a somewhat different meaning – to drive home his point.[3]

> Possibility is not reality: but it is in itself a reality. Whether a man can or cannot do a thing has its importance in evaluating what is done in reality. Possibility means 'freedom'. The measure of freedom enters into the concept of man. That the objective possibilities exist for people not to die of hunger and that people do die of hunger, has its importance, or so one would have thought. But the existence of objective conditions, of possibilities or of freedom is not yet enough: it is necessary to 'know' them, and know how to use them. And to want to use them. Man, in this sense, is concrete will, that is, the effective application of the abstract will or vital impulse to the concrete means which realise such a will.
>
> (SPN: 360)

It is because this kind of progressive will does not come into being spontaneously, because human history is not programmed towards some single *telos*, that the problem of culture loomed so large for Gramsci, and that he was so interested in the role of intellectuals in that history. New forms of consciousness, to go back to the *Il Grido del Popolo* piece, do not emerge automatically, they are 'formed not under the brutal goad of physiological necessity, but as a result of intelligent reflection, at first by just a few people and later by a whole class, on why certain conditions exist and how best to convert the facts of vassalage into the signals of rebellion and social reconstruction'. In the description of 'intelligent reflection, at first just by a few people', there is a prefiguring of Gramsci's later focus on the role of intellectuals in bringing new 'cultures' into being. Interestingly, for Gramsci here, central to the notion of 'culture' is the ability to

3. Henri Bergson (1859–1941) was a French philosopher whose notion of the *élan vital* or 'creative impulse'as central to human history was highly influential among many thinkers of his time. See n. 4 (SPN: 325) and n. 50 (SPN: 360) for a discussion of Bergson's possible influence on Gramsci.

theorize a critique which moves beyond a narrow concern on the part of 'masses of men' with 'solving their own immediate economic and political problems for themselves', to an understanding of how these 'masses of men' are in reality linked to one another. 'It was through a critique of capitalist civilization that the unified consciousness of the proletariat was or is still being formed, *and a critique implies culture*, not simply a spontaneous and naturalistic evolution' (my emphasis). Crucial to this critique is the ability to evaluate 'facts and events' and to judge whether 'they tend to drive history backwards or forwards'. Clearly there is an underlying notion of historical progress here, but, let me stress again, the movement forward towards socialism for Gramsci is by no means inevitable; history can move backwards as well as forwards. It is true that in one Note he writes, 'in the movement of history there is never any turning back', but this is in the context of a discussion of what he termed Caesarism, that is, a situation in which the basic contending forces in society 'balance each other in such a way that a continuation of the conflict can only terminate in their reciprocal destruction' and a third force intervenes from outside. In such a situation, 'The problem is to see whether in the dialectic "revolution/restoration" it is revolution or restoration which predominates; for it is certain that in the movement of history there is never any turning back, and that restorations *in toto* do not exist' (SPN: 219–20). Gramsci's point here, however, is the impossibility of any society being able to return exactly to an earlier state. History in that sense does advance, but it does not advance to a known and predictable endpoint.

Gramsci's attitude to any kind of socialist teleology can be summed up as follows. He knew what direction he *wanted* human history to move in, but he never assumed that it would. He certainly did believe that movement in this direction was possible, and that the structural contradictions of capitalist society themselves create that possibility; but while the potential for socialist transformation may be given, its realization depends on the existence of a conscious human will that understands what is possible in any given circumstances, and is determined to bring it into existence. His life's work, both as a political activist before his imprisonment – at the time of his arrest he was, it should be remembered, one of the leaders of the Italian Communist Party – and in the prison notebooks, centred on the question of how such a conscious human will actually emerged and how to facilitate this process. In part, it is Gramsci's total rejection of any form of teleological thinking that makes the problem of 'culture' so central to his intellectual project.

Moving on now from the issue of teleology, I want to look first at some examples from the prison notebooks in which Gramsci both explicitly and implicitly explains what he understands by 'culture', going on from these to some passages that deal with the idea of cultural revolution.

Culture and Cultural Revolution in the Prison Notebooks

When Gramsci laid out his plans for study in prison in the famous 1927 letter to his sister-in-law (discussed in Chapter 2), he explained that the four topics he has outlined (Italian intellectuals, comparative linguistics, the theatre of Pirandello and the serial novel) are all in some way concerned with 'the creative spirit of the people in its diverse stages and degrees of development' (PLI: 84). And it was always this creative spirit, and the potential of a critical cultural awareness to make history, in which Gramsci was interested. Culture for Gramsci *acts* on the world. In one of the Notes on 'Americanism and Fordism'[4] he writes, for instance:

> the difference between real action on the one hand, which modifies in an essential way both man and external reality (*in other words, real culture*) and which is Americanism, and on the other hand the gladiatorial futility which is self-declared action but modifies only the word, not things, the external gesture and not the man inside.
>
> (SPN: 307, my emphasis)

In a Note in which he attacks the idea that philosophy is a strange and arcane pursuit limited to a class of professional philosophers, Gramsci makes the point that we are all philosophers in a sense 'since even in the slightest manifestation of any intellectual activity

---

4. Gramsci wrote a series of Notes under the general heading 'Americanism and Fordism' in which he examines the transformations in American productive methods after the First World War, and considers their impact on Europe. The basic question with which Gramsci was concerned in these Notes was, in the words of Hoare and Nowell Smith: 'were the changes taking place within the world of production at the time he was writing of such importance as to constitute the beginnings of a new historical epoch, or were they merely a conjunction of events of no lasting significance?' (SPN: 277).

whatever, in "language", there is contained a specific conception of the world ...' (SPN: 323). These conceptions of the world constitute cultural perspectives, as the continuation of the Note makes clear:

> ... one then moves on to the second level, which is that of awareness and criticism. That is to say, one proceeds to the question – is it better to 'think', without having a critical awareness, in a disjointed and episodic way? In other words, is it better to take part in a conception of the world mechanically imposed by the external environment, i.e. by one of the many social groups in which everyone is automatically involved from the moment of his entry into the conscious world (and this can be one's village or province; it can have its origins in the parish and the 'intellectual activity' of the local priest or ageing patriarch whose wisdom is law, or in the little old woman who has inherited the lore of the witches or the minor intellectual soured by his own stupidity and inability to act)? Or, on the other hand, is it better to work out consciously and critically one's own conception of the world and thus, in connection with the labours of one's own brain, choose one's sphere of activity, take an active part in the creation of the history of the world, be one's own guide, refusing to accept passively and supinely from outside the moulding of one's personality? ... In acquiring one's conception of the world one always belongs to a particular grouping which is that of all the social elements which share the same mode of thinking and acting. We are all conformists of some conformism or other, always man-in-the-mass or collective man.
>
> (SPN: 323–4)

The final two sentences here give us another definition of culture: cultures are particular groupings made up of 'all the social elements which share the same mode of thinking and acting' and we all belong to some form of such a grouping, 'We are all conformists of some conformism or other'. The crucial distinction Gramsci wants to draw here is between an unthinking, 'mechanical' adoption of the culture given by the social milieu into which we are born, and a critical and conscious working-out of our own 'conception of the world'. Three points to note about this passage are: firstly, Gramsci's scorn for 'the "intellectual activity" of the local priest or ageing patriarch whose wisdom is law, for the little old woman who has inherited the lore of the witches, and for the minor intellectual soured by his own stupidity and inability to act'. In the next chapter I shall have more to say about Gramsci's highly critical attitude to rural Italian society. Secondly, in contrast to the stress in anthropology on cultures as bounded entities that I explored in the previous chapter, Gramsci sees these different conceptions of the world not as constituting bounded wholes, but rather as a complex tapestry of interwoven strands. Thirdly, while we can in some sense choose to belong to a culture with the potential to 'take an active part in the creation of the history of the world', this always involves a struggle with external forces which act to 'mould' our personality. We are of necessity social beings, always already part of some social world, but through conscious, critical activity we have the potential to become part of an emerging, progressive and dynamic culture. Gramsci's stress on culture as an individual's critical engagement with the various social worlds into which they are born in such a way as to go beyond them to create a new culture is very different to anthropology's characteristic focus on actually existing cultures. Later in the same Note Gramsci talks about how new cultures are created:

> Creating a new culture does not only mean one's own individual 'original' discoveries. It also, and most particularly, means the diffusion in a critical form of truths already discovered, their 'socialisation' as it were, and even making them the basis of vital action, an element of co-ordination and intellectual and moral order. For a mass of people to be led to think coherently and in the same coherent fashion about the real present world, is a 'philosophical' event far more important and 'original' than the discovery by some philosophical 'genius' of a truth which remains the property of small groups of intellectuals.

> (SPN: 325)

For Gramsci, Marxism itself should be seen as a new cultural synthesis that captured the theoretical, the economic and the political 'moments' of the capitalist era in all its contradictions. He writes:

> It is affirmed that the philosophy of praxis [the normal way Gramsci refers to Marxism in the prison notebooks[5]] was born on

5. See Chapter 2, p. 22 for a discussion of the significance of this terminology.

the terrain of the highest development of culture in the first half of the nineteenth century, this culture being represented by classical German philosophy, English classical economics and French political literature and practice. These three cultural movements are at the origin of the philosophy of praxis. But in what sense is the affirmation to be understood? That each of these movements has contributed respectively to the elaboration of the philosophy, the economics and the politics of the philosophy of praxis? Or that the philosophy of praxis has synthesised the three movements, that is, the entire culture of the age, and that in the new synthesis, whichever 'moment' one is examining, the theoretical, the economic, or the political, one will find each of the three movements present as a preparatory 'moment'? This is what seems to me to be the case. And it seems to me that the unitary 'moment' of synthesis is to be identified in the new concept of immanence, which has been translated from the speculative form, as put forward by classical German philosophy, into a historicist form with the aid of French politics and English classical economics.

(SPN: 399–400)

Among other things, Marxism represented for Gramsci the cultural expression of a revolution in thought and practice which, as he saw it, was tearing apart the established certainties of the bourgeois world and painfully and slowly, with many missteps, giving birth to a new post-capitalist order. A key dimension of this cultural revolution was the formation of new kinds of human beings. Gramsci rejected completely any notion of autonomous individual subjectivity as existing, in any sense, outside a particular time and place. For him the individual necessarily comes to consciousness in the context of a particular constellation of power relations, and cannot be imagined outside that historical location. Rather, as he in writes in a Note on 'Progress and Becoming', 'man' should be 'conceived of as the *ensemble* of social relations ... man is also the *ensemble* of his conditions of life ...' (SPN: 359, Gramsci's emphasis). In another Note he writes:

Conformism has always existed: what is involved today is a struggle between 'two conformisms', i.e. a struggle for hegemony, a crisis of civil society. The old intellectual and moral leaders of society feel the ground slipping from under their feet; they perceive that their 'sermons' have become precisely mere sermons, i.e. external to reality, pure form without any content, shades without a spirit. This is the reason for their reactionary and conservative tendencies; for the particular form of civilisation, culture and morality which they represented is decomposing, and they loudly proclaim the death of all civilisation, all culture, all morality; they call for repressive measures by the State, and constitute resistance groups cut off from the real historical process, thus prolonging the crisis, since the eclipse of a way of living and thinking cannot take place without a crisis. The representatives of the new order in gestation, on the other hand, inspired by 'rationalistic' hatred for the old, propagate utopias and fanciful schemes. What is the point of reference for the new world in gestation? The world of production; work. The greatest utilitarianism must go to found any analysis of the moral and intellectual institutions to be created and of the principles to be propagated. Collective and individual life must be organised with a view to the maximum yield of the productive apparatus. The development of economic forces on new bases and the progressive installation of the new structure will heal the contradictions which cannot fail to exist, and, when they have created a new 'conformism' from below, will permit new possibilities for self-discipline, i.e. for freedom, including that of the individual.

(SPN: 242)

What is involved here is the collapse of an existing cultural order whereby 'the old intellectual and moral leaders of society' can no longer rely on the old cultural consensus as to how society should be run and how people should live, and 'loudly proclaim the death of all civilisation, all culture, all morality'. Since they can no longer rule by consensus they look to force to preserve their way of life and call for repression by the state. It is worth noting how, while Gramsci is clearly on the side of the 'new order in gestation', he is keenly aware of the prevalence of romantic delusions among its representives, who are prone to 'propagate utopias and fanciful schemes'.

The revolution that he saw as in progress in his own time was for him equivalent to the revolution that had demolished the feudal order and brought into being the bourgeois world. And this earlier revolution too had necessarily involved a radical cultural transformation. In the prison notebooks he devotes a good deal of space to the exploration of the nature and history of that earlier bourgeois revolution – particularly as it played itself out in an ultimately arrested form in Italy – and the lessons that contemporary socialists could learn from that history. In a Note headed 'Humanism and Renaissance', Gramsci's main concern is to attack careless and over-generalizing summaries of the Renaissance as 'discovering "man"', but the Note also shows how he saw the Renaissance as a 'great cultural revolution':

> What does it mean that the Renaissance discovered 'man', that it made him the centre of the universe, etc.? Does it mean that before the Renaissance 'man' was not the centre of the universe? One could say that the Renaissance created a new culture or civilization, in opposition to the preceding ones or as a development of them, but one must 'limit' or 'specify' the nature of this culture. Is it really true that before the Renaissance 'man' was nothing and then became everything or is it that a process of cultural formation was developed in which man tended to become everything? It seems that we must say that before the Renaissance the transcendent formed the basis of medieval culture; but were those who represented this culture 'nothing' or was not perhaps that culture their way of being 'everything'? If the Renaissance was a great cultural revolution, it is not because everybody began to think that he was 'everything' instead of 'nothing'. It is because this way of thinking became widespread, became universal leaven. Man was not 'discovered', rather a new form of culture was initiated, a new effort to create a new type of man in the dominant classes.

> (SCW: 217)

Note here how Gramsci is careful to characterize the 'great cultural revolution' of the Renaissance as concerned with the creation of 'a new type of man in the *dominant* classes'. For Gramsci the humanism of the Renaissance was an essentially elitist cultural movement that did not spread beyond the dominant classes. The Reformation, by contrast, he saw as representing a cultural revolution that did extend to the non-elite. In a Note headed 'The Philosophy of Praxis and Modern Culture' he writes:

> In the history of cultural developments, it is important to pay special attention to the organisation of culture and the personnel through whom this organisation takes concrete form ... [The intel-

lectuals of the Reformation, such as Erasmus] gave way in the face of persecution and the stake. *The bearer of the Reformation was therefore the German people itself in its totality, as undifferentiated mass, not the intellectuals.* It is precisely this desertion of the intellectuals in the face of the enemy which explains the 'sterility' of the Reformation in the immediate sphere of high culture, until, by a process of selection, the people, which remained faithful to the cause, produced a new group of intellectuals culminating in classical philosophy.

(SPN: 397, my emphasis)

Note here also how it is 'the people' who Gramsci sees as having producing 'a new group of intellectuals'. I will come back to this point in Chapter 6.

An article by the literary historian Vittorio Rossi prompted the following reflection on language and how the Renaissance as cultural revolution has to be seen as involving conflict between radically different conceptions of the world:

Rossi is quite right to say that 'the use a people makes of one language rather than another for disinterested intellectual ends is not an individual or collective whim, but the spontaneous act of a peculiar inner life, springing out in the only form that is suited to it.' In other words, every language is an integral conception of the world and not simply a piece of clothing than can fit indifferently as form over any content. Well then? Does not this mean that [during the Renaissance] two conceptions of the world were in conflict: a bourgeois-popular one expressing itself in the vernacular and an aristocratic-feudal one expressing itself in Latin and harking back to Roman antiquity? And is not the Renaissance characterized by this conflict rather than by the serene creation of a triumphant culture?

(SCW: 226)

It is important to stress that cultural revolution, like culture itself, was never for Gramsci simply the 'reflection' of some more profound economic underpinning. The linguistic struggle between the vernacular and Latin described here, for instance, was for Gramsci an integral part of the economic and political struggle for bourgeois hegemony.

It is also important here to clarify what Gramsci means when he insists that 'every language is an integral conception of the world and not simply a piece of clothing than can fit indifferently as form over any content', and that during the Renaissance there were two distinct and conflicting 'conceptions of the world'. At the end of the last chapter I stressed that Gramsci does not approach cultures as logical, coherent systems, and yet is he not here identifying two cultural logics? The difference, I would argue, is that for Gramsci the logical coherence of these two 'conceptions of the world' derives from a meshing with the respective 'needs' of two distinct, and very broadly defined, class positions, which gives each a very general orientation, while allowing for considerable heterogeneity and contradiction. Gramsci was always as interested in contradictions and conflict as in coherence. But, lest I be accused of functionalism, let me clarify what I mean by 'needs' here. I do not mean that those conceptions of the world were generated in any mechanical way to rationalize particular forms of exploitation, rather that those who are located economically in specific ways are likely to find plausible accounts of the world they inhabit which in some sense mesh with their experience of their economic positioning. Over time, if those economic locations are, as Gramsci puts it, fundamental, each will tend to give rise to accounts of the world as it appears from that particular vantage point. It should be noted, however, that producing *coherent* accounts involved in Gramsci's view the emergence of intellectuals organically linked to that class position.[6] Very importantly, for Gramsci such broad cultural clusters are profoundly historical phenomena entangled with fundamental economic relations; he never approached them as anything like autonomous, purely cultural 'systems'. What Gramsci is ultimately concerned with in mapping out what persists, and what does not, is the persistence, change or transformation not of 'conceptions of the world' in themselves, but of the basic power relations of which such conceptions are, to use Gramscian terminology, an organic part.

The final section of this chapter gathers together a series of passages in which Gramsci expands on the complex entanglement of economic relations and cultural expression. In these elaborations we can begin to trace out just how Gramsci locates 'culture' in

6. Gramsci's concept of the organic intellectual, and how he saw the role of intellectuals generally in society is discussed at length in Chapter 6.

'history'. First, however, it is important to clarify Gramsci's position as regards economic determination.

'The *Ultimately* Determining Factor in History'

As I explained in Chapter 2, Gramsci's starting point was a clearly Marxist one in which basic economic relations provide the ultimate dynamic of history. At the same time Gramsci was never an economic determinist. Like so many Marxists both before and after him Gramsci drew attention to two famous letters of Engels, one to Joseph Bloch (21 September 1890) and one to Heinz Starkenburg (25 January 1894) in which Engels cautions against a crudely economistic reading of the work of Marx and himself. As Gramsci puts it, 'Engels' statement too should be recalled, that the economy is only the mainspring of history "in the last analysis" ...' (SPN: 162). This caution, it seems, cannot be reiterated too often given the regularity with which this charge continues to be made. It is useful to recall Engels' careful phrasing.

> According to the materialist conception of history, the *ultimately* determining factor in history is the production and reproduction of real life. Neither Marx nor I have ever asserted more than this. Hence if somebody twists this into saying that the economic factor is the *only* determining one, he transforms the proposition into a meaningless, abstract, absurd phrase.
>
> (Marx and Engels, 1975: 394, Engels' emphasis)

Now, of course, just what we should take 'ultimately', or 'in the last analysis', to mean remains a question. Indeed, one way of seeing Gramsci's intellectual project is as the exploration of just what that slippery 'ultimately' might mean in practice. Nonetheless, since the Gramsci extracts in this section for the most part present a Gramsci emphasizing the role of economic factors in history, it is important to be clear as to the limits he saw to this shaping power.

It is also worth quoting another couple of sentences from later in the Bloch letter in which Engels accepts that Marx and he are to some extent responsible for an overemphasis on the economic by their followers.

Marx and I are ourselves partly to blame for the fact that the younger people sometimes lay more stress on the economic side than is due to it. We had to emphasise the main principle *vis-à-vis* our adversaries, who denied it, and we had not always the time, the place or the opportunity to give their due to the other factors involved in the interaction.

(Marx and Engels, 1975: 396)

This is a useful point to remember when trying to tease out just where Gramsci stood on certain questions (such as the role of basic economic relations) given, as I discussed in Chapter 2, his characteristic dialogic style. In his writings Gramsci tends always to be engaging, explicitly or implicitly, with an opposing point of view. This is as true of the prison notebooks as of his earlier more straightforwardly polemical journalism. Writing more than a generation after Marx and Engels, and writing primarily for an audience of leftists, Gramsci's concern was more with combating dogmatic economism than with asserting the importance of the economic. His focus on factors other than the economic is in part a reflection of his debates with his leftist adversaries, but only in part. It should also be stressed that Gramsci is elaborating a political theory that *does* take fully into account those 'other factors' that Marx and Engels were not able to treat adequately. The fact that he does so should not be taken to mean that he rejected the basic Marxist premise that it is the economic 'structure' in the form of the classes brought into being on that structural terrain that is the ultimate dynamic of history. Indeed, he continually comes back to the need for an analysis of this structure, as in this note on Machiavelli:

> One of the first sections [of *The Modern Prince*[7]] must precisely be devoted to the 'collective will', posing the question in the following terms: 'When can the conditions for awakening and developing a national-popular collective will be said to exist?' *Hence an historical (economic) analysis of the social structure of the given country* and a 'dramatic' representation of the attempts made

7. Just as Machiavelli had theorized the emergence of an Italian national state under a single Prince, so in the modern period it was necessary to theorize a new socialist hegemony capable of replacing the existing bourgeois one. This new hegemony, however, could not find embodiment in a single individual; the equivalent of Machiavelli's Prince, in other words, the modern prince, would be the Communist Party.

in the course of the centuries to awaken this will, together with the reasons for the successive failures.

(SPN: 130, my emphasis)

In Chapter 6 I shall discuss what Gramsci meant by a national-popular collective will (see pp. 152–5); here I just want to draw attention to Gramsci's assumption that if we want to know what potential there is in a given society for the emergence of any form of collective political will, then we need to map out its economic and social structure and how this has developed over time.

Gramsci's careful discussion of those known in Italy as *morti di fame* (glossed by the SPN editors as, 'Literally "starveling[s]", the term has overtones of both pity and contempt' (SPN: 272)) is a good example of how in practice he approached the analysis of the relationship between a particular economic situation and political consciousness.

The *morti di fame* are not a homogeneous stratum, and serious mistakes can be made if they are identified abstractly. In the village, and in the small urban centres of certain agricultural regions, there exist two distinct strata of *morti di fame:* the day-labourers, and the petty intellectuals. The essential characteristic of the day-labourers is not their economic situation but their intellectual and moral condition. The typical peasant of these regions is the smallholder or the more primitive share-cropper (whose rent takes the form of a third, half, or even two-thirds of his crop, depending on the fertility and location of his holding), who owns a few tools, a pair of oxen, and a cottage which he has often built himself on days when he is not working, and who has obtained the necessary capital either by emigrating for a few years, or by spending a few years 'down the pits' or serving in the *carabinieri*,[8] etc., or as a servant for a big landowner – i.e. by 'contriving' and saving. The day-labourer on the other hand, unable or unwilling to 'contrive', possesses nothing, is a *morto di fame*, because day labour is scarce and irregular.

The petit-bourgeois *morto di fame* came originally from the rural bourgeoisie. Property gets broken up among large families until it vanishes altogether, but the members of this class are not prepared

---

8. The *carabinieri* is in effect a police force, but one that is organized on military lines and is independent from the ordinary police force.

to work with their hands. In this way there is formed a famished stratum of aspirants to minor municipal appointments, as clerks, messengers, etc. This stratum constitutes a disruptive element in the life of the countryside, always thirsting for changes (elections, etc.), and furnishes the local 'subversive'; since it is fairly numerous, it has a certain importance. It allies itself especially with the rural bourgeoisie against the peasantry, and organises the *morti di fame* to serve its interests.

(SPN: 273–4)

Structure and Superstructure

In the prison notebooks Gramsci often wrestles with 'the problem of the relations between structure and superstructure', as in the Note 'Analysis of Situations. Relations of Force'. Gramsci argues here that it is important to distinguish between the various 'moments or levels' of 'relations of forces' existing in society. The first level, essentially the level of 'structure', is

A relation of social forces which is closely linked to the structure, objective, independent of human will, and which can be measured with the systems of the exact or physical sciences. The level of development of the material forces of production provides a basis for the emergence of the various social classes, each one of which represents a function and has a specific position within production itself. This relation is what it is, a refractory reality: nobody can alter the number of firms or their employees, the number of cities or the given urban population, etc. By studying these fundamental data it is possible to discover whether in a particular society there exist the necessary and sufficient conditions for its transformation – in other words, to check the degree of realism and practicability of the various ideologies which have been born on its own terrain, on the terrain of the contradictions which it has engendered during the course of its development.

(SPN: 180–1)

Note that it is 'the level of development of the material forces of production' which is the 'basis for the emergence of the various social classes' and that each of these classes 'represents a function and has a specific position within production itself'. Also, very importantly, for Gramsci this is an objective, 'refractory reality' that 'is what it is'. A second level or moment is 'the relation of political forces; in other words, an evaluation of the degree of homogeneity, self-awareness, and organisation attained by the various social classes' (SPN: 181). The distinction Gramsci is making here is essentially the same as Marx makes between 'class-in-itself' and 'class-for-itself',[9] between that is, the *potential* created by certain structural relations for a class with a consciousness of itself as a class to emerge, and the *actuality* of a class with such a consciousness having come into being. And indeed, the progress, or lack of it, from one to the other is Gramsci's central concern.

Gramsci goes on to analyse the various levels within this second political level, laying out the broad path by which he sees certain fundamental economic interests as becoming progressively more conscious of themselves as political actors until finally they are able to achieve a hegemony over the whole society. I have emphasized certain phrases and sentences which make it clear that what Gramsci is talking about here is a process (which may or may not be realized; what is at issue here is a historical *possibility* not a certainty) driven ultimately by economic realities, the 'structure' of society. These various levels correspond

> to the various moments of collective political consciousness, as they have manifested themselves in history up till now. *The first and most elementary of these is the economic-corporate level*: a tradesman feels *obliged* [Gramsci's italics] to stand by another tradesman, a manufacturer by another manufacturer, etc., but the tradesman does not yet feel solidarity with the manufacturer; in other words, the members of the professional group are conscious of its unity and homogeneity, and of the need to organise it, but in the case of the wider social group this is not yet so. *A second moment is that in which consciousness is reached of the solidarity of interests among all the members of a social class – but still in the purely economic field*. Already at this juncture the problem of the State is posed – but only in terms of winning politico-juridical equality

9. This distinction is to be found in *The Poverty of Philosophy* (Marx, 1963: 173). While the terminology has been attacked, it seems to me that, leaving aside the Hegelian language, it does capture the often wide gap between certain 'objective' realities of how people live, and how they understand those realities.

with the ruling groups: the right is claimed to participate in legis-
lation and administration, even to reform these – but within the
existing fundamental structures. *A third moment is that in which one
becomes aware that one's own corporate interests, in their present and
future development, transcend the corporate limits of the purely
economic class, and can and must become the interests of other subordinate groups too. This is the most purely political phase, and marks the
decisive passage from the structure to the sphere of the complex superstructures*; it is the phase in which previously germinated ideologies
become 'party', come into confrontation and conflict, until only
one of them, or at least a single combination of them, tends to
prevail, to gain the upper hand, to propagate itself throughout
society – bringing about not only a unison of economic and
political aims, but also intellectual and moral unity, posing all the
questions around which the struggle rages not on a corporate but
on a 'universal' plane, and thus creating the hegemony of a fundamental social group over a series of subordinate groups. It is true
that the State is seen as the organ of one particular group, destined
to create favourable conditions for the latter's maximum
expansion. But the development and expansion of the particular
group are conceived of, and presented, as being the motor force of
a universal expansion, of a development of all the 'national'
energies. In other words, the dominant group is co-ordinated
concretely with the general interests of the subordinate groups,
and the life of the State is conceived of as a continuous process of
formation and superseding of unstable equilibria (on the juridical
plane) between the interests of the fundamental group and those
of the subordinate groups – equilibria in which the interests of the
dominant group prevail, but only up to a certain point, i.e.
stopping short of narrowly corporate economic interest.

(SPN: 181–2, my emphasis except where indicated)

It is clear from this extract that, for Gramsci as for Marx, the
primary actors in human history are *classes*. This is not to say, of
course, that Gramsci saw classes as the *only* actors in history, just
that for him it is these kinds of large grouping, occupying a similar
economic position in a given society, that ultimately explain large
and genuinely revolutionary epochal changes, such as the
emergence of the bourgeois world out of feudalism, or the possibility of the overthrow of capitalist society. The problem faced by those,

like Gramsci, working to bring about the latter was that the potentially revolutionary class under capitalism had not managed to
achieve the same level of political development as had the bourgeoisie by the time of the French Revolution.

> ... the crisis of today is more acute than that of the Middle Ages;
> the latter lasted several centuries, up to the French Revolution,
> when the social grouping that had been economically the motor
> force in Europe throughout the millennium was able to present
> itself as an integral 'State', possessing all the intellectual and moral
> forces it needed to organise a complete and perfect society.

> (SPN: 270–1)

While Gramsci, as in the Note on Machiavelli quoted previously,
was centrally concerned with the question of how a political consciousness capable of *effectively* opposing that of dominant bourgeois
society could be 'awakened and developed', he was insistent that any
such 'cultural reform' is necessarily linked to economic reform, as
when he writes towards the end of the Machiavelli Note:

> Can there be cultural reform, and can the position of the
> depressed strata of society be improved culturally, without a
> previous economic reform and a change in their position in the
> social and economic fields? Intellectual and moral reform has to
> be linked with a programme of economic reform – indeed the
> programme of economic reform is precisely the concrete form in
> which every intellectual and moral reform presents itself.

> (SPN: 133)

In another Note Gramsci characterizes politics and economics as
both distinct from each other but also interdependent. It is
economic life that provides the 'permanent and organic terrain', and
unless politics is, as it were, a genuine outgrowth of that terrain, it
is doomed to be merely transient.

> Politics becomes permanent action and gives birth to permanent
> organisations precisely in so far as it identifies itself with
> economics. But it is also distinct from it, which is why one may
> speak separately of economics and politics, and speak of 'political
> passion' as of an immediate impulse to action which is born on

the 'permanent and organic' terrain of economic life but which transcends it, bringing into play emotions and aspirations in whose incandescent atmosphere even calculations involving the individual human life itself obey different laws from those of individual profit, etc.

(SPN: 139–40)

A group crucial to the achievement of the passage from the 'permanent and organic terrain of economic life' to effective political organization for Gramsci is that of the intellectuals. In Chapter 6 I shall explore what he meant by intellectuals – a usage that is rather different from how the term is commonly used. Here I just want to draw attention to the fact that for Gramsci ultimately it is intellectuals as distinct groups who articulate the perspective of specific classes. He writes, for example:

Every social group, coming into existence on the original terrain of an essential function in the world of economic production, creates together with itself, organically, one or more strata of intellectuals which give it homogeneity and an awareness of its own function not only in the economic but also in the social and political fields.

(SPN: 5)

A class which is unable to produce its own intellectuals is unable to transform itself into a hegemonic force.

[A] class, often, *as an economic fact (which is what every class is essentially)* might not enjoy any intellectual or moral prestige, i.e. might be incapable of establishing its hegemony, hence of founding a State. Hence the function of monarchies, even in the modern era; hence, too, in particular, the phenomenon (especially in England and in Germany) whereby the leading personnel of the bourgeois class organised into a State can be constituted by elements of the old feudal classes, who have been dispossessed of their traditional economic predominance (Junkers and Lords), but who have found new forms of economic power in industry and in the banks, and who have not fused with the bourgeoisie but have remained united to their traditional social group.

(SPN: 269–70, my emphasis)

Note that the achievement of hegemony by a class here is linked to the 'founding of a State'. For Gramsci part of what hegemony means is that a class, or an alliance of classes, has succeeded in transcending its own narrow corporate interests, and has incorporated at least some of the interests of subordinate classes so that it appears to represent the interests of society as a whole. It has, that is, 'become organised as a State' so that its de facto dominance is embodied in the formal institutions of the state. This is the 'third moment' referred to in the Note quoted above (p. 93), the one that 'marks the decisive passage from the structure to the sphere of the complex superstructures'. A crucial element here is the political party. Classes may be the key actors in human history, but to act in a conscious way they need parties. Party was a key term for Gramsci which he used to refer to both formal and informal political organisations. '[I]n any given society nobody is disorganised and without party, provided that one takes organisation and party in a broad and not a formal sense' (SPN: 264).

In a Note on the weakness of Italian political parties Gramsci reveals something of the tight web of interconnections he saw as threading through and binding together economic and political life in as much as this is embodied in political parties.

In fact, if it is true that parties are only the nomenclature for classes, it is also true that parties are not simply a mechanical and passive expression of those classes, but react energetically upon them in order to develop, solidify and universalise them ...

... Classes produce parties, and parties form the personnel of State and government, the leaders of civil and political society. There must be a useful and fruitful relation in these manifestations and functions. There cannot be any formation of leaders without the theoretical, doctrinal activity of parties, without a systematic attempt to discover and study the causes which govern the nature of the class represented and the way in which it has developed. Hence, scarcity of State and government personnel; squalor of parliamentary life; ease with which the parties can be disintegrated, by corruption and absorption of the few individuals who are indispensable. Hence, squalor of cultural life and wretched inadequacy of high culture. Instead of political history, bloodless erudition; instead of religion, superstition; instead of books and great reviews, daily papers and broadsheets; instead of serious politics, ephemeral quarrels and personal clashes. The universities, and all the institutions which develop intellectual and technical abilities, since they were not permeated by the life of the parties, by the living realities of national life, produced apolitical national cadres, with a purely rhetorical and non-national mental formation.

(SPN: 227–8)

I shall return to Gramsci's stress on the importance of the political party in Chapter 6.

In beginning to map out the terrain culture occupies in Gramsci's writings this chapter has focused on how he approached the problem of culture and history. Central here, as I hope this chapter has shown, is the key role Gramsci gives to classes in the process of historical development. For Gramsci, as for Marx, at the heart of recorded human history is class struggle, with classes emerging as conscious actors out of basic economic relations and vying with each other for domination. A dominant class or alliance of classes is one that has succeeded in bringing into being a hegemonic culture that in fact embodies their world-view, but that appears to represent not simply their interests but those of society as a whole. It should be stressed, however, that no hegemonic culture, no matter how complete its power appears to be, is ever totally stable and free from contradictions; its reproduction can never be taken for granted. Any hegemony represents no more than a particular moment in the ceaseless onrush of history with its contending forces. Nonetheless, to those within it, an existing hegemony can appear dauntingly impregnable. What possibilities does Gramsci see for the dominated, or – to use the terminology introduced by Gramsci – the subaltern, to assert a different world-view and a different way of living? It is this question that the next chapter explores.

5   Subaltern Culture

Subaltern classes are subject to the initiatives of the dominant classes, even when they rebel; they are in a state of anxious defense.

(PNII: 21)

This chapter focuses on Gramsci's mapping of the cultural worlds inhabited by the subordinate and the subaltern. Gramsci's concern here is to trace out both the power relations that maintain their subordination and the cracks and fissures that could potentially lead to their overcoming it. In other words, what keeps the subaltern subaltern, and how might their subalternity be overcome?

In a much quoted passage in the Preface to *The Making of the English Working Class*, E. P. Thompson declared he was 'seeking to rescue the poor stockinger, the Luddite cropper, the "obsolete" hand-loom weaver, the "utopian" artisan, and even the deluded follower of Joanna Southcott, from the enormous condescension of posterity' (1968: 13) – a sentiment that resonates with many anthropologists who have often spent much of their working lives attempting to rescue marginalized lives from the condescension of modernity. This was not, however, why Gramsci devoted so much space in the prison notebooks to the culture of peasant and other subaltern peoples. Not that Gramsci did not have respect for the kind of peasant culture that he himself had grown up in, but at the same time, probably precisely because he knew it so well, he was never sentimental about it, seeing it both as narrow and parochial, and needing to be transcended; but also as possessing a certain hard-nosed realism about the nature of power. Contained within the chaotic eclecticism of popular 'common sense', as he put it in 'Relation between Science, Religion and Common Sense' (I quote from this Note again below, see p. 111) there was a 'healthy nucleus ... which deserves to be made more unitary and coherent' (SPN: 328). The concept of common sense (a term which does not have the same connotations of practical, down to earth good sense in Italian that it does in English) is at the heart of Gramsci's theorization of popular consciousness and deserves a section to itself. But, first, it is necessary to spend some time with one of Gramsci's most basic concepts: hegemony.

Hegemony

Exactly what Gramsci meant by hegemony has been much argued over,[1] but what is not in dispute is that it is a concept that Gramsci uses to explore relationships of power and the concrete ways in which these are lived. The realities of power are central to Gramsci's theorization of subaltern culture and consciousness. For him that consciousness could not but be an impoverished and *unsystematic* one, precisely because of the subaltern's relative powerlessness. Here, in a Note to which I shall return, we find Gramsci arguing for folklore to be approached as a way of discovering how the subaltern sees the world:

> One can say that until now folklore has been studied primarily as a 'picturesque' element ... Folklore should instead be studied as a 'conception of the world and life' implicit to a large extent in determinate (in time and space) strata of society and in opposition (also for the most part implicit, mechanical and objective) to 'official' conceptions of the world (or in a broader sense, the conceptions of the cultured parts of historically determinate societies) that have succeeded one another in the historical process. (Hence the strict relationship between folklore and 'common sense', which is philosophical folklore.) *This conception of the world is not elaborated and systematic because, by definition, the people (the sum total of the instrumental and subaltern classes of every form of society that has so far existed) cannot possess conceptions which are elaborated, systematic and politically organized and centralized* in their albeit contradictory development.
>
> (SCW: 188–9, my emphasis)

In a Note on the term 'subversive' (*sovversivo*), Gramsci elaborates on a characteristic consciousness that is found in rural Italy. It should be noted, as the editors of the SPN explain, that *sovversivo* has more positive connotations than those of the English term (see SPN: 272).

The purely Italian concept of 'subversive' can be explained as follows: a negative rather than a positive class position – the

---

1. See Chapter 7 for a discussion of this debate as it relates to the use of Gramsci by anthropologists.

'people' is aware that it has enemies, but only identifies them empirically as the so-called *signori*. Contained in the concept of *signore* there is much of the old dislike of country for town; dress is a fundamental element of distinction. There is also dislike of officialdom – the only form in which the State is perceived. The peasant, and even the small farmer, hates the civil servant; he does not hate the State, for he does not understand it. He sees the civil servant as a *'signore'*, even if he is himself in fact better off economically; hence the apparent contradiction whereby the *signore* is often at the same time a *morto di fame*[2] as far as the peasant is concerned. This 'generic' hatred is still 'semi-feudal' rather than modern in character, and cannot be taken as evidence of class consciousness – merely as the first glimmer of such consciousness, in other words, merely as the basic negative, polemical attitude. Not only does the people have no precise consciousness of its own historical identity, it is not even conscious of the historical identity or the exact limits of its adversary. *The lower classes, historically on the defensive, can only achieve self-awareness via a series of negations, via their consciousness of the identity and class limits of their enemy; but it is precisely this process which has not yet come to the surface, at least not nationally.*

(SPN: 272–3, my emphasis)

For Gramsci, the basic character of subaltern culture derives from their being 'historically on the defensive'; the question of power is at the heart of his theorization of culture. This is in fact why he makes so much use of the term 'subaltern' in his discussions of the mentality of the subordinated. It is their subordination, their subaltern character, that shapes how they see the world. As I hope the last chapter made clear, it is not that Gramsci rejected Marx's insistence on basic economic relations as the *ultimate* dynamic of history, but rather that his intellectual project was focused on the question of how at particular historical moments, within certain broad economic parameters, specific political landscapes, with their specific possibilities for transformation, come into being. It may be true that basic economic relations, whether those of feudalism or capitalism, contain within them contradictions which *may* tear them apart, but just as it is impossible to know exactly when and where

---

2. See above, Chapter 4 (pp. 90–1) for Gramsci's discussion of this term.

the seismic faults created by colliding tectonic plates will produce earthquakes or volcanic eruptions, so too with the seismic upheavals of human societies. And, moreover, unlike the inanimate world of geophysics, the social world depends on human volition for its earthquakes and volcanoes. Gramsci's concern was with how the potential energy of subordinated classes – an energy given by its objective exploitation – could realize itself as a historical force. Holding this force in check, as long as a particular constellation of class forces exists, is the power exercised by the dominant groups. This power, however, is not simple brute coercion. If it were it would be impossible to understand how small elites are able to dominate large masses; crucial to any long-term domination is gaining the 'consent' of the dominated. One of the most helpful ways of approaching Gramsci's admittedly difficult concept of hegemony is as a way of thinking about the complicated way consent and coercion are entangled with one another, rather than as the delineation of a specific kind of power.

Gramsci himself never provided a neat capsule definition of hegemony – in part, I would argue, precisely because it does not describe any kind of easily delineated relationship. Rather, it is a way of marking out ever-shifting, highly protean relationships of power which can assume quite different forms in different contexts. It is important to remember, as Buttigieg has pointed out,[3] that Gramsci did not begin elaborating hegemony as a theoretical concept; it is a concept he arrived at as result of his attempts to understand the dynamics of Italian state formation during and immediately after the Risorgimento.[4] As a way of helping to clarify what Gramsci meant by hegemony, I have brought together here a series of passages from the prison notebooks which show something of the shifting way the term is used by Gramsci. This lack of consistency, I would argue, should be seen not as some confusion on Gramsci's part as to what he meant by hegemony but as a reflection of the way in which actual power relations can take very different forms in different contexts.

For Gramsci power relations can be seen as occupying a continuum with direct coercion through brute force at one pole and willing consent at the other. In a discussion of the formation of intel-

---

3. Oral presentation, New School of Social Research, 12 December 1995.
4. The movement which led to the unification of Italy as an independent state with its capital at Rome in 1870.

lectuals, for instance, Gramsci does apparently give us a rather straightforward definition of hegemony:

> What we can do, for the moment, is to fix two major superstructural 'levels': the one that can be called 'civil society', that is the ensemble of organisms commonly called 'private', and that of 'political society' or 'the State'. These two levels correspond on the one hand to the function of 'hegemony' which the dominant group exercises throughout society and on the other hand to that of 'direct domination' or command exercised through the State and 'juridical' government. The functions in question are precisely organisational and connective. The intellectuals are the dominant group's 'deputies' exercising the subaltern functions of social hegemony and political government. These comprise:
> 1. The 'spontaneous' consent given by the great masses of the population to the general direction imposed on social life by the dominant fundamental group; this consent is 'historically' caused by the prestige (and consequent confidence) which the dominant group enjoys because of its position and function in the world of production.
> 2. The apparatus of state coercive power which 'legally' enforces discipline on those groups who do not 'consent' either actively or passively. This apparatus is, however, constituted for the whole of society in anticipation of moments of crisis of command and direction when spontaneous consent has failed.
>
> (SPN: 12)

Here it would seem hegemony is defined as *consent* organized by the organizations of civil society as opposed to the state with its apparatus of *coercive* power. It is important, however, to remember that hegemony here is being defined in the context of a discussion of the role of intellectuals. I shall come back to this passage in the next chapter.

Elsewhere, however, Gramsci does not oppose civil society/ hegemony and the state/coercion in this way. In one Note, for instance, hegemony, or the organization of consent, is *included* as one of the activities of the state. Here Gramsci writes that 'the State is the entire complex of practical and theoretical activities with which the ruling class not only justifies and maintains its dominance, but manages to win the active consent of those over whom it rules' (SPN: 244). And in another Note we find him referring to '... the State (in its integral meaning: dictatorship + hegemony) ...' (SPN: 239). The basic point to grasp in these shifting definitions of the state is that sometimes in order to understand a particular manifestation of power, such as that exercised by intellectuals, it is helpful to distinguish between 'two superstructural "levels"', one representing hegemony and consent, and the other coercion and force. At other times it is necessary to focus on how the state encompasses both force and consent, as when Gramsci criticizes a book by Danièl Halévy because,

> For Halévy, 'State' is the representative apparatus; and he discovers that the most important events of French history from 1870 until the present day have not been due to initiatives by political organisms deriving from universal suffrage, but to those either of private organisms (capitalist firms, General Staffs, etc.) or of great civil servants unknown to the country at large, etc. But what does that signify if not that *by 'State' should be understood not only the apparatus of government, but also the 'private' apparatus of 'hegemony' or civil society?*
>
> (SPN: 261, my emphasis)

In one of his many Notes attacking economism Gramsci makes the same point, prefacing it with the very helpful clarification that the distinction between political society (force) and civil society (hegemony) should be seen simply as a methodological one. The state and civil society, that is, do not represent two bounded universes, always and for ever separate, but rather a knot of tangled power relations which, depending on the questions we are interested in, can be disentangled into different assemblages of threads. It should also be stressed that for Gramsci, just because civil society in general represents consent rather than force, it by no means follows that civil society is, therefore, necessarily benign. This seems a particularly important point to stress in the contemporary political climate.

> The ideas of the Free Trade movement are based on a theoretical error whose practical origin is not hard to identify; *they are based on a distinction between political society and civil society which is made into and presented as an organic one, whereas in fact it is merely methodological.* Thus it is asserted that economic activity belongs to civil society, and that the State must not intervene to regulate

it. But since *in actual reality civil society and State are one and the same*, it must be made clear that *laissez-faire* too is a form of State 'regulation', introduced and maintained by legislative and coercive means. It is a deliberate policy, conscious of its own ends, and not the spontaneous, automatic expression of economic facts.

(SPN: 159–60, my emphasis)

While hegemony, as in these passages, is frequently associated with consent and opposed to force or coercion, it can also encompass force, as when Gramsci writes in the context of a discussion of the Jacobins: 'The "normal" exercise of hegemony on the now classical terrain of the parliamentary regime is characterised by the combination of force and consent, which balance each other reciprocally, without force predominating excessively over consent' (SPN: 80). It is clear that hegemony in Gramsci is a highly fluid and flexible term with no one single definition. The reason for this, I would suggest, is that rather than being a precisely bounded theoretical concept, hegemony for Gramsci simply names the problem – that of how the power relations underpinning various forms of inequality are produced and reproduced – that he is interested in exploring. What in any given context constitutes hegemony can only be discovered through careful empirical analysis.

A key dimension of inequality for Gramsci is the inability of subaltern people to produce coherent accounts of the world they live in that have the potential to challenge the existing hegemonic accounts (which by definition see the world from the perspective of the dominant) in any *effective* way. I stress 'effective' here since Gramsci certainly never denied that subaltern peoples had their own conceptions of the world, he just sees these as inherently fragmentary, incoherent and contradictory, and as lacking the kind of clear, rigorous insight into how local environments of oppression are located within larger economic and political realities, which is essential if a subaltern account is to have any hope of becoming genuinely counter-hegemonic. As far as Gramsci is concerned, subaltern people may well be capable of seeing the little valley they inhabit very clearly, but they remain incapable of seeing beyond their valley walls and understanding how their little world fits into the greater one beyond it. Gramsci's discussions of subaltern culture begin from the assumption that it is unable to produce effective, genuinely transformative, political movements. He saw even

Marxism (the philosophy of praxis), which he believed had the potential to develop into a genuinely counter-hegemonic conception of the world, as still in the process of formation, still struggling to create its own intellectuals capable of elaborating it in such a way that it could become a shared mass culture.

> [C]reating a group of independent intellectuals is not an easy thing; it requires a long process, with actions and reactions, coming together and drifting apart and the growth of very numerous and complex new formations. [The philosophy of praxis] is the conception of a subaltern social group, deprived of historical initiative, in continuous but disorganic expansion, unable to go beyond a certain qualitative level, which still remains below the level of the possession of the State and of the real exercise of hegemony over the whole of society which alone permits a certain organic equilibrium in the development of the intellectual group.
>
> (SPN: 395–6)

The point here is that because Marxism represents 'the conception of a subaltern social group' it cannot advance beyond a certain level. Its development as a mass, hegemonic culture can only come about together with the emergence to power of the subaltern group whose world-view it represents. There is, therefore, a complex reciprocal interaction between the advance of this new mass culture and the advance of the social group out of whose experience it has emerged, where each is dependent on the other. What Gramsci wants to understand in his explorations of subaltern culture is how the various relationships of subordination work. What is it about the conditions of subaltern life, and the relationship of subalterns to the dominant groups in society, that keep them subaltern? In other words, what does hegemony actually look like in concrete historical contexts, and how might it be overcome?

Folklore

One of the ways Gramsci approaches the question of subaltern culture, as in the extract from 'Observations on Folklore' quoted above (p. 99), is through the notion of folklore. The category folklore, defined by the *Oxford English Dictionary* as 'The traditional beliefs, legends, and customs, current among the common people;

the study of these', emerged throughout Europe in the nineteenth century out of the same intellectual and political currents as the modern notion of nationalism. Folklore was often celebrated by those who collected and studied it as an expression of the spirit of 'the people'. There was in fact a romanticism bound up with the whole notion of folklore that saw it as an 'authentic' reflection of the 'soul' of a nation. Gramsci, as we might expect, was totally opposed to any fuzzy romanticism of this kind. Folklore, for him, was essentially something that needed to be combated.

In 'Observations on Folklore' Gramsci makes a number of points that are central to his understanding of subaltern culture which are worth quoting at length. The extract given here begins with the short section included at the beginning of this chapter.

> One can say that until now folklore has been studied primarily as a 'picturesque' element ... Folklore should instead be studied as a 'conception of the world and life' implicit to a large extent in determinate (in time and space) strata of society and in opposition (also for the most part implicit, mechanical and objective) to 'official' conceptions of the world (or in a broader sense, the conceptions of the cultured parts of historically determinate societies) that have succeeded one another in the historical process. (Hence the strict relationship between folklore and 'common sense', which is philosophical folklore.) This conception of the world is not elaborated and systematic because, by definition, the people (the sum total of the instrumental and subaltern classes of every form of society that has so far existed) cannot possess conceptions which are elaborated, systematic and politically organized and centralized in their albeit contradictory development. It is, rather, many-sided – not only because it includes different and juxtaposed elements, but also because it is stratified, from the more crude to the less crude – if, indeed, one should not speak of a confused agglomerate of fragments of all the conceptions of the world and of life that have succeeded one another in history. In fact, it is only in folklore that one finds surviving evidence, adulterated and mutilated, of the majority of these conceptions.
>
> Philosophy and modern science are also constantly contributing new elements to 'modern folklore' in that certain opinions and scientific notions, removed from their context and more or less distorted, constantly fall within the popular domain and are 'inserted' into the mosaic of tradition. *(La scoperta de l'America* by

C. Pascarella shows how notions about Christopher Columbus and about a whole set of scientific opinions, put about by school textbooks and the 'Popular Universities', can be strangely assimilated.) Folklore can be understood only as a reflection of the conditions of cultural life of the people, although certain conceptions specific to folklore remain even after these conditions have been (or seem to be) modified or have given way to bizarre combinations.

Certainly, there is a 'religion of the people', especially in Catholic and Orthodox countries, which is very different from that of the intellectuals (the religious ones) and particularly from that organically set up by the ecclesiastical hierarchy. One could claim, though, that all religions, even the most refined and sophisticated, are 'folklore' in relation to modern thought. But there is the essential difference that religions, in the first place Catholicism, are 'elaborated and set up' by the intellectuals (as above) and the ecclesiastical hierarchy. Therefore, they present special problems. (One should see if such an elaboration and set-up may not be necessary to keep folklore scattered and many-sided: the conditions of the Church before and after the Reformation and the Council of Trent and the different historico-cultural development of the Reformed and Orthodox countries after the Reformation and Trent are highly significant elements.) Thus it is true that there is a 'morality of the people', understood as a determinate (in space and time) set of principles for practical conduct and of customs that derive from them or have produced them. Like superstition, this morality is closely tied to real religious beliefs. Imperatives exist that are much stronger, more tenacious and more effective than those of official 'morality'. In this sphere, too, one must distinguish various strata: the fossilized ones which reflect conditions of past life and are therefore conservative and reactionary, and those which consist of a series of innovations, often creative and progressive, determined spontaneously by forms and conditions of life which are in the process of developing and which are in contradiction to or simply different from the morality of the governing strata.

(SCW: 188–90)

The first point to note here is how Gramsci sees the study of folklore as valuable because of the opportunities it offers us to observe something of potentially oppositional 'conceptions of the world and life' of subaltern people which have otherwise left no record. 'It is only in folklore that one finds surviving evidence, adulterated and mutilated, of the majority of these conceptions.' As these, however, are implicit rather than explicitly worked out, the most we can hope for are glimpses. One of the fundamental characteristics of subaltern thought for Gramsci is its incoherence and contradictoriness. It is 'a confused agglomerate of fragments of all the conceptions of the world and of life that have succeeded one another in history'. 'Folklore' for Gramsci does not represent some primordial tradition handed down unchanged from the pre-modern world. Rather, 'philosophy and modern science are also constantly contributing new elements' and being 'inserted into the mosaic of tradition'. In another Note on folklore Gramsci writes how 'folklore has always been tied to the culture of the dominant class and, in its own way, has drawn from it the motifs which have then become inserted into combinations with the previous traditions ... there is nothing more contradictory and fragmentary than folklore' (SCW: 194).

It is also worth noting here how far this approach to non-elite cultures is from the search for 'patterned wholes' with their own systematic logics that, as Chapter 3 explored, has been such a dominant theme in mainstream anthropology; and how it eschews any simple notion of a basic opposition between 'tradition' and 'modernity'. What Gramsci stresses is how folklore can be seen as representing an essentially *oppositional* culture (albeit one that is 'implicit, mechanical', and not an explicit, conscious critique), one that is 'in opposition ... to "official" conceptions of the world'. In other words, the key relationship is between the dominant and the dominated, not between the traditional and the modern.

The instability of folklore and its readiness to absorb elements from the dominant culture are important in that they give folklore a potentially progressive quality. Gramsci stresses the need to distinguish between 'fossilized' and 'therefore conservative and reactionary' strata and 'those which consist of a series of innovations, often creative and progressive, determined spontaneously by forms and conditions of life which are in the process of developing and which are in contradiction to or simply different from the morality of the governing strata'.

Gramsci's basic attitude to religion, in particular the Catholicism that so permeated the Italian society of his time, is revealed very clearly in this passage. As a committed secularist, for him 'all religions, even the most refined and sophisticated are "folklore" in relation to modern thought', but with the difference – indicated by the quotation marks given to 'folklore' – that the great religions are 'elaborated and set up' by intellectuals and organized religious institutions. The next chapter examines in detail the enormous importance Gramsci attached to the role of intellectuals in the dynamic of human history.

At the end of 'Observations on Folklore' Gramsci argues that one of the reasons why folklore needs to be taken so seriously is that in its reactionary aspects it represents a conception of the world which progressive educators need to 'uproot'.

> [T]he state [here Gramsci is imagining a progressive state] is not agnostic but has its own conception of life and has the duty of spreading it by educating the national masses. But this formative activity of the state, which is expressed particularly in the education system, as well as in political activity generally, does not work upon and fill up a blank slate. In reality, the state competes with and contradicts other explicit and implicit conceptions, and folklore is not among the least significant and tenacious of these; hence it must be 'overcome'. For the teacher, then, to know 'folklore' means to know what other conceptions of the world and of life are actually active in the intellectual and moral formation of young people, in order to uproot them and replace them with conceptions which are deemed to be superior ...
>
> It is clear that, in order to achieve the desired end, the spirit of folklore studies should be changed, as well as deepened and extended. Folklore must not be considered an eccentricity, an oddity or a picturesque element, but as something which is very serious and is to be taken seriously. Only in this way will the teaching of folklore be more efficient and really bring about the birth of a new culture among the broad popular masses, so that the separation between modern culture and popular culture of folklore will disappear. An activity of this kind, thoroughly carried out, would correspond on the intellectual plane to what the Reformation was in Protestant countries.
>
> (SCW: 191)

Note that the conclusion of Gramsci's argument here is that 'folklore' should neither be preserved as a 'picturesque element', nor totally rooted out. What is needed is a recognition of its positive aspects so as to 'bring about the birth of a new culture among the broad popular masses' which will effectively erase 'the separation between modern culture and popular culture of folklore'.

A key term in Gramsci's explorations of subaltern mentality is 'common sense', which in Italian is a more neutral term than in English. That which he saw as clearly positive within common sense, Gramsci referred to as good sense. The next section focuses on Gramsci's notions of common sense and good sense.

Common Sense and Good Sense

Common sense for Gramsci, as he explains in this passage, occupies a position somewhere between folklore and the knowledge produced by specialists.

> Every social stratum has its own 'common sense' and its own 'good sense', which are basically the most widespread conception of life and of man. Every philosophical current leaves behind a sedimentation of 'common sense': this is the document of its historical effectiveness. *Common sense is not something rigid and immobile, but is continually transforming itself, enriching itself with scientific ideas and with philosophical opinions which have entered ordinary life.* 'Common sense' is the folklore of philosophy, and is always half-way between folklore properly speaking and the philosophy, science, and economics of the specialists. Common sense creates the folklore of the future, that is as a relatively rigid phase of popular knowledge at a given place and time.

> (SPN: 326, my emphasis)

Another key category, of course, is religion. In the following Note, quoted in full, Gramsci succinctly describes how he sees the relationship between common sense, religion and philosophy.

> Philosophy is intellectual order, which neither religion nor common sense can be. It is to be observed that religion and common sense do not coincide either, but that religion is an element of fragmented common sense. Moreover common sense is a collective noun, like religion: there is not just one common sense, for that too is a product of history and a part of the historical process. Philosophy is criticism and the superseding of

religion and 'common sense'. In this sense it coincides with 'good' as opposed to 'common' sense.

(SPN: 325–6)

In a Note entitled 'Relation between science, religion and common sense' Gramsci expands on the difference between philosophy and common sense:

> Perhaps it is useful to make a 'practical' distinction between philosophy and common sense in order to indicate more clearly the passage from one moment to the other. In philosophy the features of individual elaboration of thought are the most salient: in common sense on the other hand it is the diffuse, uncoordinated features of a generic form of thought common to a particular period and a particular popular environment. But every philosophy has a tendency to become the common sense of a fairly limited environment (that of all the intellectuals). It is a matter therefore of starting with a philosophy which already enjoys, or could enjoy, a certain diffusion, because it is connected to and implicit in practical life, and elaborating it so that it becomes a renewed common sense possessing the coherence and the sinew of individual philosophies. But this can only happen if the demands of cultural contact with the 'simple' are continually felt.

(SPN: 330)

We will come back to Gramsci's insistence on the importance of those attempting to bring a 'renewed common sense' into being, never losing sight of the need to remain in touch with the 'simple' [*simplice*].[5]

In the prison notebooks Gramsci devoted considerable space to a detailed critique of Nikolai Bukharin's attempt to provide a popular guide to Marxism, *The Theory of Historical Materialism, A Manual of Popular Sociology*. The following passage describes what common sense means to Gramsci and how he sees it as related to 'high' culture and to Catholicism.

> A work like the *Popular Manual*, which is essentially destined for a community of readers who are not professional intellectuals,

---

5. In Italian *simplice* does not have the derogatory associations that the term 'simple' used of people has in English.

should have taken as its starting point a critical analysis of the philosophy of common sense, which is the 'philosophy of non-philosophers', or in other words the conception of the world which is uncritically absorbed by the various social and cultural environments in which the moral individuality of the average man is developed. Common sense is not a single unique conception, identical in time and space. It is the 'folklore' of philosophy, and, like folklore, it takes countless different forms. Its most fundamental characteristic is that it is a conception which, even in the brain of one individual, is fragmentary, incoherent and inconsequential,[6] in conformity with the social and cultural position of those masses whose philosophy it is. At those times in history when a homogeneous social group is brought into being, there comes into being also, in opposition to common sense, a homogeneous – in other words coherent and systematic – philosophy.

The first mistake of the *Popular Manual* is that it starts, at least implicitly, from the assumption that the elaboration of an original philosophy of the popular masses is to be opposed to the great systems of traditional philosophy and the religion of the leaders of the clergy – i.e. the conception of the world of the intellectuals and of high culture. In reality these systems are unknown to the multitude and have no direct influence on its way of thinking and acting. This does not mean of course that they are altogether without influence but it is influence of a different kind. These systems influence the popular masses as an external political force, an element of cohesive force exercised by the ruling classes and therefore an element of subordination to an external hegemony. This limits the original thought of the popular masses in a negative direction, without having the positive effect of a vital ferment of interior transformation of what the masses think in an embryonic and chaotic form about the world and life. The principal elements of common sense are provided by religion, and consequently the relationship between common sense and religion is much more intimate than that between common sense and the philosophical systems of the intellectuals. But even

6. The Italian term that the editors of the SPN translate as inconsequential here is *inconseguente* which in this context means rather inconsistent. I am grateful to Frank Rosengarten for drawing my attention to this mistranslation.

within religion some critical distinctions should be made. Every religion, even Catholicism (indeed Catholicism more than any, precisely because of its efforts to retain a 'surface' unity and avoid splintering into national churches and social stratifications), is in reality a multiplicity of distinct and often contradictory religions: there is one Catholicism for the peasants, one for the *petits-bourgeois* and town workers, one for women, and one for intellectuals which is itself variegated and disconnected. But common sense is influenced not only by the crudest and least elaborated forms of these sundry Catholicisms as they exist today. Previous religions have also had an influence and remain components of common sense to this day, and the same is true of previous forms of present Catholicism – popular heretical movements, scientific superstitions connected with past cults, etc. In common sense it is the 'realistic', materialistic elements which are predominant, the immediate product of crude sensation. This is by no means in contradiction with the religious element, far from it. But here these elements are 'superstitious' and acritical. This, then, is a danger of the *Popular Manual,* which often reinforces, instead of scientifically criticising, these acritical elements which have caused common sense to remain Ptolemaic, anthropomorphic and anthropocentric.

(SPN: 419–20)

This Note reveals very clearly one of the basic threads which runs through all of Gramsci's writings; the opposition between coherent and incoherent conceptions of the world, and an insistence that any potentially counter-hegemonic ones must be coherent. Elaborating such a coherent counter-hegemonic narrative demands a rigorous critical analysis of the hegemonic narratives it must supplant. In the case of the broad masses of the population, who live immersed in the 'fragmentary, incoherent and inconsistent [see n. 7]' world of common sense, it is precisely this world of common sense that has to be overcome, not 'the great systems of traditional philosophy and the religion of the leaders of the clergy' since 'these systems are unknown to the multitude and have no direct influence on its way of thinking and acting'. This is why Gramsci is so critical of Buhkarin for not having taken as his starting point in a text specifically intended for a non-specialist mass audience, 'a critical analysis of the philosophy of common sense'. What people need to be made self-consciously and *critically* aware of is the incoherence and inadequacy of the taken-for-granted, common sense assumptions which they have simply absorbed uncritically and, as it were, mechanically, from the 'social and cultural environments' within which they have grown up. It is this task with which the *Popular Manual* should have concerned itself in Gramsci's view.

Once again in this Note Gramsci discusses the close connection between religion and common sense, arguing that 'the principal elements of common sense are provided by religion'. This is a slightly different emphasis to that of the Note quoted above where 'religion is an element of fragmented common sense', religion, that is, is there incorporated *within* common sense. Also stressed, however, is that every religion, especially Catholicism, 'is in reality a multiplicity of distinct and often contradictory religions: there is one Catholicism for the peasants, one for the *petits-bourgeois* and town workers, one for women, and one for intellectuals which is itself variegated and disconnected'. In other words, this mosaic of Catholicisms is *incoherent*.

For those who are interested in radical social change, common sense, apart from its nucleus of good sense, is something to be opposed. It is what any emerging counterhegemonic narrative has to struggle to overcome. At the same time, however, common sense does also contain elements of 'good sense', and these constitute an important part of the raw material out of which counterhegemonic narratives develop. But, given that, according to Gramsci, the subaltern condition itself prevents subalterns from developing 'conceptions which are elaborated, systematic and politically organized and centralized', how is it possible for 'good sense' to develop into an effective counterhegemonic conception of the world? The first point to emphasize here is the dynamic, 'historical' nature of the incoherent bundle of fragments that constitute common sense. Common sense exists in history. As Gramsci writes in the short Note I have already quoted (see pp. 110–11), '... common sense is a collective noun, like religion: there is not just one common sense, for that too is a product of history and a part of the historical process' (SPN: 325–6). In other words neither religion nor common sense should be seen as fossilized, static tradition; they are continually being modified and adapted, often in unpredictable ways, as the contexts in which they exist shift and change.

A very important argument in Gramsci's critique of the *Popular Manual* is that the emergence of new, counterhegemonic philosophies and the emergence of new classes are closely linked. It is at those moments in history when a major new class (in one of the prison notebooks' euphemisms, 'a homogeneous social group') emerges that 'there comes into being also, in opposition to common sense, a homogeneous – in other words coherent and systematic – philosophy'. As fundamentally new locations come into being on the basic economic terrain – in other words, new classes – new conceptions of the world, reflecting how the world appears from those locations, also emerge. Let me stress, while this is possible it is not inevitable; we are not talking about a teleology. If such conceptions are to emerge and achieve hegemonic dominance, as for example in the case of the bourgeois accounts of the world that supplanted the old feudal ones, the new class must be able to bring into being its own 'organic' intellectuals who are capable of elaborating and giving coherence to its embryonic imaginings. The next chapter looks at Gramsci's notion of the organic intellectual in detail; for the moment I just want to stress that at its heart is the idea of an ever-continuing dialogue between those who actually live a particular class experience and those who, because of their particular skills and training, are able to articulate this experience as a coherent narrative. Very important here is the difference between explicit and implicit conceptions of the world.

Explicit and Implicit Conceptions of the World

In a number of Notes Gramsci explores the difference between conceptions of the world which take an explicit, verbal form, and those that while they are not articulated, are implicit in how people act. In the Note 'Relation between science, religion and common sense', from which I have already quoted, Gramsci writes:

> Philosophy in general does not in fact exist. Various philosophies or conceptions of the world exist, and one always makes a choice between them. How is this choice made? Is it merely an intellectual event, or is it something more complex? And is it not frequently the case that there is a contradiction between one's intellectual choice and one's mode of conduct? Which therefore would be the real conception of the world: that logically affirmed as an intellectual choice? or that which emerges from the real activity of each man, which is implicit in his mode of action? And since all action is political, can one not say that the real philosophy of each man is contained in its entirety in his political action?

This contrast between thought and action, i.e. the co-existence of two conceptions of the world, one affirmed in words and the other displayed in effective action, is not simply a product of self-deception [*malafede*]. Self-deception can be an adequate explanation for a few individuals taken separately, or even for groups of a certain size, but it is not adequate when the contrast occurs in the life of great masses. In these cases the contrast between thought and action cannot but be the expression of profounder contrasts of a social historical order. It signifies that the social group in question may indeed have its own conception of the world, even if only embryonic; a conception which manifests itself in action, but occasionally and in flashes – when, that is, the group is acting as an organic totality. But this same group has, for reasons of submission and intellectual subordination, adopted a conception which is not its own but is borrowed from another group; and it affirms this conception verbally and believes itself to be following it, because this is the conception which it follows in 'normal times' – that is when its conduct is not independent and autonomous, but submissive and subordinate. Hence the reason why philosophy cannot be divorced from politics. And one can show furthermore that the choice and the criticism of a conception of the world is also a political matter.

(SPN: 326–7)

A point to note here is the basic assumption that 'all action is political'. In other words, as I stressed in Chapter 2, for Gramsci all social relations involve power. One consequence of this is the fact that how subalterns see the world is in part a product of their subordinate and dominated position. Their world-view necessarily comes into being in the context of lives lived in conditions of subordination and of hegemonic accounts reflecting how the world appears from the perspective of society's dominant groups. It is out of the lived experience of subordination, however, that over time counter-hegemonic accounts of reality may begin to emerge, albeit at first no more than 'embryonic' ones. In this passage Gramsci stresses how such a counter-hegemonic conception is likely to emerge in the course of struggle: it 'manifests itself in action, but occasionally and in flashes – when, that is, the group is acting as an organic totality'. Once that spasm of action is over, the hegemonic forces are likely to reassert themselves, driving the embryonic new consciousness back into an inarticulate embodiment in action, although with perhaps some memory of its emergence. One way of describing what Gramsci is talking about here is as one aspect of the often long and fraught process by which (to use Marx's terminology from *The Poverty of Philosophy*) a 'class-in-itself' becomes a 'class-for-itself' (see above, Chapter 4, n. 9).

Later in the same Note Gramsci goes on to describe how articulated, verbal conceptions that have been 'inherited from the past and uncritically absorbed', can stifle the emergence of a new consciousness in an articulated form in the individual, even though this is already 'implicit in his activity' and it 'in reality unites him with all his fellow-workers in the practical transformation of the real world'.

> The active man-in-the-mass has a practical activity, but has no clear theoretical consciousness of his practical activity, which nonetheless involves understanding the world in so far as it transforms it. His theoretical consciousness can indeed be historically in opposition to his activity. One might almost say that he has two theoretical consciousnesses (or one contradictory consciousness): one which is implicit in his activity and which in reality unites him with all his fellow-workers in the practical transformation of the real world; and one, superficially explicit or verbal, which he has inherited from the past and uncritically absorbed. But this verbal conception is not without consequences. It holds together a specific social group, it influences moral conduct and the direction of will, with varying efficacity but often powerfully enough to produce a situation in which the contradictory state of consciousness does not permit of any action, any decision or any choice, and produces a condition of moral and political passivity.
>
> (SPN: 333)

Once again the problem, as Gramsci sees it, is particularly the *uncritical* absorption of an existing conception of the world. In another Note, entitled 'What is Man?', Gramsci elaborates on the need to acquire a critical understanding of the relationships in which one is involved.

> I mean that one must conceive of man as a series of active relationships (a process) in which individuality, though perhaps the most important, is not, however, the only element to be taken into

account. The humanity which is reflected in each individuality is composed of various elements: 1. the individual; 2. other men; 3. the natural world. But the latter two elements are not as simple as they might appear. The individual does not enter into relations with other men by juxtaposition, but organically, in as much, that is, as he belongs to organic entities which range from the simplest to the most complex. Thus Man does not enter into relations with the natural world just by being himself part of the natural world, but actively, by means of work and technique. Further: these relations are not mechanical. They are active and conscious. They correspond to the greater or lesser degree of understanding that each man has of them. So one could say that each one of us changes himself, modifies himself to the extent that he changes and modifies the complex relations of which he is the hub. In this sense the real philosopher is, and cannot be other than, the politician, the active man who modifies the environment, understanding by environment the *ensemble* of relations which each of us enters to take part in. If one's own individuality is the *ensemble* of these relations, to create one's personality means to acquire consciousness of them and to modify one's own personality means to modify the *ensemble* of these relations.

(SPN: 352, Gramsci's italics)

One of the important differences, Gramsci argues, between Catholicism (which after all has always had its own intellectuals, and often of a very high calibre) and Marxism is that while both of them are concerned with not losing touch with the broad masses, their attitudes to critical thinking on the part of those broad masses are diametrically opposed.

'Politically' the materialist conception is close to the people, to 'common sense'. It is closely linked to many beliefs and prejudices, to almost all popular superstitions (witchcraft, spirits, etc.). This can be seen in popular Catholicism, and, even more so, in Byzantine orthodoxy. Popular religion is crassly materialistic, and yet the official religion of the intellectuals attempts to impede the formation of two distinct religions, two separate strata, so as not to become officially, as well as in reality, an ideology of restricted groups. But from this point of view it is important not to confuse the attitude of the philosophy of praxis with that of

Catholicism. Whereas the former maintains a dynamic contact and tends continually to raise new strata of the population to a higher cultural life, the latter tends to maintain a purely mechanical contact, an external unity based in particular on the liturgy and on a cult visually imposing to the crowd. Many heretical movements were manifestations of popular forces aiming to reform the Church and bring it closer to the people by exalting them. The reaction of the Church was often very violent: it has created the Society of Jesus; it has clothed itself in the protective armour of the Council of Trent; although it has organised a marvellous mechanism of 'democratic' selection of its intellectuals, they have been selected as single individuals and not as the representative expression of popular groups.

(SPN: 396–7)

Whereas Marxism, in Gramsci's view, strives 'continually to raise new strata of the population to a higher cultural life', Catholicism is interested in 'a purely mechanical contact' with its flock, based on the unquestioning acceptance of 'the liturgy and on a cult visually imposing to the crowd', saving its sophisticated theological analyses for an intellectual elite.

While Gramsci could be harsh on the blinkered parochialism of subaltern culture, at the same time he was fascinated by it and believed that much could be learnt from it. It was there, for instance, and often only there, that one could find, as he put in one of the Notes on folklore quoted above, 'surviving evidence' albeit 'adulterated and mutilated' of historical subaltern conceptions of the world. One very interesting Note, which discusses the case of the nineteenth-century peasant visionary rebel, Davide Lazzaretti,[7] is worth quoting at length. In this Note Gramsci is responding to a 1928 article by Domenico Bulferetti which referred to a number of books and articles about Lazzaretti by various authors, including Giacomo Barzellotti. Gramsci's primary concern may not be to rescue Lazzaretti 'from the enormous condescension of posterity', but he does take him very seriously. What he is interested in is what the Lazzaretti case tells us about subaltern culture in this particular place at this particular time, and very importantly, how that culture was moulded and shaped by the dominant culture.

---

7. Lazzaretti is also discussed by Eric Hobsbawm in his *Primitive Rebels*.

Davide Lazzaretti

Lazzaretti was born in 1834 in a remote part of Tuscany. He was a carter by trade and served as a volunteer in the national army in 1860. In 1868 he began a career as a religious visionary, retiring to a cave from which he emerged periodically to prophesy about the coming of a new order of which he was the messiah. He attracted an extensive following which alarmed the local authorities and in 1878 he was shot dead by the Carabinieri as he came down from his mountain to proclaim the establishment of the republic of God. The specific details of the Lazzaretti episode are less important for the purposes of this chapter than what the Note reveals about Gramsci's approach to this kind of event. Gramsci is especially interested in how Lazzaretti's movement can be seen as reflecting the 'general discontent that existed in Italy', while using the rhetoric and imagery of popular religion, but a popular religion that was closely linked to contemporary Italian politics. Gramsci mentions in particular the Vatican's hostile attitude to the newly unified and secular Italian state. In 1871, ten years after the establishment of that state, the Vatican declared that it was 'not expedient' (*non expedit*), in effect a prohibition, for Catholics to participate in national elections. Gramsci insists that Lazzaretti must be understood in relation to the culture of his time, and not that of some age-old cultural traditions handed down from a distant past. Lazzaretti, for instance, took his visions not, as Barzellotti wanted to believe, from some fourteenth-century legends, but from a contemporary historical novel.

> It seems to me that Barzellotti's book, which has shaped public opinion on Lazzaretti, is nothing more than a manifestation of the 'patriotic' (for love of country!) tendency that spawned the efforts to conceal the causes of the general discontent that existed in Italy by providing narrow, individual, pathological, etc., explanations of single explosive incidents. The same thing happened with Davide Lazzaretti as did with the 'brigandage' of the South and Sicily. The politicians have not concerned themselves with the fact that the killing of Lazzaretti was savage in its cruelty and coldly premeditated (it would be interesting to know what instructions the government sent to the local authorities). In spite of the fact that Lazzaretti died exalting the republic (the republicanism of Lazzaretti's movement must have had a special impact on the

government's determination to assassinate him), even the repub-
licans ignored the issue – maybe because the republicanism of
Lazzaretti's movement had religious and prophetic ingredients.
Nevertheless, in my view, this is precisely the main distinctive
feature of the Lazzaretti incident, which was politically related to
the Vatican's *non expedit* and revealed the kind of subversive-
popular-rudimentary tendency that could arise out of the
abstentionism of the priests. (In any case, one needs to find out
whether those who were in the opposition at the time adopted a
stance on the issue: one must bear in mind that it was a
government of the left that had just come into power, and this
may also help to explain the lack of enthusiasm for supporting a
struggle against the government inspired by the criminal murder
of someone who could be portrayed as a reactionary, a supporter
of the papacy, a clericalist, etc.)

Bulferetti observes that Barzellotti did not conduct research on
the formation of the culture he refers to. He would have noticed
that an abundance of leaflets, pamphlets, and popular books
printed in Milan was reaching even Monte Amiata at that time (!
but how does Bulferetti know this?). Lazzaretti was an insatiable
reader of these materials, which his occupation as a carter enabled
him to procure. Davide was born in Arcidosso on 6 November
1834 and worked at his father's occupation until 1868, when he
converted from his blasphemous ways and went into seclusion to
do penance in a cave in Sabina where he 'saw' the ghost of a
warrior who 'revealed' himself to be Lazzaretti's ancestral father,
Manfredo Pallavicino, from Denmark, the illegitimate son of a
French king, etc. Doctor Emilio Rasmussen, from Denmark,
discovered that Manfredo Pallavicino is the main character in a
historical novel by Giuseppe Rovani entitled, precisely, *Manfredo
Pallavicino*. The plot and episodes in the novel are transmitted
intact in the 'revelation' in the cave, and out of these revelations
comes the beginning of Lazzaretti's religious propaganda. Barzellotti, however, had thought Lazzaretti was influenced by legends
from the fourteenth century (the adventures of the Sienese king
Giannino), and Rasmussen's discovery persuaded him only to
insert in the last edition of his book a vague allusion to Lazzaretti's
reading – but without mentioning Rasmussen and leaving
untouched the section of the book devoted to King Giannino.
Nevertheless, Barzellotti examines the subsequent development
of Lazzaretti's mind, his travels in France, and the influence
exercised on him by the Milanese priest Onorio Taramelli, a man

of fine intelligence and wide learning who had been arrested in Milan – and later escaped to France – for having written against the monarchy. Davide got his republican impulse from Taramelli. Davide's flag was red, with the inscription 'The republic and the Kingdom of God.' During the procession in which he was killed, on 18 August 1878, Davide asked his followers whether they wanted the republic. To their loud yes, he responded: 'The republic begins from this time forth in the world, but it will not be the republic of 1848; it will be the Kingdom of God, the law of Justice that has succeeded the law of Grace.' (Davide's response contains some interesting elements that must be connected to his memory of Taramelli's words: his desire to differentiate himself from 1848, which had not left good memories among the peasants in Tuscany; the distinction between Justice and Grace, etc. Remember that the priests and peasants involved with Malatesta in the trial of the gangs of Benevento had somewhat similar ideas. At any rate, in the case of Lazzaretti, literary impressionism should be replaced by some political analysis.)

(PNII: 19–20)

Lazzaretti's cultural world – or what we can glean of it from the fragments that have come down to us through the official record – is, in Gramsci's eyes, very characteristic of subaltern people. It is in many ways 'a confused agglomerate of fragments of all the conceptions of the world and of life that have succeeded one another in history' (see above pp. 106–8) Nonetheless, Lazzaretti was able to fashion from this bundle of fragments a subversive narrative that could be seen as providing something like a critique, albeit an embryonic, incoherent one, of the new Italian state. This critique moreover was one that, given the mass following that Lazzaretti was able to attract, clearly resonated with precisely those people whom any counterhegemonic view of the world needed to persuade. At the beginning of this Note Gramsci draws attention to how such embryonic, popular critiques of power are normally dismissed by intellectuals, commenting with reference to a book about Lazzaretti entitled *The Insane and The Abnormal* by the then celebrated, and now notorious, criminologist, Cesare Lombroso, 'this was the custom of the time: instead of studying the origins of a historical event, one would find the protagonist to be a madman' (PNII: 18). For Gramsci, it was crucial that progressive intellectuals should pay serious attention to the critiques produced by figures like Lazzaretti precisely because they emanated from subalterns themselves and captured something of how the world looked from a subaltern perspective. We should not forget that ultimately Gramsci's interest in such movements was because of his concern with the question of how a genuinely progressive *and* popular oppositional culture might be brought into being. Gramsci was always keenly aware that however articulate and logically coherent the narratives of revolutionary intellectuals may be, unless they resonate with popular understandings they are doomed to remain empty phrasemongering.

Gramsci's writings on subaltern culture have often been drawn on by those interested in colonised peoples and the hegemonic structures associated with colonialism. Let me end this chapter with some brief reflections on Gramsci's relevance here, leaving a more detailed consideration of how Gramsci has been used by anthropologists for Chapter 7.

Colonialism and Subalternity

The current popularity of referring to subordinated groups in society as 'subaltern' is largely due to the work of the hugely influential Subaltern Studies group. The Subaltern Studies collective was founded by Ranajit Guha and other Indian historians and social theorists concerned to shift the debate around colonialism, the nationalist struggle and the emergence of modern India. In their view the role of non-elite groups had been sidelined and they castigated historians of India for their 'failure to acknowledge the subaltern as the maker of his own destiny' (*Subaltern Studies III*, p. vii). In an effort to theorize the place of the subaltern in the making of Indian history more adequately they turned to Gramsci, particularly the Notes on Italian history. In addition to their adoption of the term subaltern, the Preface to their first collection of essays, *Subaltern Studies I*, by Guha, explicitly linked their project to that of Gramsci, writing, 'It will be idle of us, of course, to hope that the range of contributions to this series may even remotely match the six-point project envisaged by Antonio Gramsci in his "Notes on Italian History"' (Guha and Spivak, 1988: 35).[8] Subsequently the

8. The relevant paragraph in the prison notebooks, in a Note headed 'History of the Subaltern Classes: Methodological Criteria', reads as follows:

> The subaltern classes, by definition, are not unified and cannot unite until they are able to become a 'State': their history, therefore, is intertwined with that of civil society, and thereby with the history of States

Subaltern Studies historians moved away from Gramsci and began to draw increasingly on Foucault and various deconstructionists and postcolonial theorists, but the term subaltern as a way of referring to colonized peoples and subordinated groups in the postcolonial world remains popular.

Gramsci's approach to the analysis of subaltern peoples can, I believe, provide useful insights for the analysis of colonialism and the postcolonial world but it is important to bear in mind that Gramsci's Notes on subalterns deal overwhelmingly with Italian realities and Italian history. As I stressed in Chapter 2, Gramsci's approach was always one grounded in specific places and specific history. He wrote a lot about peasants and peasant society but the realities he was writing about were very much Italian ones, not some generic and abstract 'peasant society' applicable to all times and places. We need to be careful about taking the conclusions he came to based on his understanding of Italian conditions and applying them to quite different parts of the world with possibly very different configurations of power. For instance, the peasants of rural Italy had been subordinate elements within larger societies – Italy as a unified whole may not have existed before the nineteenth century but regional power blocs did – for many centuries, during which time the Catholic Church had been a powerful and pervasive local presence. The stifling effect of the Church on the emergence of an oppositional subaltern consciousness was, as we have seen, a common theme for Gramsci. A situation, as in many parts of Africa, in which a colonizing power occupied a region for no more than a couple of generations, and for much of that time may have been in

---

and groups of States. Hence it is necessary to study: 1. the objective formation of the subaltern social groups, by the developments and trans- formations occurring in the sphere of economic production; their quantitative diffusion and their origins in pre-existing social groups, whose mentality, ideology and aims they conserve for a time; 2. their active or passive affiliation to the dominant political formations, their attempts to influence the programmes of these formations in order to press claims of their own, and the consequences of these attempts in determining processes of decomposition, renovation or neo-formation; 3. the birth of new parties of the dominant groups, intended to conserve the assent of the subaltern groups and to maintain control over them; 4. the formations which the subaltern groups themselves produce, in order to press claims of a limited and partial character; 5. those new formations which assert the autonomy of the subaltern groups, but within the old framework; 6. those formations which assert the integral autonomy, ... etc.

(SPN: 52)

cultural terms a rather peripheral presence, is likely to constitute a rather different kind of hegemonic landscape. The history of British colonialism in India, and of the complex mosaic of local power constellations with which the British Raj had such complicated, and varied relations, is again a very different one to that of Italy. Indeed, while it is true that no colonizing power can rule through direct coercion alone – apart from anything else, those they rule always outnumber them – the balance between consent and coercion is likely to have a fundamentally different character in a colonial situation. Guha makes this point forcefully, using Gramscian language, in his 1997 volume, *Dominance without Hegemony*:

[T]he colonial state in Asia was very unlike and indeed fundamentally different from the metropolitan bourgeois state which had sired it. The difference consisted in the fact that the metropolitan state was hegemonic in character with its claim to dominance based on a power relation in which the moment of persuasion outweighed that of coercion, whereas the colonial state was non-hegemonic with persuasion outweighed by coercion in its structure of dominance ... We have defined the character of the colonial state therefore as *dominance without hegemony*.

(Guha, 1997: xii)

This characterization, as might be expected from a scholar who has immersed himself as deeply in Gramsci as Guha, is very much in line with Gramsci's own writings on colonialism. In 'Analysis of Situations. Relations of Force', for example, in which Gramsci lays out his view of how analysis of the relationship between basic economic relations and political events should be approached, he discusses the various levels of analysis and how the different relations act in history.[9] The third moment identified by Gramsci is that of those historical moments in which events are played out through direct military force. Gramsci then makes a further differentiation within this third moment between 'the military level in the strict or technical military sense, and the level which may be termed politico-military', going on to say how 'In the course of history these two levels have appeared in a great variety of combi-

9. See Chapter 4 (pp. 91–3) for another extract from this Note.

nations'. He then uses the example of a struggle for national independence as an example of the closest thing to pure coercion.

> A typical example, which can serve as a limiting case, is the relation involved in a State's military oppression of a nation seeking to attain its national independence. The relation is not purely military, but politico-military; indeed this type of oppression would be inexplicable if it were not for the state of social disintegration of the oppressed people, and the passivity of the majority among them; consequently independence cannot be won with purely military forces, it requires both military and politico-military. If the oppressed nation, in fact, before embarking on its struggle for independence, had to wait until the hegemonic State allowed it to organise its own army in the strict and technical sense of the word, it would have to wait quite a while. (It may happen that the claim to have its own army is conceded by the hegemonic nation, but this only means that a great part of the struggle has already been fought and won on the politico-military terrain.)
>
> (SPN: 183)

In general it seems safe to say that in the modern era of nationalism and nation states, the acceptance of the legitimacy, or at least inevitability, of colonial rule is likely to have shallower roots than those of a sovereign nation state. For those interested in the analysis of postcolonial societies and the South generally, perhaps the most important lesson that Gramsci has to teach is that of paying careful attention to the specificities of local histories, attempting to read the fragmentary narratives left by the subaltern in their own terms while never forgetting to pay equal attention to how these local realities belong simultaneously to larger worlds.

I began this chapter by saying that Gramsci's concern was not primarily with rescuing the subaltern 'from the enormous condescension of posterity'. He did believe, however, as the Note on Lazzaretti demonstrates, that the fragmentary accounts of subordinate world-views to be glimpsed in the shadows of the official accounts should be taken seriously and treated with a respect that those accounts denied them. Let me end the chapter with a brief extract that seems to me to capture the essence of what Gramsci was concerned with in his explorations of subaltern culture, namely to disinter the rough beginnings of a genuine counterhegemony from the accumulated dross of common sense. It also captures his characteristically unsentimental realism as to the nature of subaltern culture which he saw, at one and the same time, as backward and misguided *and* the true, and only, source of a consciousness capable of overcoming the harsh brutality of capitalist hegemony.

> Is it possible that a 'formally' new conception can present itself in a guise other than the crude, unsophisticated version of the populace? And yet the historian, with the benefit of all necessary perspective, manages to establish and to understand the fact that the beginnings of a new world, rough and jagged though they always are, are better than the passing away of the world in its death-throes and the swan-song that it produces.
>
> (SPN: 342–3)

For Gramsci the task of transforming such rough and jagged beginnings into coherent, powerful and plausible cultures fell to intellectuals. Just what Gramsci meant by intellectuals and how he saw their role in the work of cultural production is explored in the next chapter.

6 Intellectuals and the Production of Culture

I greatly amplify the idea of what an intellectual is and do not confine myself to the current notion that refers only to the preeminent intellectuals ... this conception of the function of the intellectuals helps to cast light on the reason or one of the reasons for the fall of the medieval Communes, that is, of the government of an economic class that was unable to create its own category of intellectuals and thus exercise hegemony and not simply dictatorship ...

(PLII: 67)

In 1920, looking back at the founding of *L'Ordine Nuovo*, Gramsci wrote the following:

When in the month of April 1919, three or four or five of us got together and decided to begin publishing this review *L'Ordine Nuovo* ... none of us (perhaps) thought in terms of changing the face of the world, of renewing the hearts and minds of the human multitudes, of starting a new historical cycle. None of us (perhaps: some dreamed of 6,000 subscribers in a few months) entertained rosy illusions as to the success of the enterprise. Who were we? What did we represent? Of what new tidings were we the bearers? Ah well! *The only sentiment that united us, in those meetings of ours, was the sentiment aroused by a vague passion for a vague proletarian culture.* We wanted to do something. We felt desperate, disoriented, immersed in the excitement of life in those months after the Armistice, when the cataclysm in Italian society appeared imminent. Ah well!

(SPWI: 291, my emphasis)

For Gramsci part and parcel of the successful achievement of any socialist revolution is the creation of a proletarian culture. The nature of this culture cannot be foreseen, however, only that it will represent a radical break with bourgeois culture. A few months later, again in *L'Ordine Nuovo*, he wrote in a piece on the futurist Marinetti:

> The battlefield for the creation of a new civilization is, on the other hand, absolutely mysterious, absolutely characterized by the unforeseeable and the unexpected. Having passed from capitalist power to workers' power, the factory will continue to produce the same material things that it produces today. But in what way and under what forms will poetry, drama, the novel, music, painting and moral and linguistic works be born? It is not a material factory that produces these works. It cannot be reorganized by a workers' power according to a plan. One cannot establish its rate of production for the satisfaction of immediate needs, to be controlled and determined statistically. Nothing in this field is foreseeable except for this general hypothesis: *there will be a proletarian culture (a civilization) totally different from the bourgeois one* and in this field too class distinctions will be shattered. Bourgeois careerism will be shattered and there will be a poetry, a novel, a theatre, a moral code, a language, a painting and a music peculiar to proletarian civilization, the flowering and ornament of proletarian social organization.
>
> (SCW: 50, my emphasis)

I have chosen to begin this chapter on intellectuals and culture with these two extracts from the pre-prison writings, because it is important to stress how 'culture' for Gramsci is not something that simply persists through time, handed down from one generation to another, culture is both tightly bound to basic economic relations and, particularly for a group or a class attempting to win hegemony, has to be *actively* created. It is also important to note that, as these two passages suggest, for Gramsci the meaning of culture embraces Williams' whole complex of senses, indicating 'a complex argument about the relations between general human development and a particular way of life, and between both and the works and practices of art and intelligence' (see Chapter 3, p. 41). Williams' gloss here is particularly relevant since the problem of the relationship between these different senses of culture is at the heart of Gramsci's explorations of culture.

In Gramsci's eyes, intellectuals are crucial to the process whereby a major new culture, one that represents the world-view of an emerging class, comes into being. It is intellectuals who transform the incoherent and fragmentary 'feelings' of those who live a particular class position into a coherent and reasoned account of the world as it appears from that position. A Note on the relationship between knowing, understanding and feeling, which we shall meet again below, provides a good introduction to the kind of relationship that Gramsci believed had to exist between intellectuals and 'the popular element'.

> The popular element 'feels' but does not always know or understand; the intellectual element 'knows' but does not always understand and in particular does not always feel ... The intellectual's error consists in believing that one can know without understanding and even more without feeling and being impassioned (not only for knowledge in itself but also for the object of knowledge): in other words that the intellectual can be an intellectual (and not a pure pedant) if distinct and separate from the people-nation, that is, without feeling the elementary passions of the people, understanding them and therefore explaining and justifying them in the particular historical situation and connecting them dialectically to the laws of history and to a superior conception of the world, scientifically and coherently elaborated – i.e. knowledge. One cannot make politics-history without this passion, without this sentimental connection between intellectuals and people-nation.
>
> (SPN: 418)

As Gramsci writes in 'Spontaneity and Conscious Leadership', the theory produced by progressive intellectuals cannot be in opposition to the 'feelings' of those they would represent.

> [C]an modern theory be in opposition to the 'spontaneous' feelings of the masses? ('Spontaneous' in the sense that they are not the result of any systematic educational activity on the part of an already conscious leading group, but have been formed through everyday experience illuminated by 'common sense', i.e. by the traditional popular conception of the world – what is unimaginatively called 'instinct', although it too is in fact a primitive and elementary historical acquisition.) It cannot be in opposition to them. Between the two there is a 'quantitative' difference of degree, not one of quality.
>
> (SPN: 198–9)

Intellectuals have the job of producing knowledge but for those intellectuals interested in the revolutionary transformation of society, knowledge must be based on a genuine understanding of the conditions of life experienced by 'the popular element'. But how exactly does Gramsci define the term 'intellectual'?

What Defines the Intellectual?

An intellectual is commonly defined as 'an intellectual being; a person possessing or supposed to possess superior powers of intellect' (*OED*). Gramsci's definition runs significantly counter to this.

> What are the 'maximum' limits of acceptance of the term 'intellectual'? Can one find a unitary criterion to characterise equally all the diverse and disparate activities of intellectuals and to distinguish these at the same time and in an essential way from the activities of other social groupings? *The most widespread error of method seems to me that of having looked for this criterion of distinction in the intrinsic nature of intellectual activities, rather than in the ensemble of the system of relations in which these activities (and therefore the intellectual groups who personify them) have their place within the general complex of social relations.* Indeed the worker or proletarian, for example, is not specifically characterised by his manual or instrumental work, but by performing this work in specific conditions and in specific social relations ... And we have already observed that the entrepreneur, by virtue of his very function, must have to some degree a certain number of qualifications of an intellectual nature although his part in society is determined not by these, but by the general social relations which specifically characterise the position of the entrepreneur within industry.
>
> (SPN: 8, my emphasis)

What defines the intellectual, therefore, is not that s/he possesses 'superior powers of intellect', but that they have in society a responsibility to produce knowledge and/or to instill that knowledge into others. The function of intellectuals is, above all, 'directive and organisational, i.e. educative, i.e. intellectual' (SPN: 16, see p. 150 for the context of this statement). Intellectuals are not merely those who think, but those whose thoughts are considered to have a certain weight and authority. Gramsci stresses that it is not the fact that someone thinks that makes them an intellectual; every sentient being thinks. 'There is no human activity from which every form of intellectual participation can be excluded: *homo faber* cannot be separated from *homo sapiens*' (SPN: 9). The point is that while 'all men are intellectuals' in so far as they think, 'not all men have in society the function of intellectuals' (SPN: 9). As Gramsci adds in a footnote here, 'Thus, because it can happen that everyone at some time fries a couple of eggs or sews up a tear in a jacket, we do not necessarily say that everyone is a cook or a tailor' (SPN: 9).

Gramsci also widens the standard definition of intellectual by including all those with a responsibility to instill knowledge into others and ensure, in however minor a way, that a given way of seeing the world is reproduced. As he writes in the letter to Tatiana from which I took the epigraph for this chapter, 'I greatly amplify the idea of what an intellectual is and do not confine myself to the current notion that refers only to the preeminent intellectuals' (PLII: 67). Included within his category of intellectual, for instance, are those who perform organizational tasks, as here in one of the Notes on Italian history:

> By 'intellectuals' must be understood not those strata commonly described by this term, but in general the entire social stratum which exercises an organisational function in the wide sense – whether in the field of production, or in that of culture, or in that of political administration. They correspond to the NCOs and junior officers in the army, and also partly to the higher officers who have risen from the ranks.
>
> (SPN: 97)

Relevant here is Gramsci's enormous stress on the importance of organization, as for instance in the two early articles quoted at the beginning of Chapter 4. It is subaltern classes' inability to organize that he sees as perhaps their most fundamental weakness, preventing them from overcoming their subordination. For any group to achieve dominance and to make its conception of the world hegemonic, and then to reproduce that hegemony, demands organization. The work of organization is for Gramsci an integral part of the production of knowledge that is able to act in the world, while knowledge that does not act in the world is no more than sterile pedantry.

Standard definitions of the intellectual, as with the *OED*'s quoted above, assume that what we are talking about are individuals. Gramsci, however, shifts the focus from the intellectual as individual to 'the ensemble of the system of relations' within which knowledge is produced, and how this activity is located 'within the general complex of social relations'. In other words, he is interested in the institutions and practices that produce socially recognized knowledge and how individuals are situated within these, rather than in lone individual thinkers. A very important consequence of this is that 'the intellectual' in Gramsci may well be a group rather than a single individual. In a Note on Marxism as philosophy, for instance, Gramsci writes how Marxism as a particular consciousness is

> full of contradictions, in which *the philosopher himself, understood both individually and as an entire social group,* not only grasps the contradictions, but posits himself as an element of the contradiction and elevates this element to a principle of knowledge and therefore of action.
>
> (SPN: 405, my emphasis)

As an example of the kind of new intellectual that an effective working class movement must create, Gramsci draws on his experience of the *L'Ordine Nuovo* editorial collective, of which he was one of the leading members. He describes 'what happens on the editorial committees of some reviews, when these function at the same time both as editorial committees and as cultural groups', explaining how

> The group criticises as a body, and thus helps to define the tasks of the individual editors, whose activity is organised according to a plan and a division of labour which are rationally arranged in advance. By means of collective discussion and criticism (made up of suggestions, advice, comments on method, and criticism which is constructive and aimed at mutual education) in which each individual functions as a specialist in his own field and helps to complete the expertise of the collectivity, the average level of the individual editors is in fact successfully raised so that it reaches the altitude or capacity of the most highly-skilled – thus not merely ensuring an ever more select and organic collaboration for the review, but also creating the conditions for the emergence of a homogeneous group of intellectuals, trained to produce a

regular and methodical 'writing' activity (not only in terms of occasional publications or short articles, but also of organic, synthetic studies).

(SPN: 28)

In Chapter 4 I stressed how absolutely central to Gramsci's definition of 'the intellectual' is the assumption that intellectuals, in so far as they play a significant role in history, are fundamentally linked to particular classes.

Every social group, coming into existence on the original terrain of an essential function in the world of economic production, creates together with itself, organically, one or more strata of intellectuals which give it homogeneity and an awareness of its own function not only in the economic but also in the social and political fields. The capitalist entrepreneur creates alongside himself the industrial technician, the specialist in political economy, the organisers of a new culture, of a new legal system, etc.

(SPN: 5)

Note here how the specific economic and political character of a given class shape the kind of intellectuals it produces. Capitalists, for instance, produce 'the industrial technician, the specialist in political economy', as well as 'the organisers of a new culture' and 'a new legal system'.

In one of the Notes on Italian history Gramsci argues that while intellectuals may seem at times to constitute their own autonomous group, this autonomy is illusory.

[T]here does not exist any independent class of intellectuals, but every social group has its own stratum of intellectuals, or tends to form one; however, the intellectuals of the historically (and concretely) progressive class, in the given conditions, exercise such a power of attraction that, in the last analysis, they end up by subjugating the intellectuals of the other social groups; they thereby create a system of solidarity between all the intellectuals, with bonds of a psychological nature (vanity, etc.) and often of a caste character (technico-juridical, corporate, etc.).

(SPN: 60)

I shall return to this point in the next section where I discuss Gramsci's distinction between organic and traditional intellectuals.

In 'Aspects of the Southern Question', on which Gramsci was working at the time of his arrest, he discusses, among other topics, the empirical reality of the class composition of the South and the place of various groups of intellectuals within this. This passage provides a good example of the careful, and always historically grounded, way Gramsci approaches the analysis of 'the intellectual'.

> Southern society is a great agrarian bloc, made up of three social layers: the great amorphous, disintegrated mass of the peasantry; the intellectuals of the petty and medium rural bourgeoisie; and the big landowners and great intellectuals. The Southern peasants are in perpetual ferment, but as a mass they are incapable of giving a centralized expression to their aspirations and needs. The middle layer of intellectuals receives the impulses for its political and ideological activity from the peasant base. The big landowners in the political field and the great intellectuals in the ideological field centralize and dominate, in the last analysis, this whole complex of phenomena. Naturally, it is in the ideological sphere that the centralization is most effective and precise. Giustino Fortunato[1] and Benedetto Croce thus represent the keystones of the Southern system and, in a certain sense, are the two major figures of Italian reaction.
>
> The Southern intellectuals are one of the most interesting and important social strata in Italian national life. One only has to think of the fact that more than three fifths of the State bureaucracy is made up of Southerners to convince oneself of this. Now, to understand the particular psychology of the Southern intellectuals, it is necessary to keep in mind certain factual data.
>
> 1. In every country, the layer of intellectuals has been radically modified by the development of capitalism. The old type of intellectual was the organizing element in a society with a mainly peasant and artisanal basis. To organize the State, to organize commerce, the dominant class bred a particular type of intellectual. Industry has introduced a new type of intellectual: the technical organizer, the specialist in applied science. In the societies where the economic forces have developed in a capitalist

1. Fortunato was a liberal conservative who had written on the Southern Question.

direction, to the point where they have absorbed the greater part of national activity, it is this second type of intellectual which has prevailed, with all his characteristics of order and intellectual discipline. In the countries, on the other hand, where agriculture still plays a considerable or even preponderant role, the old type has remained predominant. It provides the bulk of the State personnel; and locally too, in the villages and little country towns, it has the function of intermediary between the peasant and the administration in general. In Southern Italy this type predominates, with all its characteristic features. Democratic in its peasant face; reactionary in the face turned towards the big landowner and the government: politicking, corrupt and faithless. One could not understand the traditional cast of the Southern political parties, if one did not take the characteristics of this social stratum into account.

2. The Southern intellectual mainly comes from a layer which is still important in the South: the rural bourgeois. In other words, the petty and medium landowner who is not a peasant, who does not work the land, who would be ashamed to be a farmer, but who wants to extract from the little land he has – leased out either for rent or on a simple share-cropping basis – the wherewithal to live fittingly; the wherewithal to send his sons to a university or seminary; and the wherewithal to provide dowries for his daughters, who must marry officers or civil functionaries of the State. From this social layer, the intellectuals derive a fierce antipathy to the working peasant – who is regarded as a machine for work to be bled dry, and one which can be replaced, given the excess working population. They also acquire an atavistic, instinctive feeling of crazy fear of the peasants with their destructive violence; hence, they practise a refined hypocrisy and a highly refined art of deceiving and taming the peasant masses.

(SPWII: 454–5)

Note here how closely Gramsci links the different intellectuals with particular economic and social bases. His three 'great social levels' are made up of firstly, 'the great amorphous, disintegrated mass of the peasantry', who do not produce their own intellectuals since, 'as a mass they are incapable of giving a centralized expression to their aspirations and needs'. Gramsci's insistence that peasants do not produce their own intellectuals – for which he has often been attacked – is a point to which I shall return in the next section. The second level consists of 'the intellectuals of the petty and medium rural bourgeoisie' while the third is made up of 'the big landowners and great intellectuals'. Intellectuals speak, as it were, for the fundamental groups in society; ultimately, their polished, articulate accounts of reality are fashioned out of the raw lumps of clay given by the day-to-day experience of those groups' lives. One aspect of the close link between economic realities and intellectuals is that the rise of new classes is associated with the emergence of new types of intellectuals. For example, associated with the rise of industrial capitalism, as in the Note quoted above, is 'a new type of intellectual: the technical organizer, the specialist in applied science'.

Gramsci's basic premise that ultimately it is classes that produce intellectuals underlies the fundamental distinction he makes between organic and traditional intellectuals. The next section explores these two basic Gramscian categories and where they fit in his general theorization of culture and its production.

Organic and Traditional Intellectuals

Gramsci begins his Note 'The Formation of the Intellectuals' with a question: 'Are intellectuals an autonomous and independent social group, or does every social group have its own particular specialised category of intellectuals?' To answer this question, which 'is a complex one, because of the variety of forms assumed to date by the real historical process of formation of the different categories of intellectuals' (SPN: 5), Gramsci begins by distinguishing between what he sees as the two most important of these forms: organic and traditional intellectuals. Gramsci's general use of the term 'organic' to describe any relationship he saw as fundamental and structural, not merely fortuitous or secondary (see Chapter 2, pp. 23–4 is important here.

Organic intellectuals for Gramsci are those with fundamental, structural ties to particular classes. As a class becomes a self-conscious entity, as it moves from being merely a class-in-itself to being a class-for-itself, it brings into being its own intellectuals. In the case of the category of organic intellectuals,

It can be observed that the 'organic' intellectuals which every new class creates alongside itself and elaborates in the course of its development, are for the most part 'specialisations' of partial aspects of the primitive activity of the new social type which the new class has brought into prominence.

(SPN: 6)

This organic relationship between classes as economic entities and their intellectuals is, however, a mediated one.

> The relationship between the intellectuals and the world of production is not as direct as it is with the fundamental social groups but is, in varying degrees, 'mediated' by the whole fabric of society and by the complex of superstructures, of which the intellectuals are, precisely, the 'functionaries'. It should be possible both to measure the 'organic quality' [*organicità*] of the various intellectual strata and their degree of connection with a fundamental social group, and to establish a gradation of their functions and of the superstructures from the bottom to the top (from the structural base upwards).

(SPN: 12)

This 'organic quality' essentially has to do with the role played by different intellectuals in maintaining an already dominant class's dominance, or in the case of an emerging, potentially dominant class – and Gramsci's concern here, of course, is with the working class – in enabling that class to achieve dominance. Gramsci divides the functions performed by intellectuals into two broad types, 'social hegemony', which has to do with winning consent, and 'political government', which falls back on coercion when consent cannot be achieved. The two broad types of functions are defined as follows.

> 1. The 'spontaneous' consent given by the great masses of the population to the general direction imposed on social life by the dominant fundamental group; this consent is 'historically' caused by the prestige (and consequent confidence) which the dominant group enjoys because of its position and function in the world of production.[2]
>
> 2. The apparatus of state coercive power which 'legally' enforces discipline on those groups who do not 'consent' either actively or passively. This apparatus is, however, constituted for the whole of

---

2. This definition is one of the most frequently quoted glosses of hegemony.

society in anticipation of moments of crisis of command and direction when spontaneous consent has failed.

(SPN: 12)

It is important to stress that the 'organicity' of intellectuals depends on the degree to which they are part of the process by which the hegemony (understood in its broad sense as both force and consent; see, for instance, SPN: 80) of a particular class is produced. There is no necessary connection between this and the individual class origins of particular intellectuals.

Gramsci's broad understanding of the role of intellectuals has important implications for his definition of what constitutes an intellectual. As important as the creative, original and 'superior' quality of thought commonly associated with the idea of the intellectual, is the transmission and reproduction of particular conceptions of the world. The point here is that what Gramsci is ultimately interested in is regimes of power and their reproduction or transformation; and binding together any such regime, and crucial to its functioning, are certain conceptions of reality. That free-market mechanisms are the best and most practical way of producing and distributing goods and services, for example, is an assumption on which – leaving aside the question of whether or not it is true – modern capitalist societies depend. Gramsci recognizes that his definition of intellectual is a departure from accepted usage. Having described the two types of functions performed by intellectuals he continues:

This way of posing the problem has as a result a considerable extension of the concept of intellectual, but it is the only way which enables one to reach a concrete approximation of reality. It also clashes with preconceptions of caste. The function of organising social hegemony and state domination certainly gives rise to a particular division of labour and therefore to a whole hierarchy of qualifications in some of which there is no apparent attribution of directive or organisational functions. For example, in the apparatus of social and state direction there exist a whole series of jobs of a manual and instrumental character (non-executive work, agents rather than officials or functionaries). It is obvious that such a distinction has to be made just as it is obvious that other distinctions have to be made as well. Indeed, intellectual activity must also be distinguished in terms of its intrinsic characteristics ... at the highest level would be the creators of the various sciences, philosophy, art, etc., at the lowest the most humble 'administrators' and divulgators of pre-existing, traditional, accumulated intellectual wealth.

(SPN: 12–13)

Gramsci goes on in the same Note to consider the role played by bourgeois organic intellectuals in the maintenance of political domination.

In the modern world the category of intellectuals, understood in this sense, has undergone an unprecedented expansion. The democratic-bureaucratic system has given rise to a great mass of functions which are not all justified by the social necessities of production, though they are justified by the political necessities of the dominant fundamental group.

(SPN: 13)

A concrete example of ruling-class organic intellectuals in Italian history for Gramsci was the Moderates, a political party with its origins in the liberal Catholicism of the early nineteenth century that developed into a rightist party after the Unification of Italy. What interests Gramsci was how the Moderate Party had managed to become the governing party after the establishment of the Italian state, even though the real driving force behind Italian unification had been the more leftist Action Party. The Moderates had achieved their dominance because of their powerful presence in Italian civil society. In other words, the forces in society they represented *had* managed to produce a powerful group of intellectuals which meant the Moderates were in a position not merely to rule but to lead. Gramsci writes of the Moderates:

Moderates were intellectuals already naturally 'condensed' by the organic nature of their relation to the social groups whose expression they were. (As far as a whole series of them were concerned, there was realised the identity of the represented and the representative; in other words, the Moderates were a real, organic vanguard of the upper classes, to which economically they belonged. They were intellectuals and political organisers, and at the same time company bosses, rich farmers or estate managers, commercial and industrial entrepreneurs, etc.)

(SPN: 60)

If organic intellectuals make up the first category of intellectuals, the second category consists of the traditional intellectuals. Traditional intellectuals did originally have organic links to particular classes but they have developed over time into 'a crystallised social group ... which sees itself as continuing uninterruptedly through history and thus independent of the struggle of groups'[3] (SPN: 452). They are the pre-existing intellectual groups that the organic intellectuals of any newly emerging class must confront.

> However, every 'essential' social group which emerges into history out of the preceding economic structure, and as an expression of a development of this structure, has found (at least in all of history up to the present) categories of intellectuals already in existence and which seemed indeed to represent an historical continuity uninterrupted even by the most complicated and radical changes in political and social forms.
>
> (SPN: 6–7)

Gramsci then gives examples of such traditional intellectuals. In Italy an enormously important group of intellectuals have been the ecclesiastics, 'who for a long time ... held a monopoly of a number of important services: religious ideology, that is the philosophy and science of the age, together with schools, education, morality, justice, charity, good works, etc.'. In their time the ecclesiastics had themselves been organic intellectuals, 'organically bound to the landed aristocracy' (SPN: 7), but over time these traditional intellectuals had developed a sense of themselves 'as autonomous and independent of the dominant social group'. As Gramsci sees it,

> This self-assessment is not without consequences in the ideological and political field, consequences of wide-ranging import. The whole of idealist philosophy can easily be connected with this position assumed by the social complex of intellectuals and can be defined as the expression of that social utopia by which the intellectuals think of themselves as 'independent', autonomous, endowed with a character of their own, etc.
>
> (SPN: 7–8)

3. By 'the struggle of groups' Gramsci means class struggle. This is another of his characteristic euphemisms used to avoid arousing the suspicions of the prison censors.

The reason why the question of the linkage between intellectuals and specific economic groups, posed by Gramsci at the beginning of 'The Formation of the Intellectuals', is such a complex one is that although all intellectual groups may have their *ultimate* origin in basic economic relations, in the course of history things get a lot messier. As the discussion of traditional intellectuals makes clear, once a group of intellectuals, such as those associated with the church or, to give another example used by Gramsci, with royal courts, becomes established, and gains control of institutions such as schools or legal courts, there is a tendency for it to develop over time at least a degree of autonomy, and sometimes much more than this.

A crucial task for any new class struggling to give birth to its own organic intellectuals is to win over and assimilate the existing traditional intellectuals. Using the example of *L'Ordine Nuovo*, Gramsci explains how he sees these linked processes.

> The problem of creating a new stratum of intellectuals consists therefore in the critical elaboration of the intellectual activity that exists in everyone at a certain degree of development, modifying its relationship with the muscular-nervous effort towards a new equilibrium, and ensuring that the muscular-nervous effort itself, in so far as it is an element of a general practical activity, which is perpetually innovating the physical and social world, becomes the foundation of a new and integral conception of the world. The traditional and vulgarised type of the intellectual is given by the man of letters, the philosopher, the artist. Therefore journalists, who claim to be men of letters, philosophers, artists, also regard themselves as the 'true' intellectuals. In the modern world, technical education, closely bound to industrial labour even at the most primitive and unqualified level, must form the basis of the new type of intellectual.
>
> On this basis the weekly *L'Ordine Nuovo* worked to develop certain forms of new intellectualism and to determine its new concepts, and this was not the least of the reasons for its success, since such a conception corresponded to latent aspirations and conformed to the development of the real forms of life. The mode of being of the new intellectual can no longer consist in eloquence, which is an exterior and momentary mover of feelings and passions, but in active participation in practical life, as constructor, organiser, 'permanent persuader' and not just a simple orator (but superior at the same time to the abstract mathemat-

ical spirit); from technique-as-work one proceeds to technique-as-science and to the humanistic conception of history, without which one remains 'specialised' and does not become 'directive' (specialised and political).

Thus there are historically formed specialised categories for the exercise of the intellectual function. They are formed in connection with all social groups, but especially in connection with the more important, and they undergo more extensive and complex elaboration in connection with the dominant social group. One of the most important characteristics of any group that is developing towards dominance is its struggle to assimilate and to conquer 'ideologically' the traditional intellectuals, but this assimilation and conquest is made quicker and more efficacious the more the group in question succeeds in simultaneously elaborating its own organic intellectuals.

(SPN: 9–10)

The most important point to grasp about the basic distinction between organic and traditional intellectuals is that Gramsci's concern is always with the *process* by which power is produced and reproduced or transformed, and how intellectuals fit within this, rather than with individual intellectuals themselves.

Having sketched out the broad outlines of Gramsci's theorization of intellectuals, I want to end this section by returning to the question of why he thought that peasants do not produce their own organic intellectuals. He is quite clear on this point.

[I]t is to be noted that the mass of the peasantry, although it performs an essential function in the world of production, does not elaborate its own 'organic' intellectuals, nor does it 'assimilate' any stratum of 'traditional' intellectuals, although it is from the peasantry that other social groups draw many of their intellectuals and a high proportion of traditional intellectuals are of peasant origin.

(SPN: 6)

This passage has often been read[4] as if Gramsci here is making a blanket pronouncement about *all* peasants everywhere. However, as

---

4. See, for example, Steven Feierman's *Peasant Intellectuals* (1990) which explores the history of peasant discourse in one region of Tanzania.

I think is apparent from the reference to 'a high proportion of traditional intellectuals' being 'of peasant origin', Gramsci here is talking about *Italian* peasants, not some general theoretical category, 'peasant'. In the long passage from 'Aspects of the Southern Question' quoted above, Gramsci carefully elaborates the different social and economic realities that produce 'Southern intellectuals' (of whom Croce was a pre-eminent example), whom he saw as 'one of the most interesting and important social strata in Italian national life' in part because 'more than three fifths of the State bureaucracy is made up of Southerners' (SPWII: 454). It is clear here, I think, that what interests Gramsci and what he wants to explain is a very specific situation that was the result of a very specific Italian history. The Italian peasants Gramsci is talking about when he claims that 'the mass of the peasantry does not elaborate its own organic intellectuals' had lived for centuries as a subordinated element within larger political entities, and as a subordinated element that had been throughout those centuries, as it were, 'disciplined' by the pervasive, and highly effective, institutional network of the Catholic Church.

The fundamental reason, however, why Gramsci believes that the Italian peasantry is incapable of producing its own organic intellectuals is that while 'it performs an essential function in the world of production', it is not an 'essential social group' that has emerged 'into history out of the preceding economic structure ... as an expression of the development of this structure' (see above, p. 141). In this respect Gramsci is very much the orthodox Marxist. It is the historical development of the forces of production that creates particular economic locations or classes-in-themselves. Gramsci, who was always concerned with combating crude, overly determinist versions of Marxism, may have stressed the need to build political will, but he never believed that pure will alone was enough. For him, not all classes-in-themselves have the potential to become classes-for-themselves, that is, self-aware, political entities striving to make their understanding of reality – an understanding that derives ultimately from how the world appears from their economic location – hegemonic. A class's organic intellectuals are both a product of the economic realities of that class, but also – it is important to remember here Gramsci's very wide definition of intellectual – the means by which it emerges as a class-for-itself. The Italian peasantry for Gramsci simply did not have the potential, in an era of modern capitalism, to be the bearer of an *effective* counterhegemony. By definition, therefore, it could not produce its own organic intellectuals. It was only in alliance with the working class, and with the working class as the leading force, that the Italian peasantry could ever hope to overcome its subaltern status.

To avoid any misunderstanding let me add that in saying that peasants did not produce their own organic intellectuals, Gramsci is not saying that individuals from a peasant background could not become intellectuals. Indeed, the church had historically provided just such an opportunity of upward mobility for individuals of peasant origin, but this in Gramsci's view merely tied peasants more firmly to the existing dominant classes. 'The peasant always thinks that at least one of his sons could become an intellectual (especially a priest), thus becoming a gentleman and raising the social level of the family by facilitating its economic life through the connections which he is bound to acquire with the rest of the gentry' (SPN: 14). Inevitably such intellectuals would be socialized into the world-view of the intellectual stratum they were joining. Given the long history of peasant subordination none of the traditional strata of Italian intellectuals, of course, represented a peasant view of the world.

In the untidy confusion of real history the relationship between traditional and organic intellectuals is often a very complicated one. The next section gathers together passages in which Gramsci explores this relationship, particularly in the context of the political party.

Intellectuals and the Political Party

As I mentioned in Chapter 4 (see pp. 96–7), a key concept in Gramsci's theorization of the achievement of hegemony by 'fundamental social groups' is that of the political party. It is important here to clarify what Gramsci means by 'party' since once again Gramsci's usage is more inclusive than standard definitions. His Note 'Organisation of National Societies' explains both what he means by party, and how he sees parties as the bearers of particular cultures. In this Note Gramsci uses the term totalitarian, a term which nowadays conjures up visions of the concentration camp and the Stalinist *gulag*. It should be stressed, as the editors of the SPN point out, that for Gramsci, 'it is a quite neutral term ... meaning approximately "all-embracing and unifying"' (SPN: 147). In the SPN it is sometimes translated as 'global'.

I have remarked elsewhere that in any given society nobody is disorganised and without party, provided that one takes organisation and party in a broad and not a formal sense. In this multiplicity of private associations (which are of two kinds: natural, and contractual or voluntary) one or more predominates relatively or absolutely – constituting the hegemonic apparatus of one social group over the rest of the population (or civil society): the basis for the State in the narrow sense of the governmental-coercive apparatus.

It always happens that individuals belong to more than one private association, and often to associations which are objectively in contradiction to one another. A totalitarian policy is aimed precisely: 1. at ensuring that the members of a particular party find in that party all the satisfactions that they formerly found in a multiplicity of organisations, i.e. at breaking all the threads that bind these members to extraneous cultural organisms; 2. at destroying all other organisations or at incorporating them into a system of which the party is the sole regulator. This occurs: 1. when the given party is the bearer of a new culture – then one has a progressive phase; 2. when the given party wishes to prevent another force, bearer of a new culture, from becoming itself 'totalitarian' then one has an objectively regressive and reactionary phase, even if that reaction (as invariably happens) does not avow itself, and seeks itself to appear as the bearer of a new culture.

(SPN: 264–5)

Gramsci's apparent hostility to pluralism here – even if we replace 'totalitarian' by 'global' – is likely to offend contemporary sensibilities. It is important to remember, however, that for Gramsci societies are not neutral playing fields in which different, autonomous cultures happily coexist; they are fields of struggle, in which those espousing radically different conceptions of the world strive for primacy. At any one time, there are certain groups that are hegemonic, although it should be stressed that however hegemonic a particular power regime may appear, hegemony is never total; it is always, although to varying degrees, a struggle in process. Those groups that have power act, often in extremely subtle ways, to stifle the emergence of understandings of the world that challenge their accounts of reality. We also need to remember that Gramsci's primary interest is in the struggle between the *fundamental* social groups or classes. Within any such group there is always considerable heterogeneity, which is one of the reasons why cultures are never bounded, homogeneous entities for Gramsci. His concern, however, is with the broad contours that separate certain fundamental interests. In this connection it is relevant to note how in his political practice Gramsci demonstrated a commitment to inclusiveness and alliance building, and a scorn for narrow, sectarian dogmatism. At the same time he recognized the limits to co-operation; any attempt at building a rapprochement with Mussolini and the Fascists, for example, would have been absurd.

A passage from towards the end of 'Aspects of the Southern Question' provides a good example of Gramsci's political practice, and how undogmatic and open he was when it came to those who, while not communists, or even Marxists, did share certain 'main principles'. It also suggests the enormous importance he attached to the role of intellectuals in political struggle. We can see here, in this essay written on the eve of his imprisonment, why Gramsci was so interested in the problem of intellectuals – so interested in fact as to make it the core of his project in the prison notebooks as this was outlined in the famous letter to Tatiana. At this point Gramsci is responding to criticisms from some inside the Italian Communist Party that he and others allied with him had not denounced the liberal Piero Gobetti. Gobetti was the founder of the journal *La Rivoluzione Liberale*. He died in exile in 1926 from the after-effects of a savage beating by Fascist vigilantes.

> We could not fight against Gobetti, because he developed and represented a movement which should not be fought against, at least so far as its main principles are concerned.
>
> Not to understand that, means not to understand the question of intellectuals and the function which they fulfil in the class struggle. Gobetti, in practice, served us as a link: 1. with those intellectuals born on the terrain of capitalist techniques who in 1919–20 had taken up a left position, favourable to the dictatorship of the proletariat; 2. with a series of Southern intellectuals who through more complex relationships, posed the Southern question on a terrain different from the traditional one, by introducing into it the proletariat of the North ... Why should we have fought against the *Rivoluzione liberale* movement? Perhaps because it was not made up of pure communists who had accepted our programme and our ideas from A to Z? This could not be asked of them, because it would have been both politically and historically a paradox.
>
> *Intellectuals develop slowly, far more slowly than any other social group, by their very nature and historical function. They represent the*

entire cultural tradition of a people, seeking to resume and synthesize all of its history. This can be said especially of the old type of intellectual: the intellectual born on the peasant terrain. To think it possible that such intellectuals, *en masse,* can break with the entire past and situate themselves totally upon the terrain of a new ideology, is absurd. It is absurd for the mass of intellectuals, and perhaps it is also absurd for very many intellectuals taken individually as well – notwithstanding all the honourable efforts which they make and want to make.

Now, we are interested in the mass of intellectuals, and not just in individuals. It is certainly important and useful for the proletariat that one or more intellectuals, individually, should adopt its programme and ideas; should merge into the proletariat, becoming and feeling themselves to be an integral part of it. *The proletariat, as a class, is poor in organizing elements. It does not have its own stratum of intellectuals, and can only create one very slowly, very painfully, after the winning of State power.* But it is also important and useful for a break to occur in the mass of intellectuals: a break of an organic kind, historically characterized. For there to be formed, as a mass formation, a left tendency, in the modern sense of the word: i.e. one oriented towards the revolutionary proletariat.

The alliance between proletariat and peasant masses requires this formation. It is all the more required by the alliance between proletariat and peasant masses in the South. *The proletariat will destroy the Southern agrarian bloc insofar as it succeeds, through its party, in organizing increasingly significant masses of poor peasants into autonomous and independent formations. But its greater or lesser success in this necessary task will also depend upon its ability to break up the intellectual bloc that is the flexible, but extremely resistant, armour of the agrarian bloc.* The proletariat was helped towards the accomplishment of this task by Piero Gobetti, and we think that the dead man's friends will continue, even without his leadership, the work he undertook. This is gigantic and difficult, but precisely worthy of every sacrifice (even that of life, as in Gobetti's case) on the part of those intellectuals (and there are many of them, more than is believed) – from North and South – who have understood that *only two social forces are essentially national and bearers of the future: the proletariat and the peasants.*

(SPWII: 461–2, my emphasis)

For Gramsci, as the sentences I have emphasized indicate, the working class has to create its own organic intellectuals, but this is a long and difficult process that can only come to full fruition *after* 'the winning of State power'. At the same time state power can only be won by a group, such as the bourgeoisie at an earlier period in history, that has already begun to create its own intellectuals. This is saved from being a catch-22 situation in part by the relationship between the embryonic, newly emerging organic intellectuals and the existing traditional intellectuals, hence the crucial importance of building alliances with intellectuals like Gobetti. In the prison notebooks, in 'The Formation of the Intellectuals', Gramsci discusses in a more theoretical, and less empirical way the role of the organic intellectuals of an emergent class vis-à-vis traditional intellectuals.

> [T]here are historically formed specialised categories for the exercise of the intellectual function. They are formed in connection with all social groups, but especially in connection with the more important, and they undergo more extensive and complex elaboration in connection with the dominant social group. One of the most important characteristics of any group that is developing towards dominance is its struggle to assimilate and to conquer 'ideologically' the traditional intellectuals, but this assimilation and conquest is made quicker and more efficacious the more the group in question succeeds in simultaneously elaborating its own organic intellectuals.
>
> (SPN: 10)

In another Note comparing urban and rural intellectuals, Gramsci describes how traditional intellectuals are welded together with organic ones within the political party.

> The political party, for all groups, is precisely the mechanism which carries out in civil society the same function as the State carries out, more synthetically and over a larger scale, in political society. In other words it is responsible for welding together the organic intellectuals of a given group – the dominant one – and the traditional intellectuals. The party carries out this function in strict dependence on its basic function, which is that of elaborating its own component parts – those elements of a social group which has been born and developed as an 'economic' group – and of turning them into qualified political intellectuals, leaders

[*dirigenti*] and organisers of all the activities and functions inherent in the organic development of an integral society, both civil and political. Indeed it can be said that within its field the political party accomplishes its function more completely and organically than the State does within its admittedly far larger field. An intellectual who joins the political party of a particular social group is merged with the organic intellectuals of the group itself, and is linked tightly with the group.

(SPN: 15–16)

It is important to remember here Gramsci's focus on the institutions that produce knowledge rather than on individual intellectuals. In a sense, the political party itself can be seen as a collective organic intellectual. We find, for example, Gramsci writing a little later in the same passage:

That all members of a political party should be regarded as intellectuals is an affirmation that can easily lend itself to mockery and caricature. But if one thinks about it nothing could be more exact. There are of course distinctions of level to be made. A party might have a greater or lesser proportion of members in the higher grades or in the lower, but this is not the point. What matters is the function, which is directive and organisational, i.e. educative, i.e. intellectual.

(SPN: 16)

If organic intellectuals are the bearers of a particular class's understanding of reality or conception of the world, then it is in the context of the political party that this conception of the world becomes a historical force. As Gramsci writes in 'Relation between Science, Religion and Common Sense',

One should stress the importance and significance which, in the modern world, political parties have in the elaboration and diffusion of conceptions of the world, because essentially what they do is to work out the ethics and the politics corresponding to these conceptions and act as it were as their historical 'laboratory'. The parties recruit individuals out of the working mass, and the selection is made on practical and theoretical criteria at the same time. The relation between theory and practice becomes even closer the more the conception is vitally and radically innovatory and opposed to old ways of thinking. For this reason one can say that the parties are the elaborators of new integral and totalitarian[5] intelligentsias and the crucibles where the unification of theory and practice, understood as a real historical process, takes place.

(SPN: 335)

A group's organic intellectuals, those who articulate and systematize its conception of the world, are crucial to leadership through persuasion. Creating such intellectuals, however, and bringing into being what is in essence a new 'culture', is not easy. Gramsci puts it this way:

A human mass does not 'distinguish' itself, does not become independent in its own right without, in the widest sense, organising itself; and there is no organisation without intellectuals, that is without organisers and leaders, in other words, without the theoretical aspect of the theory–practice nexus being distinguished concretely by the existence of a group of people 'specialised' in conceptual and philosophical elaboration of ideas. But the process of creating intellectuals is long, difficult, full of contradictions, advances and retreats, dispersals and regroupings, in which the loyalty of the masses is often sorely tried. (And one must not forget that at this early stage loyalty and discipline are the ways in which the masses participate and collaborate in the development of the cultural movement as a whole.)

The process of development is tied to a dialectic between the intellectuals and the masses. The intellectual stratum develops both quantitatively and qualitatively, but every leap forward towards a new breadth and complexity of the intellectual stratum is tied to an analogous movement on the part of the mass of the 'simple', who raise themselves to higher levels of culture and at the same time extend their circle of influence towards the stratum of specialised intellectuals, producing outstanding individuals and groups of greater or less importance.

(SPN: 334–5)

5. See p. 145 for a discussion of the meaning this term had for Gramsci.
6. See n. 6, Chapter 5.

This continual back and forth movement between intellectuals and 'simple'[6] is central to Gramsci's approach to the problem of how cultures emerge and are, or are not, reproduced.

To get a sense of how Gramsci locates intellectuals in the production of culture it is useful to begin by returning to the notion of 'national-popular collective will', which I referred to in Chapter 4 but did not discuss.

Creating a National-Popular Collective Will

Gramsci poses the question: 'When can the conditions for awakening and developing a national-popular collective will be said to exist?' (SPN: 130) in the context of a Note discussing the form a modern revolutionary movement should take. The first point to make is that for Gramsci any movement capable of genuinely challenging a modern capitalist state like that of Italy, has to be a *mass* movement. There must be a *collective* sense of purpose. It is not enough simply to seize the formal state apparatuses of coercion. This might have worked in Russia in 1917 since there, as Gramsci put it, 'the State was everything, civil society was primordial and gelatinous', but it was not an appropriate strategy in Italy.

> [I]n the West, there was a proper relation between State and civil society, and when the State trembled a sturdy structure of civil society was at once revealed. The State was only an outer ditch, behind which there stood a powerful system of fortresses and earthworks ...
>
> (SPN: 238)

If there is to be a radical transformation of society those fortresses and earthworks must be undermined; civil society itself needs to be transformed. In other words, an emergent group needs to achieve a degree of hegemony prior to becoming politically dominant. As Gramsci writes in one of the Notes on Italian History,

> A social group can, and indeed must, already exercise 'leadership' [*direzione*] before winning governmental power (this indeed is one of the principal conditions for the winning of such power); it subsequently becomes dominant when it exercises power, but even if it holds it firmly in its grasp, it must continue to 'lead' [*dirigere*] as well.
>
> (SPN: 57–8)

The editors of the SPN draw attention to the problems of translating the Italian *'dirigere'* (direct, lead, rule) and its compounds, such as *direzione,* into English (see n. 5, SPN: 55–7). Probably the most important point to grasp is Gramsci's basic distinction between the exercise of power that relies on force, and power based on persuasion. Something of what Gramsci understood by leadership comes out in a Note on elective systems of government, in which he writes:

One of the most banal commonplaces which get repeated against the elective system of forming State organs is the following: that in it numbers decide everything, and that the opinions of any idiot who knows how to write (or in some countries even of an illiterate) have exactly the same weight in determining the political course of the State as the opinions of somebody who devotes his best energies to the State and the nation, etc. But the fact is that it is not true, in any sense, that numbers decide everything, nor that the opinions of all electors are of 'exactly' equal weight. Numbers, in this case too, are simply an instrumental value, giving a measure and a relation and nothing more. And what then is measured? *What is measured is precisely the effectiveness, and the expansive and persuasive capacity, of the opinions of a few individuals, the active minorities, the élites, the avant-gardes, etc.* – i.e. their rationality, historicity or concrete functionality. Which means it is untrue that all individual opinions have 'exactly' equal weight. Ideas and opinions are not spontaneously 'born' in each individual brain: *they have had a centre of formation, of irradiation, of dissemination, of persuasion – a group of men, or a single individual even, which has developed them and presented them in the political form of current reality.* The counting of 'votes' is the final ceremony of a long process, in which it is precisely those who devote their best energies to the State and the nation (when such they are) who carry the greatest weight. If this hypothetical group of worthy men, notwithstanding the boundless material power which they possess, do not have the consent of the majority, they must be judged either as inept, or as not representative of 'national' interests – which cannot help being decisive in inflecting the national will in one direction rather than in another.

(SPN: 192–3, my emphasis)

The sentences I have emphasized describe very well the kind of leadership that Gramsci believes intellectuals should provide. The role of intellectuals – it is important here to remember the inclusiveness of Gramsci's definition of the intellectual – is so crucial for Gramsci precisely because of his rejection of the notion that individuals are essentially autonomous and 'free'. The whole passage in fact can be read as a radical critique of the self-contained individual as the basis of society or the motor of history. People may make history, as Marx famously said, but they do not do it as isolated individuals. They do it as members of collective political entities who share a collective political will. Gramsci goes on in this same Note to discuss the need,

> ... to study precisely how permanent collective wills are formed, and how such wills set themselves concrete short-term and long-term ends – i.e. a line of collective action. It is a question of more or less long processes of development, and rarely of sudden, 'synthetic' explosions. Synthetic 'explosions' do occur, but if they are looked at closely it can be seen that they are more destructive than reconstructive; they remove mechanical and external obstacles in the way of an indigenous and spontaneous development ...
>
> It would be possible to study concretely the formation of a collective historical movement, analysing it in all its molecular phases – a thing which is rarely done, since it would weigh every treatment down. Instead, currents of opinion are normally taken as already constituted around a group or a dominant personality. This is the problem which in modern times is expressed in terms of the party, or coalition of related parties: how a party is first set up, how its organisational strength and social influence are developed, etc. It requires an extremely minute, molecular process of exhaustive analysis in every detail, the documentation for which is made up of an endless quantity of books, pamphlets, review and newspaper articles, conversations and oral debates repeated countless times, and which in their gigantic aggregation represent this long labour which gives birth to a collective will with a certain degree of homogeneity – with the degree necessary and sufficient to achieve an action which is co-ordinated and simultaneous in the time and the geographical space in which the historical event takes place.
>
> (SPN: 194)

Creating 'a national-popular collective will' in the contemporary period is seen by Gramsci as both crucial and difficult. The problem is, firstly, that while the core of this collective will derives from basic economic relations, these by no means give rise in any automatic way to a particular consciousness or conception of the world. The raw material of class experience has to be moulded into a convincing and coherent political narrative in which individuals can recognize their own situation, and that motivates them to act collectively. Secondly, to create a mass movement large enough to bring about change it is necessary for a given class to represent the aspirations of other classes as well. The bourgeoisie, for instance, achieved its hegemony in Europe by presenting itself as the representative of *all* those chafing under the inequalities of feudalism. Similarly, in the Italy of his time Gramsci saw the proletariat as doomed to failure if it was not able to ally itself with the mass of the peasantry.

Finally, there is the question of the term 'national' in 'national-popular collective will'. It is important to note that Gramsci is discussing the failure to create an Italian nation state before the mid-nineteenth century, and the legacy of that failure for the politics of his time. The political entity with which he is concerned, therefore, is the nation state; and the historical arena where an Italian national state had to be created was the Italian peninsula and its islands, a geographical area with, at least in some sense, a shared cultural tradition. In the Italian context, 'Italy' represented for Gramsci a more progressive political entity than those based on various narrow, parochial regional loyalties. The reality of Gramsci's time was that political struggles were fought within nation states – something that to a considerable extent remains the case, I would argue, even in our supposedly global world. While it is undoubtedly true that what happens within nation states is powerfully affected by all kinds of global forces – something of which Gramsci was well aware – these still tend to be mediated through the institutions of the nation state. It should be stressed, however, that, as the editors of the SPN put it, national-popular is for Gramsci, 'a cultural concept, relating to the position of the masses within the culture of the nation, and radically alien to any form of populism or "national socialism"' (n. 65, SPN: 421). What Gramsci was interested in was how the necessary mass, counterhegemonic culture might be brought into being in an Italian context. The final section of this chapter focuses on passages in which Gramsci discusses the production of culture and the role of intellectuals in this.

Creating Culture, Creating Intellectuals

The production and reproduction of culture is at the heart of what intellectuals do as a distinct stratum within the dynamic of history. It is they who produce the broad cultural conceptions of the world that underpin particular power regimes, and in the case of the organic intellectuals of an emergent class help to bring into being a new culture. It may well be that the new ideas have their 'origins in mediocre philosophical works', but this does not matter. In Gramsci's view,

> What matters is that a new way of conceiving the world and man is born and that this conception is no longer reserved to the great intellectuals, to professional philosophers, but tends rather to become a popular, mass phenomenon, with a concretely world-wide character, capable of modifying (even if the result includes hybrid combinations) popular thought and mummified popular culture.
>
> (SPN: 417)

For Gramsci, only a political movement based in a popular, mass culture could have any hope of seriously challenging the power of a modern capitalist state like Italy.

> An historical act can only be performed by 'collective man', and this presupposes the attainment of a 'cultural-social' unity through which a multiplicity of dispersed wills, with heterogeneous aims, are welded together with a single aim, on the basis of an equal and common conception of the world, both general and particular, operating in transitory bursts (in emotional ways) or permanently (where the intellectual base is so well rooted, assimilated and experienced that it becomes passion).
>
> (SPN: 349)

The creation of such a '"cultural-social" unity' demands a new kind of intellectual. Gramsci goes on to describe these new intellectuals' relationship to their social milieu, which is like the 'active and reciprocal' teacher–pupil relationship of modern pedagogical theory in which 'every teacher is always a pupil and every pupil a teacher'. In fact, according to Gramsci,

This form of relationship exists throughout society as a whole and for every individual relative to other individuals. It exists between intellectual and non-intellectual sections of the population, between the rulers and the ruled, *élites* and their followers, leaders [*dirigenti*] and led, the vanguard and the body of the army. Every relationship of 'hegemony' is necessarily an educational relationship and occurs not only within a nation, between the various forces of which the nation is composed, but in the inter-national and world-wide field, between complexes of national and continental civilisations.

One could say therefore that the historical personality of an individual philosopher is also given by the active relationship which exists between him and the cultural environment he is proposing to modify. The environment reacts back on the philosopher and imposes on him a continual process of self-criticism. It is his 'teacher'. This is why one of the most important demands that the modern intelligentsias have made in the political field has been that of the so-called 'freedom of thought and of the expression of thought' ('freedom of the press', 'freedom of association'). For the relationship between master and disciple in the general sense referred to above is only realised where this political condition exists, and only then do we get the 'historical' realisation of a new type of philosopher, whom we could call a 'democratic philosopher' in the sense that he is a philosopher convinced that his personality is not limited to himself as a physical individual but is an active social relationship of modification of the cultural environment ... The unity of science and life is precisely an active unity, in which alone liberty of thought can be realised; it is a master–pupil relationship, one between the philosopher and the cultural environment in which he has to work and from which he can draw the necessary problems for formulation and resolution. In other words, it is the relationship between philosophy and history.

(SPN: 350–1)

Gramsci frequently contrasts the role of the Catholic Church, in many ways the most powerful influence in the lives of the subaltern classes in Italy, with that of Marxist intellectuals.

The position of the philosophy of praxis is the antithesis of the Catholic. The philosophy of praxis does not tend to leave the 'simple' in their primitive philosophy of common sense, but rather to lead them to a higher conception of life. If it affirms the need for contact between intellectuals and simple it is not in order to restrict scientific activity and preserve unity at the low level of the masses, but precisely in order to construct an intellectual-moral bloc which can make politically possible the intellectual progress of the mass and not only of small intellectual groups.

(SPN: 332–3)

For Gramsci the relationship between intellectuals and the mass of the people[7] was especially problematic in Italy because, as he saw it, Italian intellectuals were so far removed from the Italian people.

In Italy the term 'national' has an ideologically very restricted meaning, and does not in any case coincide with 'popular' because in Italy the intellectuals are distant from the people, i.e. from the 'nation'. They are tied instead to a caste tradition that has never been broken by a strong popular or national political movement from below ...

What is the meaning of the fact that the Italian people prefer to read foreign writers? It means that they *undergo* the moral and intellectual hegemony of foreign intellectuals, that they feel more closely related to foreign intellectuals than to 'domestic' ones, that there is no national intellectual and moral bloc, either hierarchical or, still less, egalitarian. The intellectuals do not come from the people, even if by accident some of them have origins among the people. They do not feel tied to them (rhetoric apart), they do not know and sense their needs, aspirations and feelings. In relation to the people, they are something detached, without foundation, a caste and not an articulation with organic functions of the people themselves.

The question must be extended to the entire national-popular culture and not restricted just to narrative fiction. The same things must be said about the theatre, about scientific literature in general (the sciences of nature, history, etc.). Why do no writers like Flammarion[8] emerge in Italy? Why has no popularized

---

7. See Chapter 5, n. 6, for a clarification of the Italian term *simplice*, translated by Hoare and Nowell Smith as 'simple'.
8. Camille Flammarion (1842–1925), author of popular books on science.

scientific literature arisen as in France and other countries? These foreign books are read and sought after in translation and are often very successful. All this means that the entire 'educated class', with its intellectual activity, is detached from the people-nation, not because the latter has not shown and does not show itself to be interested in this activity at all levels, from the lowest (dreadful serial novels) to the highest – indeed it seeks out foreign books for this purpose – but because in relation to the people-nation the indigenous intellectual element is more foreign than the foreigners ...

The lay forces have failed in their historical task as educators and elaborators of the intellect and the moral awareness of the people-nation. They have been incapable of satisfying the intellectual needs of the people precisely because they have failed to represent a lay culture, because they have not known how to elaborate a modern 'humanism' able to reach right to the simplest and most uneducated classes, as was necessary from the national point of view, and because they have been tied to an antiquated world, narrow, abstract, too individualistic or caste-like.

(SCW: 208–11, Gramsci's emphasis)

It should be stressed how significant this inability, or unwillingness, of Italian intellectuals to relate to the mass of the population is for Gramsci in explaining the particular character of the Italian state. The absence in Italy of a 'national-popular collective will' means that the 'people' are effectively excluded from the life of the 'nation'. In Gramsci's view, it is this absence that lies behind the general weakness and inadequacy of the Italian state.

In the following passage from 'The Philosophy of Praxis and Modern Culture', Gramsci describes what he sees as the main tasks of Marxism in terms of cultural revolution, namely the creation of 'its own group of independent intellectuals', and the transformation of popular culture.

The philosophy of praxis had two tasks to perform: to combat modern ideologies in their most refined form, in order to be able to constitute its own group of independent intellectuals; and to educate the popular masses, whose culture was medieval. This second task, which was fundamental, given the character of the new philosophy, has absorbed all its strength, not only in quantitative but also in qualitative terms. For 'didactic' reasons, the new philosophy was combined into a form of culture which was a little higher than the popular average (which was very low) but was absolutely inadequate to combat the ideologies of the educated classes. And yet the new philosophy was born precisely to supersede the highest cultural manifestation of the age, classical German philosophy, and to create a group of intellectuals specific to the new social group whose conception of the world it was. On the other side, modern culture, especially that marked by idealism, does not manage to elaborate a popular culture or to give a moral and scientific content to its own school programmes,[9] which remain abstract and theoretical schemas. It remains the culture of a restricted intellectual aristocracy, which exercises a hold on youth only rarely and to the extent that it becomes immediate (and occasional) politics.[10]

(SPN: 392–3)

The creation of organic intellectuals is a long, hard process, and one that can be fully completed only *after* a group has achieved hegemony.

[C]reating a group of independent intellectuals is not an easy thing; it requires a long process, with actions and reactions, coming together and drifting apart and the growth of very numerous and complex new formations. [*Marxism*] *is the conception of a subaltern social group, deprived of historical initiative, in continuous but disorganic expansion*, unable to go beyond a certain qualitative level, which still remains below the level of the possession of the State and of the real exercise of hegemony over the whole of society which alone permits a certain organic equilibrium in the development of the intellectual group.

(SPN: 395–6, my emphasis)

9. According to the editors of the SPN, 'Gramsci would appear here particularly to have in mind the reform of the Italian school system carried out under the aegis of the idealist philosopher and Fascist Minister of Education, Giovanni Gentile, in 1923' (SPN: 393).
10. Gramsci's key distinction between that which is organic (an integral part of the structure) and that which is superficial and contingent (see Chapter 2, pp. 23–4) is relevant here.

Intellectuals are, therefore, both the producers and the product of class-for-itself, which brings us back to Gramsci and the *L'Ordine Nuovo* group in 1919 and their 'vague passion for a vague proletarian culture'. Their aspirations were necessarily vague since, although they saw themselves as playing a key role in shaping the seething ferment of the time into an effective political movement, exactly what that role should be and what that political and cultural movement would emerge as, depended on how the struggles between the various historical forces played themselves out.

In this and the preceding two chapters I have attempted to map out the broad contours of the terrain occupied by 'culture' in Gramsci's writings. I deliberately chose to follow the contours of Gramsci's thought rather than structuring the chapters around the differences between Gramsci's approach and that characteristic of anthropologists. I hope, however, that my mapping of the concept of culture in Gramsci has shown how little this concept resembles what culture came to mean in mainstream anthropology. And in particular the extent to which Gramsci's notion of culture runs counter to the three assumptions on which I focused in Chapter 3; namely, that cultures constitute patterned wholes of some kind, that they are discrete and bounded entities, and that one of the most fundamental structuring oppositions in the societies typically studied by anthropologists is that between 'tradition' and 'modernity'. Despite the divergence between Gramsci's understanding of culture and that of mainstream anthropology, since the publication of the prison notebooks in English Gramsci has become popular with a number of American and British anthropologists. In the next and final chapter I look at the place Gramsci has come to occupy in anthropology and also offer some tentative suggestions as to how anthropologists might most fruitfully engage with his work.

Part III

Gramsci and Anthropology

7   Gramsci Now

In general, for these last few months, I have felt more isolated and completely cut off from the life of the world. I read a lot, books and magazines; a lot in relation to the intellectual life that one can lead in prison. But I have lost much of the pleasure in reading. Books and magazines only offer general ideas, sketches (more or less successful) of general currents in the world's life, but they cannot give the immediate, direct, vivid impression of the lives of Peter, Paul, and John, of single, real individuals, and unless one understands them one cannot understand what is being universalized and generalized.

(PLI: 232–3)

In this final chapter I return to the question posed in Chapter 1: why should anthropologists read Gramsci? And, more particularly, why should they read him now? What have twenty-first-century anthropologists to gain from a sustained dialogue with Gramsci? In my Introduction I suggested that Gramsci's writings can provide anthropologists with intriguing, sometimes provocative, insights into how we might rethink the whole complex terrain of culture, class and inequality. This chapter elaborates on what a serious engagement with Gramsci's work might involve.

A good place to start is by taking a careful look at the Gramsci who, judging from his frequent appearance in anthropological bibliographies, is already firmly ensconced within anthropology. It is true that interest in Gramsci, which was at its height in the 1980s and early 1990s, seems to have waned somewhat in recent years and that the citations are fewer nowadays, but nonetheless he remains a significant figure. One of my reasons for writing this book was my belief that this Gramsci, the one who has been taken up with such enthusiasm by so many anthropologists, is not the Gramsci I found in the prison notebooks, the Gramsci whose thought this book has tried to map out. It may well be, I would argue, that it is indeed a lack of serious engagement with Gramsci's thought in all its ragged, dynamic complexity that explains, at least in part, his recent fall from favour within anthropology.

The Gramsci for whom anthropology has already found a place seems to me, all too often, a rather insubstantial creature. This is a Gramsci, in Foucault's words, cited more often than genuinely known. So far Gramsci has found a home in anthropology as little more than a name associated with the concept of hegemony, and more generally with an open, undogmatic Marxism. As one survey article on Gramsci and anthropology puts it, 'Most anthropologists rely on the ever-growing pile of secondary interpretations ... to develop a notion of hegemony that often bears little resemblance to Gramsci's idea' (Kurtz, 1996: 104). In general, anthropologists have tended to understand hegemony as a concept that describes a particular form of power, rather than, as it is in Gramsci (see Chapter 5), as a way of approaching the problem of how power is produced and reproduced; an approach that, as it were, provides us with certain questions to ask of the empirical realities of power. The fact that a somewhat misleading version of Gramsci has already found a home in anthropology means that if we want to think seriously about how anthropology might engage with Gramsci's thought, we have to begin by examining this already present Gramsci. We need to probe a little into what this name, Gramsci, has come to mean, examining the relationship between this name and the more sub-stantial figure whom I hope has begun to emerge in the course of the preceding chapters. In other words, we have to begin by defamiliar-izing a thinker many anthropologists may believe they already know.

Once this is done we can go on to look at how anthropology might enter into conversation with this more substantial, but also more problematic and challenging thinker, exploring what would happen if we as anthropologists were to engage seriously with Gramsci's theorization of culture, and his mappings of the lived realities of power. What would it look like in practice if anthropol-ogy were genuinely to open itself up to Gramsci's thought in all its dense and complicated richness? As a way of beginning to answer this question, in the second half of this chapter I look at some examples of what happens, or might happen, when we begin to ask Gramscian questions of power in specific ethnographic contexts. But first, just who is the Gramsci so many anthropologists cite?

Raymond Williams' Gramsci

While anthropologists who cite Gramsci commonly refer to such well known Gramsci commentators as Laclau and Mouffe, Femia, and Perry Anderson, by far the most influential source on Gramsci for anthropologists has been Raymond Williams. Williams' 1977 *Marxism and Literature*, particularly the section on hegemony (1977: 108–14), is the text most frequently quoted or cited as a gloss on hegemony.[1] Another important figure in the introduction of Gramsci into anthropology is a theorist with close ties to Williams, Stuart Hall. Hall has always claimed Gramsci as a central theoretical presence within cultural studies[2] (the school of social analysis of which both Williams and Hall were founders) and over the course of his career has written a number of essays specifically on Gramsci,[3] as well as many that draw heavily on Gramsci. Hall's work, which has often taken the form of collaborative projects with his Cultural Studies colleagues, has had a considerable influence on anthropologists. Nonetheless, he has not provided anthropologists with a comparable text to *Marxism and Literature* to which they can turn for succinct glosses of key Gramscian concepts such as hegemony. It is not so much Hall's reading of Gramsci himself but the Gramsci-informed work of Hall and his collaborators that has been influential among anthropologists, which is why I concentrate here on Williams rather than Hall.

The work of the political scientist James Scott should also be mentioned. Scott's rejection of the notion of hegemony, and fierce defence of the ability of subaltern groups to fashion their own autonomous accounts of power, have been highly influential among anthropologists. A number of anthropologists have based their characterization of hegemony on Scott's firmly idealist version of Gramsci's concept. For Scott, the key text is Marx and Engels' *The German Ideology* which contains the famous formulation: 'The ideas of the ruling class are in every epoch the ruling ideas' (quoted in Scott, 1985: 315). In his much cited *Weapons of the Weak*, Scott first quotes in full the passage in which the Marx and Engels formulation occurs, and then writes: 'Hegemony is simply the name Gramsci gave to this process of ideological domination' (Scott, 1985: 315). As we shall see, this kind of idealist understanding of hegemony is one many anthropologists share. It is Williams, however, to whom anthropologists have most commonly turned for their definitions

1. See, for example, Brow 1988, Fox 1989, Gill 1993, Lagos 1993, Linger 1993, Woost 1993.
2. See Hall 1994.
3. See, for example, Hall 1986a, 1986b, 1988a and 1988b.

of hegemony. The Gramsci who has become a significant presence in anthropology is very much the Gramsci of *Marxism and Literature*. It is this Gramsci on whom I want to focus here.

Williams, who died in 1988, was without doubt one of the major Marxist literary critics of the last century. His careful and sensitive explorations of the British literary tradition can be read with profit by any anthropologist, and many have done so. *Keywords*, in which Williams traces out the often complicated historical paths by which the names we use to map the social world have come to mean what they do today, is an invaluable guide for anyone interested in understanding that social world. Chapter 3 of this book drew extensively on the *Keywords* entry for culture. Williams himself, born in 1921, was the product of a working-class world in which the Marxist tradition was a powerful living presence, albeit a very populist, very British, atheoretical, even antitheoretical, version of that tradition. And Williams never lost touch with that common-sense (in the Gramscian sense) Marxism; for Williams Marxism was always about 'feeling' as well as 'knowing' (see the Note on the relationship between knowing, understanding and feeling quoted at the beginning of the last chapter). Williams, however, also engaged in a systematic and serious way both with the writings of Marx himself and with those of later Marxist theorists such as Gramsci, as well as Lucáks, Goldmann, Benjamin, Althusser and Adorno.

Marxism and Literature, written at a time when Marxism seemed to be undergoing an extraordinary intellectual revival, is the product of a man who has read widely and thought deeply and, very importantly, has digested his reading to come up with his own synthesis of what Marxism has to offer the literary critic. In *Marxism and Literature* Gramsci, who is dealt with towards the end of an account of what is in effect Williams' own intellectual journey, emerges as perhaps the most useful Marxist thinker for someone interested, as Williams is, in developing an approach to literature which is both genuinely materialist and yet does not confine 'literature' to the epiphenomenal realms of the superstructure. It is clear that Williams has read Gramsci carefully and understood how he fitted into an ongoing Marxist conversation. John and Jean Comaroff in their discussion of Gramsci and hegemony in *Of Revelation and Revolution* (a discussion to which anthropologists frequently refer), note with some surprise how Williams' much cited discussion of hegemony 'is written without a single page reference to, or quotation from, *The Prison Notebooks*' (1991: 317). An examination of this 'curious fact' (as the Comaroffs put it) provides a good starting point for thinking about why for anthropologists the Gramsci of *Marxism and Literature* may not in fact provide the best entry point into Gramsci's thought.

This 'curious fact' has to do, firstly, with the kind of scholar Williams was and the nature of his writing style; and secondly, with what Williams is trying to do in *Marxism and Literature*. Williams was a scholar and a writer who first and foremost 'wrote as a socialist, for socialism', as Francis Mulhern put it in the Preface to a posthumous collection of Williams' essays (1990: viii). While Williams was a careful and meticulous scholar, he was always concerned that his writings should not just reach a narrow coterie of academics but should be accessible to the widest possible audience. He was a refreshingly light footnoter, even by British standards, never seeming to feel the need, as some academics do, to prop his arguments up with a scaffold fashioned from every authority who has ever put pen to paper. In *Marxism and Literature*, which covers a lot of ground in a relatively short space, Williams distils his own engagement with various theorists linked to the Marxist tradition. We get the fruit of his labours, not an exhaustive account of his journeyings through the various theoretical orchards from which each fruit has been harvested. Rather than attempting a scholarly exegesis of any of the major authors, Williams provides us with a synthesis that draws together particular themes which have been selected always with the aim of developing what he terms a cultural materialist approach to literature. The range of theoretical work covered means that all the major theorists, including Gramsci, are dealt with in somewhat summary form; Williams does not have the space to do more than indicate, almost as a series of signposts, from where he has drawn the key elements of his cultural materialist approach to literature. It is this, I would suggest, that explains why, with the exception of Marx himself, there are so few direct quotations from *any* of the Marxist theorists Williams discusses. In the case of Gramsci, Williams' concern is not to provide an extended exegesis of his thought so much as to draw attention to how Gramsci's writings on hegemony can be used to 'think' power in a way that is *both* cultural and material, and that gets beyond the unhelpful base–superstructure dichotomy. In other words, how Gramsci can help us move beyond a particular theoretical impasse.

Moving to the question of Williams' project in *Marxism and Literature*, it needs to be stressed that Williams was very much a *literary* critic. While he may not have borne much resemblance to the popular image of a devotee of 'high culture', worshipping at the shrine of literature and keeping himself remote from the vulgar fray of politics, he was most certainly not an anthropologist. And the roots of his concern with culture were rather different from those of anthropologists. While the question of 'culture' may indeed have been at the heart of his project, this culture was not the same culture as that 'around which', according to Geertz, 'the whole discipline of anthropology arose' (see pp. 38, 43).

I have already quoted in Chapter 3 from *Keywords* where Williams argues that culture is such a complicated word primarily 'because it has now come to be used for important concepts in several distinct intellectual disciplines and in several distinct and incompatible systems of thought' (1983: 87). *Marxism and Literature*, published a year after the original edition of *Keywords*, also has a section tracing the complex history of the term 'culture'. Here Williams describes the complexity and the basic disciplinary cleavage as follows:

> The complexity of the concept of 'culture' is then remarkable. It became a noun of 'inner' process, specialized to its presumed agencies in 'intellectual life' and 'the arts'. It became also a noun of general process, specialized to its presumed configurations in 'whole ways of life'. It played a crucial role in definitions of 'the arts' and 'the humanities', from the first sense. It played an equally crucial role in definitions of the 'human sciences' and the 'social sciences', in the second sense. Each tendency is ready to deny any proper use of the concept to the other, in spite of many attempts at reconciliation.
>
> (1977: 17)

For Williams himself these divergent usages created an interesting but problematic tension. The passage continues:

> In any modern theory of culture, but perhaps especially in a Marxist theory, this complexity is a source of great difficulty. The problem of knowing, at the outset, whether this would be a theory of 'the arts and intellectual life' in their relations to 'society', or a theory of the social process which creates specific and different 'ways of life', is only the most obvious problem.
>
> (1977: 17–18)

Ultimately, however, while Williams stretches and challenges the concept of culture as understood in the humanities in illuminating and thought-provoking ways, *Marxism and Literature* remains primarily a work of literary theory. All too often, it seems to me, the 'literature' in Williams' title, *Marxism and Literature*, is forgotten by its anthropological readers. And yet the essence of Williams' project in the book is an exploration of what a Marxist literary practice that took both Marxism and literature equally seriously might look like. This is clear from Williams' Introduction. He begins by explaining how *Marxism and Literature* has been written 'in a time of radical change'. Twenty years earlier it might have been possible for him to treat Marxism as 'a settled body of theory or doctrine', and Literature as 'a settled body of work, or kinds of work', so that his book 'might then reasonably have explored problems of the relations between them or, assuming a certain relationship, passed quickly to specific applications. The situation is now very different.' Marxism 'has experienced at once a significant revival and a related openness and flexibility of theoretical development', while 'Literature ... has become problematic in quite new ways' (1977: 1). Williams may have interrogated and challenged the concept of 'Literature', and taken his own path through Marxism and other related theoretical traditions, but his concern remains that of developing 'a theory of the specificities of material culture and literary production within historical materialism' (1977: 5).

This is not to say that anthropologists cannot gain useful insights from reading Williams, but they need to bear in mind that when he talks about culture in *Marxism and Literature* he is part of a rather different conversation, that has different concerns and asks different questions, from the conversation (or conversations) in which anthropologists have characteristically engaged. Anthropologists, I would argue, have not always been sufficiently alert to the fact that the 'culture' with which Williams is primarily concerned is not 'culture' as it has been commonly understood in anthropology. This would not matter so much if it were not that the Gramsci who has found a home in anthropology has tended to be the Gramsci of Williams' hegemony chapter in *Marxism and Literature*. The problem with this, as I see it, is, firstly, that Gramsci is reduced to a theorist of hegemony, and secondly, that this hegemony is a thin and impoverished version of a much more complex, but also far more interesting, interrogation of power and its mechanisms. The next section examines this thin, anthropological version of hegemony in a little more detail.

'Hegemony Lite'

The main problem with how the concept of hegemony has been understood within anthropology, I would argue, is that hegemony is taken as referring not to the whole field of power, but only to the domain of beliefs and ideas. In terms of the old Marxist debates over idealist versus materialist accounts of the world, hegemony has become an essentially idealist concept. It is somewhat ironic that the Gramsci introduced into anthropology by Williams should have taken such an idealist turn, given how much Williams himself always stressed the importance of material relations. We find him writing in *Marxism and Literature*'s chapter on Ideology, for instance, how '"consciousness and its products" are always, though in variable forms, parts of the material social process itself' (1977: 61). In his discussion of hegemony, however, Williams is very much concerned with demonstrating how 'the concept of "hegemony" goes beyond "ideology"', and it is the debates around ideology as theorized in the Marxist tradition on which Williams focuses. 'What is decisive', Williams argues, 'is not only the conscious system of ideas and beliefs, but the whole lived social process as practically organized by specific and dominant meanings and values' (1977: 109). A little later he puts it like this:

> [Hegemony] is a lived system of meanings and values – constitutive and constituting – which as they are experienced as practices appear as reciprocally confirming. It thus constitutes a sense of reality for most people in the society, a sense of absolute because experienced reality beyond which it is very difficult for most members of the society to move, in most areas of their lives. It is, that is to say, in the strongest sense a 'culture', but a culture which has also to be seen as the lived dominance and subordination of particular classes.
>
> (1983: 110)

Now this is powerful and persuasive stuff, and undoubtedly captures very well an important part of what Gramsci means by hegemony, but it is only part of the story. Williams himself recognized this, writing at the beginning of his chapter on hegemony: 'Whatever the implications of [Gramsci's concept of hegemony] for Marxist political theory ... the effects on cultural theory are immediate' (1983: 108). And having in this way bracketed the question of the exercise of power more broadly, in the rest of the chapter Williams expands on the implications for a cultural theory anchored in a literary rather than an anthropological notion of culture. In the chapter on hegemony, therefore, Williams is not attempting to provide a full account of hegemony in Gramsci, he is arguing specifically against the way in which ideology has tended to be theorized within the Marxist tradition. For those who have not read Gramsci's own writings, or have found that in their search for an unambiguous, precise definition of hegemony the prison notebooks, as the Comaroffs put it, 'do not help us much' (1991: 19), Williams' formulations can seem to provide a helpful gloss. Unfortunately, however, hegemony can then all too easily be taken as referring solely to the domain of ideas, beliefs, meanings and values, even though Williams himself always stressed the importance of the material circumstances in which ideas and beliefs are embedded.

Jean and John Comaroff's discussion of hegemony provides a good example of this reading of Gramsci which understands hegemony as referring simply to ideas, beliefs, meanings and values. Since the Comaroffs' account of hegemony is, as I have already noted, one that has been frequently cited, it is worth looking at it a little more closely.

They begin by welcoming what they see as the indeterminacy of the notion of hegemony: 'The very fact that Gramsci's notion of hegemony was so unsystematically stated has made it good to think with; as a relatively empty sign, it has been able to serve diverse analytical purposes and positions' (1991: 19). A little further on they quote what they see as a passage in the prison notebooks 'where [Gramsci] comes closest to defining "hegemony"'. The quote reads: 'a conception of the world that is implicitly manifest in art, in law, in economic activity and in all manifestations of individual and collective life' (SPN: 328, quoted in Comaroff and Comaroff, 1991: 23). The context of this quotation in the prison notebooks is a discussion of the notion of ideology in a Note on the 'Connection between "common sense", religion and philosophy', and it is helpful, I think, to look at what precedes and follows the fragment (here italicized) that the Comaroffs have picked out.

But at this point [Gramsci has been discussing the problem of separating out 'scientific' philosophy from common sense] we reach the fundamental problem facing any conception of the world, any philosophy which has become a cultural movement, a 'religion', a 'faith', any that has produced a form of practical activity or will in which the philosophy is contained as an implicit theoretical 'premise'. One might say 'ideology' here, but on condition that the word is used in its highest sense of *a conception of the world that is implicitly manifest in art, in law, in economic activity and in all manifestations of individual and collective life*. This problem is that of preserving the ideological unity of the entire social bloc which that ideology serves to cement and to unify.

(SPN: 328)

Here Gramsci is indeed talking about the realm of ideas and beliefs, but he is talking about it, as the Comaroffs themselves note, in the specific context of a discussion of *ideology*, and, as far as I know, Gramsci *never* uses ideology as any kind of synonym for hegemony. A passage here that is more pertinent to the concept of hegemony is the one in the preceding sentence in which ideas are embedded in 'practical activity', 'any philosophy which has become a cultural movement, a "religion", a "faith", any that has produced a form of practical activity or will in which the philosophy is contained as an implicit theoretical "premise"'. Hegemony can indeed be seen, at least in part, as emerging out of Gramsci's struggle to get beyond the base–superstructure dichotomy, which in Marx is no more than a metaphor but which later Marxists all too often treated as the theorization of a fixed divide. Hegemony for Gramsci, as I hope the preceding chapters have made clear, always involves 'practical activity', and the social relations that produce inequality, as well as the ideas by which that inequality is justified, explained, normalized, and so on. While sometimes Gramsci may have stressed consent, and sometimes the intertwining of force and consent, he never saw hegemony simply as ideology.

An interesting question is why the Gramsci of *Marxism and Literature* has been so readily accepted into anthropology. One reason is certainly the resistance of the prison notebooks themselves to any easy summary. The difficulty here is, at least in part, that a concept like hegemony in Gramsci is a way of mapping an ever-shifting landscape of power that includes both accounts of 'reality' as these confront particular people in particular places, and the hard realities that lie outside the realm of discourse – even if that which is not reducible to discourse can only be referred to within the terms of some discourse. What constitutes a particular hegemonic landscape at any given moment – remembering that this is always only a single moment in a ceaseless power struggle where power is never totally secure – is likely to include an extremely complicated intertwining of force and consent, and of the entanglement of accounts of reality with hard realities that are more than discourse. What hegemony 'is', therefore, is necessarily extraordinarily protean. We cannot get from Gramsci the tightly specified theoretical concept that the Comaroffs, along with many others, seem to want. What we can get is a series of suggestive and illuminating questions to ask of power in particular empirical contexts, but we can only get these after a fairly extensive reading of Gramsci's own writings. Gramsci's writings demand careful and close reading; if we are to grasp fully the leitmotiv of concepts such as hegemony, rather than simply looking for more manageable definitions in 'single casual affirmations and isolated aphorisms', we need, so to speak, to travel with Gramsci, to follow the twists and turns of his debates with his sometimes explicit, but frequently implicit interlocutors. The attraction of *Marxism and Literature* is partly, therefore, that it offers a relatively brief and clear summary account of hegemony that saves us the labour of engaging with the complexities of the prison notebook in any serious way.

Simply providing a user-friendly Gramsci is not, however, enough to explain the popularity of *Marxism and Literature*, or of Williams generally, with anthropologists. A second key factor is Williams' concern in *Marxism and Literature*, and indeed in all his work, with the exploration of 'culture' and how it is both produced within various fields of power, and is itself a central element in the production and reproduction of those fields of power. For anthropologists Williams is attractive, and especially to those sympathetic to Marxist accounts of power, not only because of his focus on culture, but because of his concern with culture and power. The problem here, as I have suggested, is that anthropologists have too readily assumed that when Williams – and by extension Gramsci – talks of culture, what he is referring to is what anthropologists understand by culture. Because the concept of culture is so central to anthropology – and at the same time so taken for granted – and because the anthropological and the literary senses of culture, while divergent, remain closely linked, it is easy for anthropologists to miss the divergence. As a result, it seems to me, anthropologists have missed much that the more complex Gramsci of the prison notebooks has to offer them. The Gramsci who has found his way into anthropology is a very partial Gramsci, a Gramsci stripped of much of the prison notebooks' intense concern with the *materiality* of power.

The problem with the overly idealist Gramsci that too many anthropologists have derived from their reading of Williams is that it tends to obscure a more interesting and richer Gramsci – albeit a more awkward and uncomfortable Gramsci who challenges a number of the discipline's pieties. This less familiar Gramsci, it seems to me, holds out to anthropologists the possibility of far more interesting and fruitful dialogues than the Gramsci who has been trimmed and shaped, domesticated if you will, to fit so comfortably within anthropological mappings. In part this is precisely because of the awkwardness and uncomfortableness of this less familiar Gramsci for anthropologists. This is a Gramsci who challenges them not only by his rather different understanding of 'culture', and his highly critical attitude to subaltern culture in general, but also often by his unapologetic Marxism, which to many nowadays – for whom the fall of the Berlin Wall demolished Marxism together with communism – seems embarrassingly naive and passé, if not downright offensive. The difficulty here is that, as I have attempted to show, Gramsci's intellectual project is framed within an unambiguously Marxist problematic. As I read Gramsci, it is impossible to separate his insights from his Marxism without reducing him to 'Gramsci lite'. Engaging seriously with his work necessarily means engaging with his Marxism.

In the second half of this chapter I expand on what such an engagement might mean in practice in the context of analyses by two anthropologists which draw explicitly on Gramsci. Before doing this, however, it is helpful, I think, to reflect a little on the complicated history of Marxism's influence on anthropology. Given the impossibility of summarizing that history here, I have focused on a single, major anthropologist, Eric Wolf. Wolf, who died in 1999, was a central figure in American anthropology's turn towards Marx, and it is instructive to examine his intellectual trajectory; how he came to define the anthropological project, and how 'culture' was located within that project.

Eric Wolf and the Anthropological Project

Marx, while currently unfashionable, has had a significant, if often hidden and unacknowledged, presence within Anglo-American anthropology throughout most of its history as a modern discipline. But it was only in the aftermath of the upheavals of the 1960s that Marxism emerged from the shadows and became, at least for a few years, highly influential among American and British anthropologists. The work of a number of French Marxist anthropologists, such as Maurice Godelier, Claude Meillassoux and Emmanuel Terray, was particularly important in resurrecting Marx's writings as relevant and useful for contemporary anthropology. It was in this context of renewed interest in Marx that Gramsci's writings began to attract increasing attention.

One of my reasons for deciding to focus on Wolf here is that he was someone who in his later work very much rejected the notion of bounded cultures so central, as I argued in Chapter 3, to mainstream anthropology. In an essay originally published in 1984, for example, he stressed that cultures should not

> be seen as givens, integrated by some inner essence, organisational mainspring, or master plan. Rather, cultural sets, and sets of sets, are continuously in construction, deconstruction, and reconstruction, under the impact of multiple processes operative over wide fields of social and cultural connections.
>
> (2001: 313)

He was equally insistent that anthropologists must pay attention to history:

> What attention to history allows you to do is to look at processes unfolding, intertwining, spreading out, and dissipating over time. This means rethinking the units of our inquiries – households, localities, regions, national entities – seeing them not as fixed entities but as problematic: shaped, reshaped, and changing over time.
>
> (2001: 390)

In many ways Wolf can indeed be seen as part of an important countertradition that drew, sometimes explicitly, but often implicitly, on Marx, and that challenged the assumptions which I have argued have been so tightly bound up with anthropological concepts of culture. And yet nonetheless, I would argue, even in the case of Wolf, who challenged the assumptions of mainstream anthropology so radically, there are interesting limits to his reimagining of the anthropological project, particularly as regards his theorization of culture and his treatment of the relationship between culture and class. Tracing out these limits helps reveal both how Wolf's approach to the problem of culture differs from that of Gramsci, and how anthropologists might use Gramsci to rethink certain aspects of their concept of culture.

It is useful to begin by locating Wolf historically; I have drawn here on a brief autobiographical essay (2001) he wrote at the end of his life. Born in Vienna in 1923 to secular Jewish parents, Wolf came of age in a Europe in which Fascism was on the rise. He and his parents arrived in the United States in 1940, after the family had relocated first to Central Europe and then to Britain. During the Second World War he fought in the American army. After three years of war service he completed his first degree at Queen's College in New York, where he had already discovered anthropology prior to entering the army. This was followed by a postgraduate degree at Columbia University, at that time, in his words, 'the citadel of Boasian anthropology'. The major intellectual presence in the department by this period was Ruth Benedict, one of Boas's students. Wolf brought to his anthropology a certain European sensibility that included an awareness of the importance of intellectual history, and a broadly leftish political orientation. As an anthropologist he was always concerned with the larger political picture. At Columbia he was part of a study group of anthropology graduate students, who called themselves, half jokingly, the Mundial Upheaval Society (MUS). All of them were veterans, left-wing, and all shared a dissatisfaction with Benedict's 'culture and personality' school of anthropology, which was dominant in the Columbia department.

What the MUS group was looking for was a more materialist anthropology, and they found it in Julian Steward who joined the department in 1947. Steward, who defined himself as a cultural ecologist, was a key figure in Wolf's early development as an anthropologist. Strongly materialist, the focus of Steward's research was, in Wolf's words, 'on the comparative study of relations between environments and the technologies that permitted their human use' (2001: 4). Wolf and several of the MUS group, including Sidney Mintz, were recruited by Steward to carry out their dissertation fieldwork as part of a large multicommunity study of Puerto Rico. Wolf and Mintz both had chapters in the resulting joint-authored volume, *The People of Puerto Rico* (Steward, 1956). Wolf's research was in a coffee-growing area in the Central Highlands characterized by 'decaying and undercapitalised estates', while Mintz worked with landless agricultural labourers employed by 'the most technified, irrigation-based, rationalised, American-owned sugar plantation on Puerto Rico's southern coast' (2001: 5).

Reflecting back on the strengths and weaknesses of *The People of Puerto Rico* in 1978, 21 years after the book's publication, Wolf stressed its failure to address the issue of the embeddedness of the communities studied, and of Puerto Rico itself, in larger (ultimately global) economic structures over which they and Puerto Rico had relatively little control. Part of the reason for this failure, according to Wolf, was that 'dependency theory was then in its infancy, and had penetrated anthropology hardly at all' (1978: 23). But, as Wolf goes on to point out, dependency theory was only a particular variant of long-running debates about imperialism, colonialism, and uneven development generally, within the Marxist tradition. Given anthropology's formation around the study of societies seen as 'primitive', 'pre-modern', 'pre-capitalist' and so on, it is interesting how infrequent references to that Marxist literature were within Anglo-American anthropology until the late 1960s. From the vantage point of the late seventies it was blindingly obvious to Wolf that the different communities he and Steward's other students studied represented not, as Steward would have it, different subcultures but rather, 'particular combinations of capital and labor at a particular moment in time' (1978: 25). True to his commitment to the importance of historical analysis, Wolf concludes his reassessment by locating *The People of Puerto Rico* itself historically.

> Perhaps none of this [i.e. Wolf's 1978 reinterpretations of the Puerto Rican material] could have been said twenty-one years ago. These remarks are predicated on the renewal of political economy and the breaking down of conceptual and methodological boundaries among the various social sciences ... Re-reading the book, I was amazed how close we often came to opening paths towards this new ground, and chagrined as well that we did not go further at the time.
>
> (1978: 25)

Wolf himself, along with Mintz, was one of the pioneers of the renewal of political economy in American anthropology that began in the late 1960s. Significantly Wolf's explanation of why this renewal happened when it did and not earlier links it directly to the larger political climate. 'Perhaps it was only involvement in the turmoil of the 60s which raised new questions and new possible answers' (1978: 25). It is important to stress here that it is not that *no* earlier anthropologists challenged the dominant, essentially ahistorical approach to the study of cultures; anthropologists who rejected it, whether explicitly or implicitly, can be identified at virtually every period of the discipline's history. Two interesting early examples are, for North American anthropology, Alexander Lesser at Columbia, and for British, Godfrey Wilson at the Rhodes Livingstone Institute in then Northern Rhodesia. The point here is that the general assumptions about 'culture' that I have identified, while not unchallenged, dominated. In Gramscian terms they were part of a hegemony within the discipline which, it should be emphasized, was able to impose a particular approach to the analysis of culture not merely through a set of intellectual arguments but through control of the institutions and practices recognized as the means of producing *authoritative* anthropological knowledge.

After the Puerto Rican project, Wolf moved on to work in Mexico, where he continued to focus on the nature of peasant society, and in particular on its modes of political organization. By the end of the 1960s he had produced a string of influential publications, including in 1969 his wide ranging survey, *Peasant Wars of the Twentieth Century*. Wolf's approach to anthropology by this point was an explicitly political-economic one, based on Marx and the Marxist tradition. In the seventies, after the 'turmoil of the 60s' and the rediscovery of Marx by a whole range of academic disciplines, Wolf turned increasingly to the work of the dependency and world-systems theorists, spearheaded by Gunder Frank and Emanuel Wallerstein. A central question for Wolf was: how had long-distance trade shaped the histories of the so-called 'primitive' peoples typically studied by anthropologists? This theoretical engagement culminated in his 1982 volume, *Europe and the People without History*, in which Wolf attempted 'to delineate the general processes at work in mercantile and capitalist development, while at the same time following their effects on the micro-populations studied by the ethnohistorians and anthropologists' (1982: 23). Wolf continued to be extremely prolific right up to his death in 1999, his final major work being *Envisioning*

Power: Ideologies of Dominance and Crisis. Just before his death he had completed work on a volume collecting together a wide selection of his essays published over the previous half century. This appeared posthumously as *Pathways of Power: Building an Anthropology of the Modern World*. Wolf's body of work is extraordinarily rich. I have already drawn extensively on *Envisioning Power* in Chapter 3; here, however, my concern is simply with certain aspects of how Wolf locates 'culture' in his later work, that produced after 'the renewal of political economy and the breaking down of conceptual and methodological boundaries among the various social sciences'. My discussion is based on the three major volumes, *Europe and the People without History, Envisioning Power*, and *Pathways of Power*.

Culture and Class in the Later Wolf

As I have already stressed, Wolf insists on the importance of history, writing in the Preface to *Europe and the People without History*: 'The insights of anthropology ... have to be rethought in the light of a new, historically oriented political economy' (1982: ix). He is equally insistent that the old notion of cultures as bounded and fixed must be abandoned, writing in the Afterword: 'Once we locate the reality of society in historically changing, imperfectly bounded, multiple and branching social alignments, however, the concept of a fixed, unitary, and bounded culture must give way to a sense of the fluidity and per-meability of cultural sets' (1982: 387). As he goes on to point out,

> In the rough-and-tumble of social interaction, groups are known to exploit the ambiguities of inherited forms, to impart new evaluations or valences to them, to borrow forms more expressive of their interests, or to create wholly new forms to answer to changed circumstances. Furthermore, if we think of such interac-tion not as causative in its own terms but as responsive to larger economic and political forces, the explanation of cultural forms must take account of that larger context, that wider field of force. 'A culture' is thus better seen as a series of processes that construct, reconstruct, and dismantle cultural materials, in response to iden-tifiable determinants.
>
> (1982: 387)

In an essay entitled 'Culture: Panacea or Problem', originally delivered as a lecture in 1982, Wolf uses a similar formulation: 'In the place of separate and static, clearly bounded units, therefore, we must now deal with fields of relationships within which cultural sets are put together and dismantled' (2001: 314).

It is notable, however, that in these formulations Wolf, unlike Gramsci, seems anxious to hold on to some notion of coherence, as when he writes that the notion of 'fixed, unitary and bounded', or 'separate and static' cultures needs be replaced by one of fluid and permeable 'cultural sets', or that a culture is 'better seen as a series of processes that construct, reconstruct, and dismantle cultural materials'. And, earlier in the 'Culture: Panacea or Problem' essay, we find Wolf quoting approvingly from Alfred Kroeber: 'Perhaps we should once again adopt their [i.e. the diffusionists] distrust of the automatic or organic coherence of any culture and see a culture, any culture, in Kroeber's words, as "an accommodation of discrete parts, largely inflowing parts, into a more or less workable fit"' (2001: 313). All these formulations, while firmly rejecting any bounded, ahistorical notion of culture, nonetheless retain a sense of some coherent logic or pattern that ultimately in some way or another hangs together: culture is about cultural *sets*, it consists of discrete parts that come together into *a more or less workable fit*. In *Envisioning Power*, after calling for the redefinition of culture, Wolf is careful to stress what he sees as valuable in the anthropological concept of culture: 'We thus need to make our received concepts more flexible and operational, but we must not forget the relational value of concepts like culture, which – whatever its limits – *sought connections among phenomena*, in contrast to the earlier "custom"' (1999: 67, my emphasis).

This lingering sense that cultures *are* in some sense coherent can perhaps be linked to the way in which culture is located in Wolf's anthropological version of political economy and how this is related to the old Marxist base–superstructure dichotomy. One of the most fruitful aspects of Gramsci's approach to culture, I would argue, is the way in which it succeeds in going beyond this dichotomy. That is, while Gramsci never abandons the language of base and super-structure, in practice he transcends it. As, for example, in his problematic of hegemony. The very slipperiness of the notion of hegemony that has frustrated so many can be seen as due in part to Gramsci's refusal to define it as a phenomenon of either base or superstructure; hegemony is in Gramsci precisely a way of thinking about power that rejects this dichotomy. It is significant that Wolf, who cites Gramsci rarely but in general approvingly, shares this frustration to some extent, writing in *Envisioning Power*, 'Perhaps because Gramsci did not want to attract the attention of his prison guards, he was never explicit about how he envisaged the interplay between hegemonic processes and the state' (1999: 45). For Wolf himself, I would suggest, a dichotomy broadly analogous to that of base and superstructure remains central. In *Europe and the People without History*, for instance, once again referring back to an earlier anthropologist, Wolf makes a distinction between the instrumental and the ideological domains of culture. The particular context here is anthropologists' tendency to assume that cultures persist over time.

> Nearly fifty years ago Robert Lowie distinguished between 'matter-of-fact usage' and 'secondary interpretations' or 'rationalizations' ... The distinction is still useful. Even the simplest food-collecting group deploys an impressive array of objects, customs, and knowledge in its dealings with the world, together with a body of instructions for their use. This constitutes the matter-of-fact level of cultural phenomena. On another level, such instrumental forms – objects, acts, and ideas – appear as elements in cultural codes, which purport to define their place in the relations of human beings to one another, and of human beings to the surrounding world. Instructions about the instrumental use of cultural forms are synchronized with communications about the nature and praxis of the human situation. This is the level of interpretation, rationalization, or ideology, of assumptions and perspectives defining a particular view of the human lot. These communications are more than denotative and logical; they are often somatic, kinesthetic, affective, and aesthetic as well.
>
> Anthropologists have called particular combinations of such matter-of-fact usages and ideological rationalizations 'cultures,' dealing with them as if they possessed an inherent coherence over time.
>
> (1982: 387–8)

In an essay entitled 'Ideas and Power', written in 1985 although not published until its inclusion in *Pathways of Power*, Wolf provides a succinct formulation of this same basic distinction: 'In this essay I want to address an unresolved issue, the relation between economics and political ordering, on the one hand, and ideology, on the other' (2001: 371).

Wolf's answer, or partial answer, to this conundrum is as follows:

It is my argument that we shall find a key to signification and symbolic production in the social relations that govern a mode of production, a system of mobilizing and deploying social labor; the social power implicated in such relations becomes imprinted in symbols. Furthermore, if the social relations of production are the sources of power-laden signification, then it follows that important differences in the nature of these relations will produce very different symbolic expressions.

(2001: 375–6)

Here we have an orthodox Marxist causal relationship: ideology is the outgrowth of 'the social relations that govern a mode of production, a system of mobilizing and deploying social labor', with different modes of production producing different 'symbolic expressions'. In other words, a given mode of production's 'system of mobilizing and deploying social labor' defines fundamental relations of class, which can be seen as constituting the economic base, while distinct from this base there is the realm of symbolic expression. And this realm of symbolic expression is produced by that base.

At the same time Wolf's analyses of empirical cases, such as those in *Europe and the People without History* and *Envisioning Power*, provide rich and nuanced explorations of the complex intertwining of modes of deploying social labour and cultural forms; they are anything but crude, economic reductionism. Are Wolf's formulations about the relation between the mode of production and ideology in reality any different, therefore, from Gramsci's apparently similar adherence to the ultimate primacy of economic relations?[4] The key point here, I would argue, is that for Gramsci, it is not culture of which the economy is the mainspring 'in the last analysis', it is *history*.[5] And, very importantly, for Gramsci, this really is a case of 'in the last analysis', that is, he takes this *ultimate* priority as a given but in his actual analyses, of Italian history for instance, he does not make use of a base–superstructure hierarchy. For Gramsci, this hierarchy is not something that can be mapped onto the concrete realities of history. In the real historical landscapes of power that come into being in particular times and places, certain ways of understanding the world, or symbolic expressions, are very much, to use a Gramscian term, organic elements of that society's

4. See Chapter 4, in particular the 'Culture and History' section.
5. See SPN: 162.

economic base. In other words, Gramsci leaves to one side, or brackets, the whole base–superstructure hierarchy. One consequence of this is that the question of whether 'culture' in general is part of the superstructure or part of the base becomes, like so many general questions in Gramsci, a question which it is simply not meaningful to ask. A society's 'culture' for Gramsci consists of such a heterogeneous clutter of detritus deposited by history – certain elements of which fit together and certain elements of which do not – that it only makes sense to talk about specific cultural phenomena in specific historical contexts. In certain circumstances these phenomena are indeed structural and organic, in others not. Beyond the general assertion of the primacy of the economy 'in the last analysis', which really does not get us very far as regards the analysis of the specific and concrete, there is no general answer to the problem of 'the relation between economics and political ordering, on the one hand, and ideology, on the other'. It is the task of analysis to tease out specific links in specific times and places.

In line with his refusal to allocate culture either to the superstructure or to the base, Gramsci is not interested in making a separation between instrumental and ideological forms of culture, or distinguishing as does Lowie between 'matter-of-fact usage' and 'secondary interpretations' or 'rationalizations'. The problem with this distinction, I would argue, is that the ideological forms of culture have already been defined as in some sense derivative, as forms of 'secondary interpretations' or 'rationalizations' of ultimately determining economic relations. As a result the analysis of what might be termed 'actually existing hegemonies', with their complicated and unpredictable intertwining of the material and the ideational, risks being foreclosed prematurely. Ultimately, it seems to me, Wolf's insistence on the importance of fundamental economic relations, valuable as it is, falls back into an unhelpful dualism of base and superstructure with culture in effect being treated as a superstructural phenomenon.

There is an interesting and revealing difference between *Europe and the People without History* and *Envisioning Power* that seems to reflect that dualism. In the case studies of the former book the concept of culture scarcely appears (as was noted by a number of anthropologists when the book first appeared), while in the latter the concept of culture is given a central role. As a recent review essay puts it, 'in *Europe and the People without History*, political economy clearly is the explanatory backbone, whereas in *Envisioning Power*, culture (or ideas) is allowed to stand on its own as an independent variable' (Barrett et al., 2001: 477). It is as if in one book the analysis of class is foregrounded, and in the other, that of culture, but in neither book does Wolf seem able to integrate the basic economic relations of class with symbolic expressions in a wholly satisfactory way. In the view of Barrett et al., 'in attempting to find room for culture [i.e., in *Envisioning Power*], he seems to have crossed the line between materialism and idealism, in the process moving from Marx and closer to Weber' (2001: 477). A part of the problem here is perhaps Wolf's reluctance to theorize class in a way that fully incorporates culture, ultimately remaining committed to the concept of culture as a *distinct*, albeit fluid and shifting, domain. This can be illustrated by Wolf's discussion of the concepts of class and culture in *Envisioning Power* – a book that Wolf himself saw as growing out of *Europe and the People without History*.[6]

Wolf stresses how culture and class should not be seen as two separate totalities:

> When first introduced in the present-day senses, these concepts [class and culture] appeared to be wholly incompatible, especially when deployed in political discourse. Yet they do not exclude each other; they occur together and overlap in various ways. Both terms, in fact, claim too much and also too little. They suggest that 'classes' or 'cultures' represent totalities in their own right – homogeneous, all-embracing entities, each characterized by a common outlook and capable of collective agency.
>
> (1999: 65)

Wolf goes on to argue that the concept of class needs to be rethought in more historical and less structural terms, referring approvingly to E. P. Thompson's *Making of the English Working Class*, and its recognition that classes are 'made', and made 'out of disparate groups of people who bear diverse cultural heritages' (Wolf, 1999: 65). Culture too, in Wolf's view, needs to be rethought, and here the ghost he wants to exorcize is the Counter-Enlightenment concept of culture.

> The initial use of the concept in the service of the Counter-Enlightenment stressed a supposed inner unity, marked by a continuity through time from primordial beginnings. A 'culture'

6. See Wolf, 2001: 9.

was thus conceived as the expression of the inner spiritual force animating a people or a nation. This understanding was carried into anthropological usage, together with the implicit or explicit expectation that a culture constituted a whole, centered on certain fundamentals that distinguished it from others. It was also seen as capable of reproducing and regenerating itself and as able to repair any tears in its fabric through internal processes.

Once we abandon this view of a culture as a reified and animated 'thing,' the problem of how to understand cultural phenomena must also change. What comes to be called 'culture' covers a vast stock of material inventories, behavioral repertoires, and mental representations, put in motion by many kinds of social actors, who are diversified into genders, generations, occupations, and ritual memberships.

(1999: 65–6)

This is an important critique. I drew heavily on Wolf's account of the emergence of this notion of culture in Chapter 3. But what I want to draw attention to here is how Wolf's critique of the residues of this Counter-Enlightenment holism to be found in later anthropological concepts of culture stops short of totally rejecting the assumption of coherence and system. He concludes his discussion in *Envisioning Power* with the caution not to abandon all notion of connection, which I have already quoted but which bears repeating: 'We thus need to make our received concepts more flexible and operational, but we must not forget the relational value of concepts like culture, which – whatever its limits – sought connections among phenomena, in contrast to the earlier "custom"' (Wolf, 1999: 67). My problem with the way Wolf formulates culture here is with the underlying a priori assumption that 'cultures', while they may be heterogeneous and shifting, also have some kind of coherence. The question of whether or not certain phenomena are connected seems to me to be an empirical one that can only be answered in the context of specific studies.

At the end of *Envisioning Power*, after the case study material, Wolf has a short coda in which he argues for the usefulness of the concept of culture. Here he does indeed seem rather Weberian, as Barrett et al. suggest, claiming culture as 'a concept that allows us to capture patterned social flow in its multiple interdependent dimensions and to assess how *idea-dependent power* steers these flows over time' (Wolf, 1999: 289, my emphasis). The final sentences of the book are:

The issues posed by ideology have had too little attention in anthropology since the advent of functionalism and structural-ism. Yet they deal with what a society or culture is *about*. At this millennial transition, the human capacity to envision imaginary worlds seems to be shifting into high gear. For anthropologists and others, greater concern with how ideas and power converge seems eminently warranted.

(1999: 291)

What I find interesting here is how the concept of class seems rather to have dropped out of the equation. Taken together, *Europe and the People without History* and *Envisioning Power* could almost be said to conjure up an Escher-type paradox where it seems impossible to keep both class and culture equally in view. A careful reading of Gramsci can perhaps help us get beyond this theoretical impasse.

In my Introduction I claimed that Gramsci provides us with important insights into how we might rethink the complex terrain of culture, class and inequality, and I want now in the remaining sections of this chapter to begin sketching out some broad contours of what such a mapping might look like. In line with Gramsci's own preferred dialogic style (see pp. 33–4) I have selected two texts by anthropologists, both of which draw explicitly on Gramsci, and have tried to bring them together not just with the anthropology-friendly Gramsci lite, but with the more challenging Gramsci, whose complex mappings of the topographies of power were explored in the Part II. The texts on which I focus are a monograph by Matthew Gutmann, *The Meanings of Macho*, and an article by Roger Keesing, 'Colonial and Counter-Colonial Discourse in Melanesia'. The first of these three sections looks at Gutmann's use of the concept of class and compares it with Gramsci's rather different understanding.

Two Concepts of Class

Anthropologists, along with other social scientists and historians, have long debated the usefulness, or otherwise, of the concept of class. Nowadays, class is a distinctly unfashionable concept. One common criticism is that the theory of class is an overgeneralizing master narrative which, firstly, crams complicated and varied tapestries of inequality into a series of oversimple, overrigid boxes, and secondly, claims universality, but which has in fact been fashioned from the particularities of western European history. Castigated for ignoring issues of culture, class as a category has often been seen as particularly inadequate when it comes to theorizing inequalities of gender and race. The concept of class continues nonetheless to have its defenders, among whom I would include myself. It seems to me that while the old, crude, mechanical notions of class do indeed need to be jettisoned, getting rid of the concept altogether risks, to use the old cliché, throwing out babies as well as bathwater. If we abandon the concept of class entirely, we can all too easily find ourselves adrift amid a myriad eddies of difference, all competing for our attention, but at a loss for ways to talk about certain very large, and very real, systematic inequalities to be found in the contemporary world. And that there are glaring inequalities in our brave new, 'globalizing' world, which privilege a minority while condemning many to desperate poverty, seems difficult to deny. Since the late 1970s anthropologists grappling with the problem of how to describe that world and its inequalities began increasingly to turn to Gramsci. Gutmann is one of these.

The Meanings of Macho is based on fieldwork in Santo Domingo, a poor neighbourhood of Mexico City, where Gutmann lived for a year with his wife and baby daughter in the early 1990s. Gutmann's project was to examine 'what it means to be a man, *ser hombre*, for men and women who live in the *colonia popular* of Santo Domingo, Mexico City' (1996: 11); and he explored this through an examination of fatherhood. Haunting Gutmann's study, not surprisingly in a book about Mexican men, is the spectre of machismo. Machismo is indeed a central plank in the whole edifice of 'traditional' Mexican culture as this has been understood by anthropological and other observers. In part *The Meanings of Macho* can be read as Gutmann's attempt to escape this huge and looming presence, and to reframe the analysis of Mexican masculinity in different terms. Running through the book is a critique of the whole notion of machismo as essentially a rather tired cliché that tells us little about the way actual men and women in Santo Domingo live their lives. I shall return to Gutmann's account of machismo in the next section.

Accepting for the moment that the concept of machismo is a poor guide to the character of Mexican masculinity and fatherhood, what would be a better one? On this Gutmann is less clear. The concluding paragraph of his book, for example, begins like this:

In the *colonia popular* of Santo Domingo, Mexico City, what macho may mean and what men may do in the future are by no means apparent. What is known and what is most culturally significant today is that gender identities and relations there are characterized by inconsistency, as well as by arrogance, idealism, manipulation, discrimination, opportunism – and always by generous doses of humor. Not only nationalism but also class, ethnicity, generation, and other factors deeply brand Mexican male identities... claims about a uniform character of Mexican masculinity, a ubiquitous *macho mexicano*, should be put to rest.

(1996: 263)

The problem is, once we have buried *macho mexicano*, and, as we shall see, Gutmann very convincingly establishes that it does indeed need burying, how then to proceed? It is certainly important to draw attention to the inconsistency and confusion in the ways in which Mexican men inhabit their male identities, and to the many factors shaping those identities, but do we not also need theoretical concepts that identify which questions are the more important ones, and which the less? In other words, which specific strands in this untidy bundle of factors should we focus on? Do we not need, that is, some different problematic within which to frame our explorations of what it means to be a man in Santo Domingo? It seems to me that from time to time in *The Meanings of Macho* we do in fact catch glimpses of an alternative problematic, albeit one that Gutmann seems a little hesitant to stress too much. This is a problematic of *class*. As I read Gutmann's study, the story it tells is a story very much structured by class, even if Gutmann's own location of the class dimension of his story is somewhat diffident. And here, I would suggest, a more explicit dialogue with Gramsci is illuminating.

As a result perhaps of his concern with class – even if only as one factor theoretically equivalent to others such as ethnicity and generation – Gutmann turns to Gramsci in attempting to tell his story in terms other than those of machismo. Not that Gramsci is the only theorist Gutmann draws on, but it is Gramsci who is the primary source for what he describes as his two key theoretical concepts: contradictory consciousness and cultural creativity (1996: 14, 22). Gutmann's Gramsci, however, is a Gramsci whose theorization of power has been stripped of its fundamental narrative of class. He remains for Gutmann a theorist of the relation between the dominant and the dominated, but the ultimate class basis of that domination seems to have slipped away.

For the concept of contradictory consciousness, Gutmann cites a passage from 'Relation between science, religion and common sense' in which Gramsci writes of 'the active man-in-the-mass':

> One might almost say that he has two theoretical consciousnesses (or one contradictory consciousness): one which is implicit in his activity and which in reality unites him with all his fellow-workers in the practical transformation of the real world; and one, superficially explicit or verbal, which he has inherited from the past and uncritically absorbed.
>
> (SPN: 333, quoted in Gutmann, 1996: 14)

This same passage is quoted, at slightly greater length, above (see p. 117). Gutmann gives no specific citation for the concept of cultural creativity, just a general reference to 'Gramsci's sense of emancipatory agency'. He also refers here to Williams and *Marxism and Literature*, specifically Williams' 'remarks concerning emergent cultural practice' (1996: 23).

As regards the notion of contradictory consciousness, Gutmann writes:

> As employed in this book, *contradictory consciousness* is a descriptive phrase used to orient our examination of popular understandings, identities and practices *in relation to* dominant understandings, identities and practices. For instance, with regard to the practices of Mexican men as fathers, many are aware of a social science image of poor urban Mexican men typified by the Macho Progenitor. Yet whereas the beliefs and practices of many ordinary men do not accord neatly with this monochromatic image, ordinary men and women are themselves often acutely aware of and influenced in one way or another by the dominant, often 'traditional' stereotypes about men.
>
> (1996: 14, Gutmann's emphasis)

One reason perhaps why Gutmann turned to Gramsci and the notion of contradictory consciousness is that it enables him explicitly to reject any assumption of a *systematic* culture of Mexican masculinity. As I explored in Chapter 3 and in my discussion of

Wolf, the ghost of culture as system continues to haunt anthropology; Gutmann's clear rejection of any assumption of a coherent, systematic culture of Mexican masculinity is important and helpful, and I shall return to it in the next section. Nonetheless, using Gramsci's notion of contradictory consciousness in this way alters its meaning significantly, since what Gramsci is in fact talking about here is class.

What happens in Gutmann's usage is that what is in Gramsci a very specific concept of an implicit consciousness arising out of activity shared with 'fellow-workers in the practical transformation of the real world' becomes the rather different, and much vaguer, 'popular understandings, identities and practices'. The point here is that Gramsci's concept of contradictory consciousness in this passage is focused on a particular kind of contradiction: one between the world-view of a dominant group (whose domination rests ultimately on their dominant economic position and on the economic exploitation of those they dominate) and an implicit, as yet unarticulated, understanding of 'how things are' on the part of the dominated. Crucially, this implicit, alternative world-view stems from the very relationships that are established in the course of the practical transformation of the real world – a practical transformation that produces the surpluses that dominant groups appropriate. In other words, the contradictory consciousness that Gramsci is talking about here is not simply a matter of different, at times conflicting, 'understandings, identities and practices' (this would correspond more to Gramsci's notion of common sense as an incoherent jumble piled up over time: see the section on common sense in Chapter 5); the contradiction in this passage derives rather from a fundamental contradiction between *classes*.

An earlier, much cited passage in 'Relation between science, religion and common sense', quoted above in Chapter 5 but not cited by Gutmann, is also relevant here.

This contrast between thought and action, i.e. the co-existence of two conceptions of the world, one affirmed in words and the other displayed in effective action, is not simply a product of self-deception [*malafede*]. Self-deception can be an adequate explanation for a few individuals taken separately, or even for groups of a certain size, but it is not adequate when the contrast occurs in the life of great masses. In these cases the contrast between thought and action cannot but be the expression of profounder contrasts of a social historical order.

(SPN: 326–7, see pp. 115–16
for a more extensive quotation)

It is clear here, I think, that what Gramsci has in mind is a very specific form of contrast or contradiction, namely, a class one. At the same time, Gramsci never sees the specific forms 'contrasts between thought and action' assume in a given historical context as any kind of straightforward or mechanical expression. He only takes it as axiomatic that, following Marx and Engels, 'the *ultimately* determining factor in history is the production and reproduction of real life' (see p. 88).

Class and Gender

An important strength of Gutmann's study is the attention it pays to gender and the processes by which gendered identities come into being. His account of these processes is rich and nuanced, and contains many insights. Here, however, what I want to focus on is Gutmann's understanding of the relations between gender and class. According to him, what it meant to be a man was changing in Santo Domingo with, for example, many men doing more in the way of domestic tasks, formerly seen as women's work, than the traditional macho accounts would suggest. Understanding these changes, in Gutmann's view, demands that we look beyond the clearly demarcated 'male' spaces. A central argument of *The Meanings of Macho* is that 'men's gender identities are developed and transformed in the home and not just in sites considered to be typical male reserves, like factories, cantinas, and political forums' (1996: 147). Using Gramsci's formulation of contradictory consciousness, we might identify in Gutmann's data a basic contradiction within the young men of Santo Domingo's consciousness of themselves as men. On the one hand, there is the consciousness implicit in how they actually live their gender identity in the day-to-day lives they share with their wives and families, and on the other, the consciousness of what a Mexican man is supposed to be, a consciousness 'superficially explicit or verbal ... inherited from the past and uncritically absorbed'.

The explanation Gutmann was given as to why men were doing more at home was generally that 'in numerous families it has become economically necessary for both husband and wife to have paid work, and that this has sometimes led the husband to do some of the household tasks' (1996: 156). Gutmann adds that the women tended to emphasize that an important factor in this shift was their insistence that their menfolk take on these responsibilities, and he identifies the impact of feminist thought as one significant factor helping to bring about this shift. Another important factor for Gutmann, however, is class. He insists, for instance, that 'generalizations about universal, modern, or even national [Mexican] cultural patterns of child rearing cannot be made without taking into account the effects of class divisions and inequalities on parenting beliefs and practices' (1996: 83). At the same time, for Gutmann class would seem to be a specific form of inequality distinct from other forms, such as gender and ethnicity. He puts it this way: 'although there are many analytical similarities between the classifications of gender, class, and ethnicity – for instance, each included elements of social inequality, privilege, and organized consent – there are also particularities to each' (1996: 257). In Gutmann's view, class is essentially one factor amongst others. As should be clear to those who have read the previous three chapters, this is not how Gramsci understands class. So how might we might locate class in Gutmann's story if we were to use the concept of contradictory consciousness in a way that is closer to the spirit of Gramsci?

Like Gramsci, we would need to begin with Marx and Marx's notion of class (this is discussed above in Chapter 4). For Marx (whose notion of class is far more nuanced and complex than is often portrayed) the notion of class refers firstly, at a very general level, to how, in a given place and time, production is organized and resources and the social product are distributed; and to the patterns of inequality thus created. One of the major contributions of recent feminist thought is to widen the conventional view of production and productivity to include *all* those activities which provide for its members' needs and wants, and not just those produced within market relations. The rearing of children and care of family members may be unpaid work, but it is vital both for the day-to-day restoration of existing workers and for the rearing of the next generation; and as such it should be seen as an integral part of a society's production. How this frequently unpaid labour is organized and who is given the responsibility for performing it is an important dimension of any society's class landscape. In other words, class is always gendered. This landscape with its characteristic contours of inequality – in a capitalist system, for example, that between the buyers of labour power (employers) and the sellers of labour power (employees) – always has implicit in it certain oppositions and contradictions, such as that between capital and labour. And it is the working-out of these oppositions and contradictions, which Marx termed class struggle, that provides the basic dynamic of history. It is important to stress, however, that what is being described here is a pattern of relationships; how those relationships are inhabited by actual individuals is a separate question.

This second question, that of how, as it were, class is *lived*, is central to the prison notebooks. For instance, what it means to be a worker, or a peasant, in a particular time and place is not simply given by the basic wage-labour or other economic relation; rather, over the course of particular histories specific subaltern cultures have developed. And it is these contradictory and incoherent, subaltern cultures that inform the meaning that given class positions have as lived realities. See, for example, Gramsci's careful mapping out of the class realities of rural Italy in the passage on the nature of the *morti di fame* quoted above (pp. 90–1). How class is lived includes the ways in which different inequalities are gendered, ethnicized, or present themselves in the forms of particular national realities. It is the work of the social analyst to trace out the paths by which certain basic contradictions have led to particular lived realities. For Gramsci, as for Marx, class acts in history, but it does so through the political and social identities that previous histories have brought into being. Following Gramsci rather more closely than Gutmann does, we could see the complicated and shifting bundle of beliefs and practices bound up with 'being a man' that Gutmann encountered in 1990s Santo Domingo as how a certain kind of working-class gendered reality was lived. It is not, I would argue, that class is, as Gutmann would have it, a distinct dimension of inequality, or one factor alongside others such as nationalism, ethnicity, and generation, but rather that class should be seen as a way of analysing systematic patterns of inequality, reproduced over time, which are in various ways gendered, ethnicized, and so on.

Having considered Gutmann's and Gramsci's rather different understandings of class as a theoretical concept, I want now to turn to Gutmann's insightful critique of the concept of Mexican machismo. Here, it seems to me, Gutmann, while he does not explicitly draw on Gramsci for this aspect of his study, is far closer to Gramsci than he is in his treatment of class, where he does draw on Gramsci. Gutmann's study is a useful corrective to two of the assumptions that I have argued haunt the notion of culture that has tended to dominate in anthropology: that cultures constitute discrete and bounded entities, and that the societies of the South are characterized by a fundamental opposition between 'tradition' and 'modernity'. His critique of the concept of Mexican machismo can be read both as a rejection of anything like a single culture of Mexican masculinity, and of the widespread tendency to frame the analysis of Mexico in terms of a fundamental opposition between 'tradition' and 'modernity'. *The Meanings of Macho* in fact provides a nicely concrete illustration of the problems of seeing history through the lens of an opposition between tradition and modernity.

Tradition, Modernity and Mexican Machismo

For Gramsci subaltern cultures are, by their very condition of emergence, far from being the bounded, discrete entities that, as I argued in Chapter 3, the concept of culture in mainstream anthropology has tended, explicitly or implicitly, to assume. Gutmann's picture of the fractured, incoherent, and sometimes contradictory, bundle of ideas and practices which constitute 'being a man' in Santo Domingo is closer to Gramsci here in its clear rejection of any notion of a distinct entity that we can identify as 'Mexican culture'. *The Meanings of Macho* shows clearly that neither the Santo Domingo men's accounts of themselves, nor the implicit accounts embodied in how they actually lived their lives, can be explained in terms of some purely Mexican reality – as for example, when Gutmann argues that the realities of those lives, and how those living them understood these realities, have been shaped in part by the ideas of an international feminist movement.[7] Some anthropologists might respond that while it is true that such ideas may indeed be influential, there is nonetheless some ultimately autonomous Mexican culture on which this outside influence acts. This, for instance, is the position taken by Ortner in her 1986 article, discussed in Chapter 3, where she stresses that 'A society, even a village, has its own structure and history' (see p. 50). The point here, I think, is that

7. 1996: 94, 236.

while a place like Santo Domingo, or indeed Mexico, can certainly be seen as having its own history, to see Santo Domingo or Mexico as having their own *structure* – a structure that is, that exists separately from the larger networks of economic, political and social relationships within which both are located – is far more questionable.

A major problem Gutmann faced in his analysis of how masculinity was lived in Santo Domingo was how to deal with the concept of machismo, given the central role it has played in anthropological (and other) accounts of Mexican 'maleness'. Gutmann points to how machismo is regularly invoked as an explanation of violence: 'that phenomenon known as machismo, the ethos widely held responsible for male violence in Mexico and beyond' (1996: 220). Gutmann quotes one anthropologist of Mexico, Romanucci-Ross, author of a 1973 ethnography of rural Mexico. Signalling the importance of the concept of machismo to her argument, Romanucci-Ross uses as her epigraph to the book what she says is a village proverb, 'The macho lives as long as the coward wills it.' Describing this as a proverb, as Gutmann points out, lends it an aura of ancient wisdom, suggesting that this is something that has been handed down since time immemorial. In the book itself Romanucci-Ross writes of 'a *machismo*-centred subculture comprising the remnants of the male version of an earlier cultural horizon. That this subgroup and subculture represent a lag in the acculturative process in which the village is involved is very important' (Romanucci-Ross, quoted in Gutmann, 1996: 286). Here the roots of machismo are seen as lying in an older Mexico, one at odds with modernity, which represents 'a lag in the acculturative process'. In other words, the problem of male violence in Mexico is seen to stem from a clash between tradition and modernity. On the one hand, we have the 'traditional' macho, captured 40 years ago by Oscar Lewis, arguably the most influential anthropologist of Mexico, in three sentences quoted from one of his informants: 'In a fight I would never give up or say, "Enough," even though the other was killing me. I would try to go to my death, smiling. That is what we mean by being *"macho"*, by being manly' (quoted from Lewis 1961: 38 in Gutmann, 1996: 231). These three sentences have had an extraordinary afterlife, being employed, in Gutmann's words, 'with astonishing frequency in anthropological texts to represent all Mexican males past, present, and future' (1996: 231). Something, one feels, with which their sheer poetic power, whether this came from Lewis's informant or from

Lewis himself, has had more than a little to do. Counterposing the macho, on the other hand, we have the modern world in which such attitudes, apparently handed down unchanged from a past before modernity, are an atavistic throwback. The issue of what it means to be a man in Mexico is thus cast squarely in terms of a basic opposition between tradition and modernity.

The problem here, as Gutmann explains in a chapter he saves for the end of his book, is that this use of 'macho' is in reality rather recent. Drawing on a 1967 essay by Américo Paredes, Gutmann reveals that the apparently age-old concept of the macho who goes to his death smiling is primarily a product of the modern mass media, the Mexican radio and cinema of the 1930s and 1940s. Romanucci-Ross's 'village proverb' is in fact unlikely to have predated her research by more than a few decades since 'the use of the word *macho* in this manner is quite modern' (1996: 26). The context for this particular 'invention of tradition'[8] was the very specific one of Mexican nationalism and its struggle to define, always in the shadow of its powerful northern neighbour, an autonomous Mexican identity. Far from being some survival from an isolated past, machismo as it is understood today needs to be seen as a creation of modern Mexican history, and as owing much to the place in that history of the United States as an other against which Mexican identity had to imagine itself. Gutmann describes this context vividly.

> The consolidation of the Mexican nation, ideologically and materially, was fostered early on not only in the gun battles on the wild frontier, not only in the voting rituals of presidential politics, but also in the imagining and inventing of *lo mexicano* and *mexicanidad* in the national cinema. (Later both radio and television played starring roles in giving people throughout the Republic a sense of themselves as sharing a common history and destiny – in short a national identity.) ... it was the manly actors who most came to embody the restless and explosive potential of the emerging Mexican nation. And of all the movie stars of this era, one stood out as 'a macho among machos' ... Jorge Negrete [who] came to epitomize the swaggering Mexican nation, singing,

8. A phrase first coined by Eric Hobsbawn and Terry Ranger in their classic *Invention of Tradition* volume, see p. 54.

I am a Mexican, and this wild land is mine.
On the word of a macho, there's no land lovelier and wilder of
its kind.
I am a Mexican, and of this I am proud
I was born scorning life and death
And though I have bragged, I have never been cowed.

In the rural cantinas, the manly temples of the golden age of
Mexican cinema, the macho mood was formed.

(1996: 228)

One cannot help suspecting that Lewis's informant, who spoke so
eloquently of going to his death smiling, had either spent his fair
share of time watching such movies, or had obtained his image of
the macho, at least in part, from those who had. The point here is
not that the image of the macho was created completely from
scratch. Clearly, it drew on certain pre-existing themes that
resonated with Mexican audiences, but as a national archetype
defining the essence of what it means to be a Mexican male it is a
modern creation produced by Mexico's relatively recent history, not
a pre-existing cultural reality that explains that history.

It is interesting in this context to recall Gramsci's speculations on
the nineteenth-century Italian peasant visionary rebel, Davide
Lazzaretti (see pp. 120–2), who crafted his visionary critique using
narrative elements drawn not from age-old peasant traditions, as
most commentators assumed, but from a popular historical novel.
To understand why Lazzaretti's critique took the form it did, it is
crucial to take into account the subaltern position from which he
was speaking. It is unrealistic to expect a nineteenth-century Italian
peasant rebel to have a coherent and fully developed counter-
hegemonic account with which to oppose the hegemonic forces
confronting him. As Gramsci put it in a Note quoted in Chapter 5
(see p. 100): 'The lower classes, historically on the defensive, can
only achieve self-awareness via a series of negations' (SPN: 273). In
the final section of this chapter I want to turn to the consideration
of the concept of hegemony in the context of the work of the
anthropologist Roger Keesing.

'Hegemony Lite' and Gramsci's Hegemony

I have argued that culture for Gramsci is, in part, the ways in which
class is lived in particular time and places. A crucial dimension of

how class is lived is as specific power relations. The concept of hegemony helps us to grasp how power is lived in a given context, and how certain regimes of power – remembering that no regime is uncontested – are produced and reproduced in the day-to-day lives of individuals. Keesing's work on anticolonial struggles in the Solomon islands provides a good example of what hegemony can look like in practice.

Anthropologists, as I argued above, have for the most part taken the concept of hegemony in Gramsci as referring to struggles over how the world is described. At issue, according to this understanding of hegemony, is: whose conceptions, ideas and beliefs as to 'how the world is' win out? Typically, for the Comaroffs, 'where [Gramsci] comes closest to defining "hegemony"' is in this formulation, 'a *conception* of the world that is implicitly manifest in art, in law, in economic activity and in all manifestations of individual and collective life' (see p. 173, my emphasis). But in this formulation, as I pointed out, Gramsci is defining ideology not hegemony. To turn hegemony in this way into little more than a synonym for ideology is, as I read Gramsci, to rob the notion of hegemony of much of what makes it a productive and useful way of approaching power. Hegemony in the prison notebooks, I would suggest, is an approach to the question of power that in its exploration of empirical realities – how power is lived in particular times and places – refuses to privilege either ideas or material realities, seeing these as always entangled, always interacting with each other. It is a concept, that is, that rejects any simple base–superstructure hierarchy. I would argue that it is precisely this rejection that makes hegemony such a potentially fruitful way of approaching issues of power.

In his 1994 article, 'Colonial and Counter-Colonial Discourse in Melanesia', for which Gramsci is the main theoretical inspiration, Keesing gives us an insightful and concrete account of hegemony. There is an interesting contradiction, however, between Keesing's definition of hegemony, which is essentially 'hegemony lite', and the realities of hegemony he describes in the case-study material, where we seem to be dealing with something much closer to the spirit of Gramsci's own use of hegemony. By drawing out this difference, bringing the 'hegemony lite' of Keesing's explicit definitions into dialogue with the more substantial understanding of hegemony that seems to me implicit in the case-study material, I hope to suggest how Gramsci can help us map the complex contours of culture, class and inequality.

Interestingly Keesing is one of the few anthropologists to draw on Gramsci who refers neither to Raymond Williams nor to Stuart Hall, either in this article or in his 1992 book (from which much of the material in the later article is taken).[9] He begins by framing his article in terms of 'ideological domination', arguing that, '[T]he hegemonic processes of ideological domination were first clearly explicated by Gramsci' (1994: 41). He goes on to describe the article as an exploration of 'how colonial discourse has imposed categorical structures and specific forms on the counter-hegemonic discourse of resistance and decolonization in the southwestern Pacific' (1994: 41–2). So far, it would seem, we are very much in the realm of discourse and ideology. Once Keesing gets into his case-study material, however, the focus of the analysis shifts to the processes by which certain categorical structures have been imposed, and to how the Solomon islanders, who within the colonial order were certainly subalterns, could not but inhabit that colonial world, and had no choice but to frame their struggles with it largely in *its* terms. These were not so much struggles between different conceptions of the world as they were struggles, firstly, between the representatives of a modern state with an arsenal of modern forms of coercive force, and those whose coercive force consisted of 'warriors brandishing clubs, spears and bows and arrows' (1994: 47); and secondly, between a new order that came bearing a powerfully seductive cornucopia of new commodities and a world that could not hope to compete in technological terms. Stone axes had little chance against steel blades that could clear forests in a fraction of the time required by those stone ones, just as guns and cloth defeated clubs, spears and local fabrics. As a source of all these desirable new goods, the colonial world with its traders and its missionaries, as well as its soldiers and police, exuded a power that was a complex bundle of coercion and seduction.

Initially, when the people of the island of Malaita first began to be drawn into the orbit of an ever-expanding world capitalist system in the late nineteenth century via explorers, whalers, traders, and those bent on recruiting them as labourers for the plantations of Queensland and Fiji (Keesing, 1992: 9), they used, as we might expect, their own categorical structures and concepts in their

9. I have also drawn on Keesing's 1992 book, *Custom and Confrontation*, in what follows but since the notion of hegemony emerges more clearly in the later article, and is less encumbered with competing theoretical concepts, I have focused on the article rather than the book.

attempts to accommodate these new figures and new forces within their own known world. Like others elsewhere,[10] they attempted to make use of these newcomers to serve their own local purposes, and when that did not work, they tried to resist them by force. The Malaitans among whom Keesing worked, the Kwaio, had a history of such resistance; attacks on recruiting ships in the 1880s, the murder of the first white missionary to establish himself in the area in 1911, and the massacre of a particularly unpopular district officer and his entourage some 15 years later. Two years after Keesing arrived to carry out fieldwork in 1963 the Kwaio killed another missionary (1994: 44). These, it would appear, were not people who had quietly acquiesced in their transformation into colonial subjects.

In the 1940s, in the context of the Second World War and the upheavals it caused in the region, a more organized, explicitly anti-colonial movement emerged, Maasina Rule (The Rule of Brotherhood). Although apparently crushed by the late 1950s, the movement continued to have an underground existence. One of Maasina Rule's central demands was the recognition by the colonial state of 'Malaitan Customary Law'. At first sight this might seem to be a clear example of resistance to colonial rule; a rejection of colonial law and a demand to return to the indigenous law of pre-colonial times. In fact, however, as Keesing points out, the whole notion of what was referred to in the local language as *kastom* (custom) was itself a product of the colonial order.

It took Keesing himself some time to understand this. Arriving as a graduate student in Malaita for his first fieldwork in the early 1960s – a distant anthropological age from the vantage point of the 1990s – Keesing saw his project in conventional anthropological terms as the recording of Kwaio life and culture. The Kwaio themselves understood him to be 'writing down the custom' (1992: 135) and much to his delight they seemed as enthusiastic about his project as he was, even building a special 'Committee House' next to his, where what they called the 'Sub-District Committee' met every Tuesday and 'devoted themselves to "straightening out" *kastom*, "custom", through endless discussions, debates and sessions of litigation. *Kastom* ... was to be written down and I [Keesing] was cast as primary agent in this process' (1994: 42). Initially pleased by his reception, Keesing gradually began to realize that what his Kwaio hosts

10. This is a prominent theme in the work of Sahlins; see for example his *Islands of History* (1985).

understood by *kastom* was something rather different from the living 'culture' he had come to record, and that their *kastom* project had a distinctly political aim in view – an aim which they saw this powerful American visitor as helping them to achieve. At first, Keesing was just puzzled as to why in this rather remote corner of Malaita, where modern life seemed to have penetrated little, 'straightening out *kastom*' was seen as so important. 'Why talk endlessly about *kastom* when ancestral ways still prevailed?' (1994: 43). Even stranger, the Kwaio leaders at the Tuesday meetings were called *sifi* (chiefs) and yet outside these meetings there were no chiefs among the Kwaio.

> Furthermore, the 'lines' over which (in this context) the 'chiefs' were supposed to have authority were not the small descent groups I was mapping sociologically the rest of the week, but were the units that had been used since the 1920s by the colonial government for tax collection purposes (units that had no correspondence with indigenous groups or categories).
>
> (1994: 43)

Gradually Keesing began to recognize the profoundly colonial nature of this apparently indigenous category '*kastom*':

> The conceptualization of 'custom' (or 'law') as both the quintessential embodiment of a people's way of life and as a domain contested through the imposition of colonial law was itself a product of colonial experience and European categorization. Prior to colonial rule, Malaitans had ancestors and their rules: but they did not – could not – have *kastom*.[11]
>
> (1994: 45)

Not that colonial officials, missionaries or any of the other players on the colonial stage, such as anthropologists, had imposed this category on local people. Rather *kastom* had emerged out of struggles between colonizer and colonized as those who were now reduced to a subaltern status within the new regime of power attempted to deny the legitimacy of a colonial state, which they had already learnt they could not defeat through force, in terms that that state would

---

11. The Comaroffs make a somewhat similar point about the emergence of the Tswana concept of *setswana* (Tswana culture) (1991: 18).

recognize. This is one aspect of what hegemony means in practice; the power to determine the structuring rules within which struggles are to be fought out. That colonized peoples had 'custom', and that in certain contexts local custom could trump colonial law, was an accepted part of most colonial regimes. From the perspective of the colonized the problem was: what would the colonial authorities accept as genuine, authoritative 'custom'? How could they, the colonized, frame their demands in the language of 'custom'?

One clear reality to any non-literate colonized people, such as the Kwaio, is that within the colonial world, the written word is all powerful.

> In terms of Melanesian experience of colonial rule, the written word – canonically, in the form of the Bible and the colonial legal statutes – was a powerful instrument of subjugation. Citing chapter and verse, missionaries challenged and condemned ancestral precepts; citing colonial laws, District officers arrested and hanged men acting according to the ancestral ways, enforcing jural rights and preserving morality. To demand recognition of ancestral ways by the colonial state, it was necessary to provide an indigenous analogue of Bible and lawbook ... Kwaio leaders speak of *loa*, 'law', as well as of *kastom* in their discourse of resistance.
>
> (1994: 45–6)

In contrast to his initial rather idealist formulations of hegemony, towards the end of his article Keesing provides a good example of a very practical form of hegemony in the context of plantation labour that brought into being new groupings and categories. Hegemony here clearly involves some very material forces.

> In the Solomons as elsewhere in Melanesia, both the administrative structures and the plantation economy of the colonial state operated so as to create new categories – districts, tribes – and ethnic stereotypes – 'Malaitaman', 'Man Tanna'. Men from particular 'tribes' or islands were assigned appropriate places in a colonial division of labour according to essentialist notions of their character. What I find most striking here is not the way Islanders were led into false consciousness in attributing salience to non-existent categories and identities but rather, the way the social, political and economic structures of colonial domination

and plantation economy made these non-existent entities *real*, in terms of the experience of the Islanders. In the world of the plantations, Malaitans became a relevant social unit; Malaitans were forced to live together, work together, fight together vis-à-vis other Islanders, resist together vis-à-vis Europeans.

(1994: 50)

Ultimately the Solomon Islands achieved independence in 1978, becoming the 150th member nation of the United Nations, with all the trappings appropriate to a modern state; a parliamentary regime, a modern legal system, development plans and so on. All of which left little place for the reinstatement of *kastom* – ironically itself a product of the colonial world – hoped for by the traditionalists among whom Keesing worked. The reality was that the Kwaio now lived in a world that had been remade by forces generated by larger economic and political systems. In their struggles against the colonial order, and more recently the postcolonial one, however fierce the Kwaio's 'resistance', it was doomed to be just that, resistance. In other words, there was no possibility that the Kwaio could remake the world so that it would once again return to the old, precolonial condition. The Kwaio case seems to me a very vivid illustration of what Gramsci understood by hegemony.

Escaping Subalternity

Also relevant here is Gramsci's distinctly critical view of subaltern culture and his insistence that it is something subalterns must escape, which was discussed in Chapter 5. Subaltern culture for Gramsci is by definition confused and incoherent; however keen their awareness of local realities of power, those trapped within subaltern culture remain incapable of grasping the larger landscapes of oppression in which they are located. It is the awareness of local, parochial realities that Scott's work is so good at mapping. For Gramsci, however, it is only by transcending their subaltern culture that those who inhabit it can ever hope to overcome their subalternity. In other words, the character of subaltern cultures is both a product of their dominated condition and helps to perpetuate that domination. In Gramsci, while there is certainly compassion and respect for the suffering and exploitation of subaltern peoples, there is none of the celebration of their culture so characteristic of anthropologists' accounts. It is important to remember in this context that

Gramsci's hostility to any such easy, and potentially sentimental celebration, stems from his identity as a political activist. Ultimately, like Marx, his concern was not simply to understand the world but to change it.

But does this mean that the world view of Keesing's Kwaio traditionalists has *no* place in the brave new world of the Solomon Islands nation state? In this context it is interesting to bring into dialogue with Keesing and the Kwaio some of Gramsci's thinking about the role of intellectuals as articulators of new, potentially counter-hegemonic accounts of the world. The problem with the Kwaio traditionalists' *kastom* is that while the old precolonial narratives provided perfectly adequate accounts of that enclosed world, once this world was incorporated into the global economic and political order, those narratives became inadequate as ways of comprehending and, crucially, *mastering* the new realities of, for example, plantation and urban life. They might, it is true, be able to explain this frightening and often incomprehensible world in ways that were psychologically satisfying to individuals belonging to the old Kwaio order, but they could not furnish a superior account that had the potential to replace the existing, dominant colonial and postcolonial narratives of capitalism, modernity and development. To put it another way, the old explanations may have been capable of capturing how the Kwaio experienced their place in the new order – how they *felt* – but they could not provide a coherent, systematic explanation that would allow those oppressed by this new order to overcome it. Producing this kind of coherent and systematic understanding, Gramsci argues, is the work of intellectuals, but such intellectuals must always remain in close contact with those they represent, they must, as Gramsci says, feel and not merely think. As he put it in the Note on the relationship between knowing, understanding and feeling, quoted at p. 130,

> The popular element 'feels' but does not always know or understand; the intellectual element 'knows' but does not always understand and in particular does not always feel ... The intellectual's error consists in believing that one can know without understanding and even more without feeling and being impassioned (not only for knowledge in itself but also for the object of knowledge): in other words that the intellectual can be an intellectual (and not a pure pedant) if distinct and separate from the people-nation, that is, without feeling the elementary passions of

the people, understanding them and therefore explaining and justifying them in the particular historical situation and connecting them dialectically to the laws of history and to a superior conception of the world, scientifically and coherently elaborated – i.e. knowledge. One cannot make politics-history without this passion, without this sentimental connection between intellectuals and people-nation.

(SPN: 418)

Retaining this connection is often especially difficult for intellectuals in postcolonial societies like that of the Solomon Islands, where being an intellectual tends to be synonymous with having cut oneself off from the 'primitive' superstitions of the past and become socialized into 'modern', 'scientific' thinking and all the taken-for-granted assumptions of contemporary global capitalism. Gramsci's comments on the Italian intellectuals of his time are relevant here: '[T]he entire 'educated class', with its intellectual activity, is detached from the people-nation ... in relation to the people-nation the indigenous intellectual element is more foreign than the foreigners' (SCW: 210). While it is important not to romanticize the world-view of the traditionalist Kwaio, perhaps it is possible to discern within it, albeit in embryonic and fragmentary form, elements of a critique of the brutalizing juggernaut of capitalism on which those trying to fashion a genuine counterhegemony – one capable of offering an achievable alternative, which by definition would have to transcend the narrow confines of the Kwaio world – might draw. Such a counterhegemonic account would be more likely to be one whose truth those actually experiencing the onrushing force of the juggernaut in this particular postcolonial manifestation might recognize, and with which they could emotionally identify.

A Concluding Note

I hope in this chapter I have begun to suggest how anthropology might engage not simply with the reduced, anthropology-friendly Gramsci who has already found a place there, but with the far more complex and awkward figure who emerges from any sustained and serious reading of his writings, a figure who resists any simple summary. If this book has succeeded, it will have sent the reader back to Gramsci himself, and it seems appropriate to give Gramsci the last word. I have chosen to end with three extracts from a series of letters Gramsci wrote to his sister-in-law, Tatiana, from prison.

Gramsci could be very sharp with Tatiana, and he was merciless when he detected anything that seemed to him loose or sloppy thinking, as when in the autumn of 1931 Tatiana wrote to Gramsci about a German film she had seen called *Two Worlds*. The film told the story of a doomed love affair between a Jewish woman and an Austrian officer, and its theme was that this affair was doomed because the lovers belonged to two different worlds. Tatiana (whose mother, Gramsci's mother-in-law, was Jewish) had found this idea of two incompatible worlds persuasive and wrote as much to Gramsci. Gramsci emphatically did not, finding the whole idea typical of a certain kind of sloppy and indeed dangerous way of thinking. His letters to Tatiana on the topic betray his irritation, but in addition show yet again his utter rejection of any notion of fixed and bounded cultural entities existing across time and space. This is not to say that he thought that we can never talk about large cultural entities such as Jewish culture or Italian culture. The point for Gramsci is that 'cultures', which are ultimately the product of specific histories, are always fluid and protean entities; and that we must always remember when talking about particular 'cultures' that their particular character depends on the particular place and the particular historical moment with which we are concerned. Equally importantly, what constitutes a 'culture' depends on the specific questions with which we are concerned. For instance, in the context of this interchange with Tatiana, Gramsci is anxious to stress his cultural identity as an Italian. In other contexts, he might well have stressed the proletarian cultural identity he shared with Russian or German workers, as against the bourgeois cultural identity of the Fiat bosses. It is safe to say, I think, that Gramsci would have had little time for the concept of hybridity so popular nowadays (see Chapter 3). In short, in Gramsci context is all.

On 13 September Gramsci writes to Tatiana:

How can you possibly believe that these two worlds [i.e. as portrayed in *Two Worlds*] really exist? This way of thinking is worthy of the Black Hundreds[12] or the American Ku Klux Klan or

---

12. The Black Hundreds were bands of monarchists who, during and after the 1905 Russian Revolution, engaged in organized attacks on Jews, students and those known to be left-wing.

the German Swastikas ... The film must be of Austrian origin, a product of postwar anti-semitism.

(PLII: 71)

He continues the argument in his 5 October letter:

The mitigating remarks that you have made with regard to the problem of the so-called two worlds does not change the fundamental error of your point of view and does not diminish in any way the value of my affirmation that we have here an ideology that belongs, even though marginally, to that of the Black Hundreds, etc. I understand very well that you would not participate in a pogrom, yet for a pogrom to take place it is necessary that the ideology of 'two worlds' that are impenetrable, of different races, etc., be widespread. This forms that imponderable atmosphere that the Black Hundreds exploit by arranging the discovery of a child bled to death and accusing the Jews of having murdered it for ritual sacrifice. The outbreak of the World War has shown us how the ruling classes and groups know how to exploit these apparently innocuous ideologies in order to set in motion waves of public opinion ... What do you mean by the expression 'two worlds'? Is it a matter of two lands that cannot approach each other and enter into communication with each other? If you don't mean this, and if it is a metaphorical and relative expression, it has little meaning, because metaphorically 'worlds' are innumerable, including the one expressed in the peasant proverb: 'Take wives and oxen from your own hometown.' How many societies does each individual belong to? And doesn't each one of us make continuous efforts to unify his conception of the world in which there continues to subsist heterogeneous fragments of fossilized cultural worlds? And does there not exist a general historical process that tends to unify all of humanity continually? Don't the two of us, by writing to each other, continually discover reasons for discord and at the same time manage to come to agreement on certain questions? And doesn't each group or party or sect or religion tend to create its own 'conformism' (not understood in a herdlike or passive state)?

(PLII: 82)

And finally, on 12 October we find him writing:

I myself have no race; my father is of recent Albanian origin ... my grandmother was a Gonzalez and descended from an Italo-Spanish family from southern Italy ... my mother is Sardinian through both father and mother and Sardinia was united with Piedmont only in 1847 after having been a personal fief and patrimony of the Piedmontese princes ... Nevertheless my culture is fundamentally Italian and this is my world; I have never felt for a moment that I was torn between two worlds ...

(PLII: 87)

Bibliography

Gramsci's Own Writings

(1971) *Selections From the Prison Notebooks*, edited by Quintin Hoare and Geoffrey Nowell Smith, London: Lawrence & Wishart

(1977) *Antonio Gramsci: Selections From Political Writings 1910–1920*, edited by Quintin Hoare, London: Lawrence & Wishart

(1978) *Antonio Gramsci: Selections From Political Writings 1921–1926*, edited by Quintin Hoare, London: Lawrence & Wishart

(1985) *Antonio Gramsci: Selections From Cultural Writings*, edited by David Forgacs and Geoffrey Nowell-Smith, London: Lawrence & Wishart

(1992) *Antonio Gramsci: Prison Notebooks* (vol. I), edited by Joseph Buttigieg, New York: Columbia University Press

(1994) *Letters from Prison* (2 vols), edited by Frank Rosengarten and translated by Ray Rosenthal, New York: Columbia University Press

(1995) *Antonio Gramsci: Further Selections From the Prison Notebooks*, edited by Derek Boothman, Minneapolis: University of Minnesota Press

(1996) *Antonio Gramsci: Prison Notebooks* (vol. II), edited by Joseph Buttigieg, New York: Columbia University Press

Other References

Anderson, Perry (1976–77) 'The Antinomies of Antonio Gramsci', *New Left Review* 100 (November 1976 – January 1977): 5–78

Asad, Talal (ed.) (1973) *Anthropology and the Colonial Encounter*, London: Ithaca Press

Bailey, Garrick and James Peoples (1999) *Introduction to Cultural Anthropology*, Belmont: Wadsworth

Barrett, Stanley R., Sean Stokholm and Jeanette Burke (2001) 'The Idea of Power and the Power of Ideas: A Review Essay', *American Anthropologist*, 103(2): 468–80

Beattie, John (1964) *Other Cultures: Aims, Methods and Achievements in Social Anthropology*, London: Routledge & Kegan Paul

Brow, James (1988) 'In Pursuit of Hegemony: Representations of Authority and Justice in a Sri Lankan Village', *American Ethnologist*, 15: 311–27

Clifford, James (1997) *Routes: Travel and Translation in the Late Twentieth Century*, Cambridge, Mass.: Harvard University Press

Comaroff, Jean and John Comaroff (1991) *Of Revelation and Revolution: Christianity, Colonialism and Consciousness in South Africa* (vol. I), Chicago and London: University of Chicago Press

Crehan, Kate (1997a) *The Fractured Community: Landscapes of Power and Gender in Rural Zambia*, Berkeley: University of California Press

―――― (1997b) '"Tribes" and the People Who Read Books: Managing History in Colonial Zambia', *Journal of Southern African Studies*, 23(2) (June): 203–18

Davidson, Alastair (1977) *Antonio Gramsci: Towards an Intellectual Biography*, London: Merlin Press

Di Nola, Annalisa (1998) 'How Critical was De Martino's "Critical Ethnocentrism" in Southern Italy?', in *Italy's 'Southern Question'*, edited by Jane Schneider, Oxford and New York: Berg

Fabian, Johannes (1983) *Time and the Other: How Anthropology makes its Object*, New York: Columbia University Press

Feierman, Steven (1990) *Peasant Intellectuals: Anthropology and History in Tanzania*, Madison: University of Wisconsin Press

Femia, Joseph V. (1981) *Gramsci's Political Thought: Hegemony, Consciousness and the Revolutionary Process*, Oxford: Clarendon Press

Fiori, Giuseppe (1990) [first published Italy, 1965] *Antonio Gramsci: Life of a Revolutionary*, London and New York: Verso

Fontana, Benedetto (1993) *Hegemony and Power: On the Relation between Gramsci and Machiavelli*, Minneapolis: University of Minnesota Press

Fox, Richard (1989) *Gandhian Utopia: Experiments with Culture*, Boston: Beacon Press

Geertz, Clifford (1973a), 'Thick Description: Toward an Interpretive Theory of Culture', in *The Interpretation of Culture*, New York: Basic Books

―――― (1973b) 'Religion as a Cultural System', in *The Interpretations of Culture*, New York: Basic Books

Germino, Dante (1990) *Antonio Gramsci: Architect of a New Politics*, Baton Rouge and London: Louisiana State University Press

Gill, Leslie (1993) '"Proper Women" and City Pleasures: Gender, Class and Contested Meanings in La Paz', *American Ethnologist* 20(1): 72–88

Guha, Ranajit (1997) *Dominance without Hegemony: History and Power in Colonial India*, Cambridge, Mass. and London: Harvard University Press

Guha, Ranajit and Gayatri Chakrovarty Spivak (eds) (1988) *Selected Subaltern Studies*, New York and Oxford: Oxford University Press

Gutmann, Matthew C. (1996) *The Meanings of Macho: Being a Man in Mexico City*, Berkeley: University of California Press

Hall, Stuart (1986a) 'Gramsci's relevance for the study of race and ethnicity', *Journal of Communication Inquiry* 10(2): 5–27

―――― (1986b) 'The problem of Ideology: Marxism without guarantees', *Journal of Communication Inquiry* 10(2): 28–43

―――― (1988a) 'The Toad in the Garden: Thatcher among the Theorists', in *Marxism and the Interpretation of Culture*, edited by Lawrence Grossberg and Cary Nelson, Urbana and Chicago: University of Illinois Press

―――― (1988b) 'Gramsci and Us', in *The Hard Road to Renewal: Thatcherism and the Crisis of the Left*, London and New York: Verso

―――― (1994) 'Cultural Studies: Two Paradigms', in *Culture/Power/History: A Reader in Contemporary Social Theory*, edited by N. Dirks, G. Eley and S. Ortner, Princeton, N.J.: Princeton University Press [originally published 1980 in *Media, Culture and Society* 2: 57–72]

Haug, W. F. (1994) *Gefängnishefte* (Prison Notebooks), Vol. 6: Philosophie der Praxis (Notebooks 9 and 10), edited by W. F. Haug, with the co-operation of K. Bochmann, P. Jehle, and G. Kuck, Hamburg: Argument Verlag

—— (2000) 'Gramsci's Philosophy of Praxis', *Socialism and Democracy* 14(1) (Spring-Summer): 1–19

Hobsbawm, Eric (1965) *Primitive Rebels*, New York: Norton

Hobsbawm, Eric and Terence Ranger (eds) (1983) *The Invention of Tradition*, Cambridge: Cambridge University Press

Hymes, Dell (ed.) (1969) *Reinventing Anthropology*, New York: Pantheon Books

James, Martin (ed.) (2001) *Antonio Gramsci: Critical Assessments of Leading Political Philosophers* (4 vols) London: Routledge

Keesing, Roger M. (1974) 'Theories of Culture', *Annual Review of Anthropology*, 3: 73–97

—— (1992) *Custom and Confrontation: the Kwaio Struggle for Cultural Autonomy*, Chicago: University of Chicago Press

—— (1994) 'Colonial and Counter-Colonial Discourse in Melanesia', *Critique of Anthropology*, 14(1): 41–58

Kroeber, A. L. and C. Kluckhohn (1952) *Culture: a Critical Review of Concepts and Definitions*, Papers of the Peabody Museum of American Archaeology and Ethnology, vol. 47, Harvard

Kurtz, Donald V. (1996) 'Hegemony and Anthropology: Gramsci, exegeses, reinterpretations', *Critique of Anthropology* 16(2): 103–35

Laclau, Ernesto and Chantal Mouffe (1985) *Hegemony and Socialist Strategy: Toward a Radical Democratic Politics*, London: Verso

Lagos, Maria (1993) 'We Have to Learn to Ask: Hegemony, Diverse Experiences, and Antagonistic Meanings in Bolivia', *American Ethnologist* 20(1): 52–71

Lewis, Oscar (1961) *The Children of Sánchez: Autobiography of a Mexican Family*, New York: Vintage

Linger, Daniel (1993) 'The Hegemony of Discontent', *American Ethnologist* 20(1): 3–24

Malinowski, Bronislaw (1984) [1922] *Argonauts of the Western Pacific*, Prospect Heights: Waveland Press

Malkki, Liisa H. (1995) *Purity and Exile: Violence, Memory, and National Cosmology among Hutu Refugees in Tanzania*, Chicago: University of Chicago Press

—— (1997) 'News and Culture: Transitory Phenomena and the Fieldwork Tradition', in *Anthropological Locations: Boundaries and Grounds of a Field Science*, edited by Akhil Gupta and James Ferguson, Berkeley: University of California Press

Marx, Karl (1963) *The Poverty of Philosophy*, New York: International Publishers

—— (1970) *Contribution to the Critique of Political Economy*, London: Lawrence & Wishart

—— (1976) *Capital* (vol. I), Harmondsworth: Penguin

Marx, Karl and Frederick Engels (1975) *Selected Correspondence*, Moscow: Progress Publishers

—— (1998) [1848] *The Communist Manifesto*, London and New York: Verso

Mitchell, J.C. (1956) *The Kalela Dance: Aspects of Social Relationships among Urban Africans in Northern Rhodesia*, The Rhodes–Livingstone Papers, no. 27, Manchester 1956

Mouffe, Chantal (ed.) (1979) *Gramsci and Marxist Theory*, London: Routledge & Kegan Paul

Ortner, Sherry (1984) 'Theory in Anthropology since the Sixties', *Comparative Studies in Society and History*, 26(1): 142–66

Sahlins, Marshall (1985) *Islands of History*, Chicago and London: Chicago University Press

Sassoon, Anne Showstack (1987) (second edition) *Gramsci's Politics*, Minneapolis: University of Minnesota Press

—— (2000) 'Gramsci's Subversion of the Language of Politics', in *Gramsci and Contemporary Politics: Beyond Pessimism of the Intellect*, London and New York: Routledge

Scott, James (1985) *Weapons of the Weak: Everyday Forms of Peasant Resistance*, New Haven and London: Yale University Press

Steward, Julian H (ed.) (1956) *The People of Puerto Rico: A Study in Social Anthropology*, Urbana: University of Illinois Press

Thompson, E.P. (1968) *The Making of the English Working Class*, Harmondsworth: Penguin Books

Turner, Victor (1967) *The Forest of Symbols: Aspects of Ndembu Ritual*, Ithaca and London: Cornell University Press

Tylor, Edward (1871) *Primitive Culture*, London: John Murray

Williams, Raymond (1977) *Marxism and Literature*, Oxford: Oxford University Press

—— (1983) *Keywords: a Vocabulary of Culture and Society*, London: Fontana Paperbacks

—— (1990) *What I Came to Say*, London: Hutchinson Radius

Wolf, Eric (1969) *Peasant Wars of the Twentieth Century*, New York: Harper & Row

—— (1978) 'Remarks on *The People of Puerto Rico*', *Revista/Review Interamericana* 8: 18–25

—— (1982) *Europe and the People without History*, Berkeley: University of California Press

—— (1999) *Envisioning Power: Ideologies of Dominance and Crisis*, Berkeley: University of California Press

—— (2001) *Pathways of Power: Building an Anthropology of the Modern World*, Berkeley: University of California Press

Woost, Michael (1993) 'Nationalizing the Local Past in Sri Lanka: Histories of Nation and Development in a Sinhalese Village', *American Ethnologist* 20(3): 502–21

Index

Compiled by Sue Carlton